STANDARD REFERENCE LIBRARY
THROUGH-THE-BIBLE COMMENTARY

NEW TESTAMENT VOLUME TWO

The New Testament Church

ACTS–REVELATION

compiled by Douglas Redford

Standard®
PUBLISHING
Bringing The Word to Life

Cincinnati, Ohio

Unless otherwise noted, all Scripture quotations are from the *Holy Bible: New International Version*®, © 1973, 1978, 1984 by International Bible Society. Used by permission of Zondervan Bible Publishers. All rights reserved.

The "NIV" and "New International Version" trademarks are registered in the United States Patent Office by International Bible Society. Use of either requires permission of International Bible Society.

Library of Congress Cataloging in Publication data:

Redford, Doug, 1953-
  The New Testament church : Acts–Revelation / compiled by Douglas Redford.
     p. cm. -- (Standard reference library. New Testament ; v. 2)
  Includes bibliographical references and index.
  ISBN 0-7847-1901-2 (casebound : alk. paper)
  1. Bible. N.T.--Criticism, interpretation, etc. 2. Church history--ca. 30-100. I. Title.

BS2361.3.R43 2007
225.7'7--dc22   2006030363

Published by Standard Publishing, Cincinnati, Ohio.
www.standardpub.com

Printed in China.

Table of Contents

Introduction

UNFINISHED BUSINESS

This book constitutes the second volume in a series of commentaries from Standard Publishing—a series that aims to provide a summation of the "best of" the *Standard Lesson Commentary*® since it was first published over fifty years ago. The first volume presented a series of studies on the life of Christ, drawn from the four Gospels. This volume provides a series of studies drawn from the remaining books of the New Testament (Acts through Revelation). Our goal is to present, when this project is finished, a five-volume reference library that will consist of two New Testament volumes and three Old Testament volumes. So when one considers the title of this essay, "Unfinished Business," he may think this applies to all the work that lies ahead before this project is complete! But that is not the reason for this title.

ACTS: A "GRAND OPENING"

"Unfinished Business" calls attention to the fact that when Jesus ascended into Heaven, his "business" was "finished" in one sense; for he had accomplished his Father's holy purpose by giving his life on the cross as the perfect sacrifice for imperfect humanity. Thus he could pray to his Father, even when the cross was yet in the future but drawing ever nearer, "I have brought you glory on earth by completing the work you gave me to do" (John 17:4).

In another sense, however, Jesus' ascension marked the beginning of something very special. He had told his followers on the night before his crucifixion that his departure from them was not to be considered a tragedy; on the contrary, it was necessary for the work of Jesus' kingdom to continue: "I tell you the truth: It is for your good that I am going away. Unless I go away, the Counselor will not come to you; but if I go, I will send him to you" (John 16:7). At the beginning of the record in Acts, we see Jesus alluding to that earlier promise by telling his disciples not to leave Jerusalem but to "wait for the gift my Father promised, which you have heard me speak about" (Acts 1:4). Ten days after Jesus' ascension, the Day of Pentecost came, Peter proclaimed the first gospel sermon, and the church of which Jesus said "the gates of Hades will not overcome it" (Matthew 16:18) had begun with three thousand converts.

Several of the passages that have been selected for coverage in the studies from Acts highlight the church's steady growth, initially in the city of Jerusalem. Although at first the followers of Jesus were "enjoying the favor of all the people" (Acts 2:47), that "favor" would soon be replaced by the "fervor" of an intense opposition from the Jewish leadership in Jerusalem, especially the Sanhedrin—the very group that had sentenced Jesus to death. In addition, there were problems "from within," such as the complaints of some of the Grecian Jews that their widows were being ignored during the daily distribution of food. (Notice that Doctor Luke, the author of Acts, has not "doctored" his record of the early church; he is as honest about reporting the struggles of the first Christians as he is about reporting their successes!)

Persecution, however, produced exactly the opposite results from those desired by the instigators of the persecution. After the apostles had been flogged and threatened by the Sanhedrin, they left that meeting "rejoicing because they had been counted worthy of suffering disgrace for the Name" (Acts 5:41). Their desire to spread the message of Jesus only intensified; they refused to be silenced.

Eventually persecution, particularly the stoning of Stephen, forced the church beyond the "comfort zone" of Jerusalem into other areas in which Jesus had told the apostles to be his witnesses (Acts 1:8). "Those who had been scattered preached the word wherever they went" (Acts 8:4). Into Samaria the followers of Jesus traveled, breaking down longstanding animosity by the power of his love. Then came the conversion of the "master persecutor," Saul of Tarsus, as recorded in Acts 9:1-19. This marked a significant milestone in the progress of the church, for it was Saul whose passion to exterminate Christians was transformed into a passion to expand the message of the Christ who had so radically transformed him. A number of the texts covered in this volume's studies from Acts will highlight the impact of Paul's vision and ministry. Acts concludes, appropriately enough, with Paul in the city of Rome, having reached what was considered the heart of the Roman Empire and the world's political and cultural center at that time.

THE EPISTLES: "BUSINESS" LETTERS

As one might imagine, the task of deciding which passages to include in a work of this nature is quite intimidating. Many passages from the New Testament epistles have been covered several times within the history of the *Standard Lesson Commentary*®. The choice is similar to that confronting someone preparing to dine in a smorgasbord that features a wide variety of mouth-watering selections. So much is there that looks so good!

We have attempted in chapters 6 through 12 to present a study of passages that provide a summation of the important themes in the epistles and that demonstrate the balance that one often sees between doctrinal and practical concerns. We want to make it clear that any letters that are not included in our selections were not omitted because they are considered to be of lesser value or quality for some reason. As Paul states without reservation in 2 Timothy 3:16 and 17, "All Scripture is God-breathed and is useful for teaching, rebuking, correcting and training in righteousness, so that the man of God may be thoroughly equipped for every good work." Space limitations have governed what we are able to include, so shorter books such as Titus, Philemon, and Jude are not represented. We have, however, included a chart (see page 184) that provides information about the approximate dates of all the New Testament books and a summation of each book's contents.

REVELATION: A "GRAND FINALE"

The final chapter in this volume consists of studies from the book of Revelation. It is in that mysterious yet encouraging book that the "unfinished business" of Jesus' kingdom comes to a glorious conclusion with the description of the "wedding supper of the Lamb" (Revelation 19:9) and "the Holy City, the new Jerusalem, coming down out of heaven from God, prepared as a bride beautifully dressed for her husband" (Revelation 21:2). In this chapter, the passages we have included for study are not among the more controversial ones that have been subject to intense examination and speculation (such as Revelation 13:16-18, which mentions the "mark of the beast" and the number "666"). They are those texts that highlight the words of both warning and encouragement that are meant to instruct followers of Jesus in every century—whether first or twenty-first. Revelation's closing chapters in particular (21 and 22) have given comfort and hope with their assurance that when all is said and done, Jesus will have the last word and his church will reign triumphantly for eternity.

Our title "Unfinished Business" thus applies to more than just the book of Acts and the remaining portions of the New Testament. We today as followers of Jesus are the ones who have been called to take upon ourselves our Father's "business" and make it our passion. May the studies in this volume fortify our desire to see that the work of Jesus continues to expand "to the ends of the earth"—until he returns.

The Arrangement of Acts

Many outlines have been suggested for the study of the book of Acts. C. H. Turner's suggestion of six chronological "panels" in the book may actually come the closest to Luke's own plan as he laid out the material. Each "panel" covers a particular time and focuses on (though not exclusively) one geographical area. In addition, each one concludes with a distinct summary statement in the text.

Panel One   Acts 1:1—6:7

Location: Jerusalem

Summary: "So the word of God spread. The number of disciples in Jerusalem increased rapidly, and a large number of priests became obedient to the faith."   —Acts 6:7

Panel Two   Acts 6:8—9:31

Location: Judea and Samaria (and Galilee)

Summary: "Then the church throughout Judea, Galilee and Samaria enjoyed a time of peace. It was strengthened; and encouraged by the Holy Spirit, it grew in numbers, living in the fear of the Lord."   —Acts 9:31

Panel Three   Acts 9:32—12:24

Location: Syria; Gentiles included

Summary: "But the word of God continued to increase and spread."   —Acts 12:24

Panel Four   Acts 12:25—16:5

Location: Asia Minor

Summary: "So the churches were strengthened in the faith and grew daily in numbers."   —Acts 16:5

Panel Five   Acts 16:6—19:20

Location: Gospel introduced in Europe; churches strengthened in Asia Minor

Summary: "The word of the Lord spread widely and grew in power."   —Acts 19:20

Panel Six   Acts 19:21—28:31

Location: The church reaches Rome

Summary: "Paul . . . welcomed all who came to see him. Boldly and without hindrance he preached the kingdom of God and taught about the Lord Jesus Christ."   —Acts 28:30, 31

Chapter 1

The Church Begins
Acts 1:1-11; 2:1-4, 37-47; 4:32-37

JESUS' COMMISSION AND ASCENSION (ACTS 1:1-11)

Establishing the Groundwork

With this volume of studies, we begin with the opening verses of the New Testament book known as "The Acts of the Apostles." That title may be a bit misleading. The "acts" and words of only two apostles dominate the book: Peter in the first twelve chapters and Paul in the last sixteen. However, the focus on their ministries gives us an accurate representation of the general witness and preaching of all the apostles.

The author of Acts is Luke, the "beloved physician" and a co-worker of Paul. One of the primary pieces of evidence for this is the fact that both the Gospel of Luke and the book of Acts are addressed to the same individual, "Theophilus" (Luke 1:3; Acts 1:1). Judging from the events recorded at the end of Acts (Paul's journey to Rome and his imprisonment there), Luke probably wrote Acts around AD 62. Luke's Gospel and Acts form a two-volume presentation of the life of Christ and the first years of Christ's church. In fact, Acts forms a kind of "bridge" from the Gospels to the New Testament epistles. Without it, the letters of Paul, James, Peter, John, and Jude would be far more difficult to understand.

Examining the Text

I. A Period of Proofs (Acts 1:1-5)
A. Introduction to the Book (vv. 1, 2)

[1, 2] *In my former book, Theophilus, I wrote about all that Jesus began to do and to teach until the day he was taken up to heaven, after giving instructions through the Holy Spirit to the apostles he had chosen.*

The *former book* mentioned in this verse is the Gospel of Luke. As noted above, both Luke and Acts are addressed to *Theophilus*. (For further information on the identity of Theophilus, see the comments in the previous volume under Luke 1:3.) No doubt Luke "carefully investigated everything" in the process of compiling this record, just as he had done in writing his account of the life and ministry of Jesus (Luke 1:3). There is even an indication of Luke's personally witnessing certain events of which he writes; note the use of the pronouns *we* and *us* in Acts 16:10-17; 20:5–21:18; and 27:1–28:16.

Luke says that in his previous account (his Gospel), he *wrote about all that Jesus began to do and to teach*. That account ended with *the day he was taken up to heaven* (Luke 24:50-53). Acts, in turn, tells how Jesus' ministry continued after his ascension through his *apostles* and his church. Notice that Luke emphasizes Jesus' actions by putting *do* before *teach*. The apostles' preaching in Acts focused on Jesus' miracles, including his death for us and his resurrection, rather than his ethical teaching. The gospel that saves us centers on what Jesus did (1 Corinthians 15:1-4).

At the same time, Jesus prepared his apostles for their future task by *giving* them *instructions through the Holy Spirit*. These included his commands to preach the gospel to all nations, baptize believers, and lead those believers toward spiritual maturity (Matthew 28:18-20). This same Spirit would be promised to the apostles as their source of power in carrying out Jesus' commission to them (Acts 1:8).

B. Evidence of the Christ (v. 3)

³ After his suffering, he showed himself to these men and gave many convincing proofs that he was alive. He appeared to them over a period of forty days and spoke about the kingdom of God.

The apostles had to be utterly convinced that Jesus had overcome death. So Jesus went out of his way to make sure that they had all the *proofs* they needed. He invited them to look at his nail marks and spear wound, to touch him, to give him food to eat, and even to thrust their hands into his wounds (Luke 24:37-43; John 20:27). Notice also the list of witnesses to the resurrection found in 1 Corinthians 15:5-8. These appearances occurred at various times during the *forty days* between Jesus' resurrection and ascension.

The subject of Jesus' post-resurrection teaching was a topic that he had frequently addressed during his public ministry: *the kingdom of God* (Luke 4:43). As described in the Model Prayer, God's kingdom is present when those who are his subjects do his will here on earth as it is done in heaven (Matthew 6:10). With the establishment of Jesus' church on the Day of Pentecost, the phrase *the kingdom of God* describes both the church's present identity (Colossians 1:13) and its future goal (2 Timothy 4:18).

C. Baptism of the Spirit (vv. 4, 5)

⁴ On one occasion, while he was eating with them, he gave them this command: "Do not leave Jerusalem, but wait for the gift my Father promised, which you have heard me speak about.

Jesus had appeared to his disciples in *Jerusalem* during the evening following his resurrection (John 20:19). During the following forty days he spent some time with them in Galilee (John 21:1-23; Matthew 28:16-20). Now, as the time of his ascension drew near, he met *with them* in Jerusalem again and told them to stay there and w*ait for the gift* that had been *promised* by the *Father*. As the next verse indicates, this gift was the Holy Spirit. The Spirit was not a new subject to the apostles; they had *heard* Jesus *speak about* him on the night before his crucifixion (John 14:16, 17, 26; 15:26, 27).

⁵ "For John baptized with water, but in a few days you will be baptized with the Holy Spirit."

Jesus' words call to mind *John* the Baptist's prophecy of how Jesus' ministry, particularly his baptism, would supersede his own (Luke 3:16). People—whether John, the apostles, or any Christian—can administer baptism by *water*. But only Jesus can immerse (the meaning of the Greek word rendered baptized) people *with* (or "in") *the Holy Spirit.*

Baptism with the Holy Spirit is mentioned only seven times in the Bible. The first four are the Gospel accounts of John the Baptist's prediction that the one coming after him would baptize with the Holy Spirit (Matthew 3:11; Mark 1:8; Luke 3:16; John 1:33). The next occurrence is in the verse before us. Jesus' words point directly to the Spirit's filling of the apostles at Pentecost (Acts 2:4). The sixth reference is found in Acts 11:16, where Peter connects the Lord's promise of the Spirit's filling with events at the household of Cornelius as well as with the filling of the apostles "at the beginning" (Acts 11:15). Thus the baptism in the Spirit is historically connected with just two events—the filling of the apostles at Pentecost and the filling of Cornelius's household. These two events are pivotal, for they mark the first gospel presentations to the Jews and then to the Gentiles.

The seventh and final verse describing a Spirit baptism is found in 1 Corinthians 12:13. Here Paul notes that all Christians have been "baptized by one Spirit into one body." (The Greek word that is translated "by" is the same word that is used in the other six passages, where it is translated "with.") Here, however, Paul is not discussing the Spirit baptism that Jesus administered. Instead, he is talking about the unity of the church based on the fact that all Christians have been "baptized . . . into one body." Given the fact that there is only "one baptism" (Ephesians 4:5), it seems best to understand 1 Corinthians 12:13 as a reference to the "gift of the Holy Spirit" that accompanies the baptism in water that all Christians are to experience (Acts 2:38). Biblically, then, the promise of Jesus' baptizing in the Spirit is applied to only two important occasions in the book of Acts.

The *few days* mentioned by Jesus were ten in number. We know this because Jesus was with the apostles after his resurrection for 40 days (v. 3) and the Spirit came upon them at Pentecost—a feast held 50 days after the Passover celebration during which Jesus died and rose again.

II. A Promise of Power (Acts 1:6-11)
A. Time of the Kingdom (vv. 6, 7)

⁶ So when they met together, they asked him, "Lord, are you at this time going to restore the kingdom to Israel?"

This occasion of meeting *together* appears to be different from the one mentioned in verse 4. The one described here occurred at the Mount of Olives (v. 12). The question raised by the apostles was not an unreasonable one. Jesus had been teaching them about the kingdom of God (v. 3) and he had been promising the coming of the Holy Spirit, which Israel had always associated with the restoration of its greatness as an independent nation (Ezekiel 36:22-28). As previous studies have noted, in the first century many believed that this restoration would be accompanied by the overthrow of the Roman forces that occupied the country.

Throughout Jesus' ministry, the apostles had been interested in becoming leaders in the restored kingdom of which he spoke (Matthew 20:20-28). Their interests, however, had been tainted by the popular thinking. Even now, with Jesus' death and resurrection having taken place, the apostles' question revealed that they still held certain misunderstandings about what Jesus had taught them.

⁷ He said to them: "It is not for you to know the times or dates the Father has set by his own authority.

Jesus responded to the apostles' question by telling them that information about God's timetable was not meant for them. Such knowledge was (and is) not necessary for the followers of Jesus to have in order to complete their mission. In fact, such knowledge is reserved by God *the Father* for himself (Mark 13:32). He holds the future in his hand, and we need not try to pry it from his fingers. The focus of Jesus' teaching about the end times is not to provide us with a handy chart outlining when and how he will return. His main concern is that we be active and faithful servants, ready for the Master to return at any moment (Mark 13:33-37).

B. Power of the Witnesses (v. 8)

8 "But you will receive power when the Holy Spirit comes on you; and you will be my witnesses in Jerusalem, and in all Judea and Samaria, and to the ends of the earth."

Instead of giving the apostles a timetable, Jesus gave them a task: he told them that they were to be his *witnesses* to the entire world. Whenever God requires an action, he supplies the *power* to achieve it. Power for the apostolic mission would be provided *when the Holy Spirit* came *on* them. It is worth noting that when the apostles were baptized in the Spirit on Pentecost, they were invested with the ability to speak of "the wonders of God" to "Jews from every nation under heaven" (Acts 2:5, 11).

The apostles, however, were not to stay in Jerusalem. In fact, the verse before us may be considered the key that unlocks the development of the rest of the book of Acts. Jesus told his apostles to fulfill their task in three stages, and those stages are reflected in the events described within Acts: *in Jerusalem* (as told in Acts 1-7), *in all Judea and Samaria* (chapters 8-12), and throughout the known world (chapters 13-28). This pattern for evangelism is one that all of us still can use; we can begin with reaching those close to us, even as we keep *the ends of the earth* our ultimate goal.

The power that the apostles were to receive from the Spirit was demonstrated by three ministries in particular. One power that the Spirit gave the apostles was the ability to accurately recall and proclaim all that Jesus taught them during his three and a half years of public ministry. Furthermore, the Spirit would reveal to them any additional truths as they would need them (John 14:26; 15:26, 27; 16:13-15). A second witness power given to the apostles was the ability to perform signs and wonders to confirm that their message came from God and was true (Acts 2:43; 5:12; 2 Corinthians 12:12). The third power that accompanied the apostles' preaching was the working of the Holy Spirit on the hearts of the hearers of the gospel to convict them of their sin and of their need for a Savior (John 16:7-11). This power is still at work whenever we share the gospel with others.

The Scriptures do not indicate that the apostles expressed any shock or voiced any objections at Jesus' words. But the implications of his commission must have been staggering to these men who only a moment before were interested in the time when Jesus would "restore the kingdom to Israel." For example, they were to reach out to the Samaritans—a shocking thought to any loyal Jew. Later, the Lord provided a dramatic revelation to Peter regarding the all-inclusive nature of the gospel message (Acts 10:9-16; 11:4-18).

C. Certainty of Jesus' Return (vv. 9-11)

⁹ After he said this, he was taken up before their very eyes, and a cloud hid him from their sight.

As he had foretold, Jesus was now leaving the earth in order to return to his Father (John 16:28). He had told the apostles, "It is for your good that I am going away. Unless I go away, the Counselor will not come to you; but if I go, I will send him to you" (John 16:7). Jesus' ascension signaled that the Holy Spirit would indeed come "in a few days," as he had earlier said (v. 5).

The *cloud* into which Jesus ascended may have been simply an ordinary cloud that eventually *hid him from* the apostles' *sight*. However, it is also possible that this was the cloud of glory associated with the presence of God in the Old Testament and with Jesus at his transfiguration (Exodus 40:34; Mark 9:7).

¹⁰ They were looking intently up into the sky as he was going, when suddenly two men dressed in white stood beside them.

The *two men* who *stood beside* the apostles as Jesus ascended are not specifically identified, but their sudden appearance and their *white* clothing leave little doubt that they were angels. (See Matthew 28:2, 3; Mark 16:5; and John 20:12. Compare also Acts 10:30 and 11:13.)

¹¹ "Men of Galilee," they said, "why do you stand here looking into the sky? This same Jesus, who has been taken from you into heaven, will come back in the same way you have seen him go into heaven."

The gentle angelic rebuke seems to say, *"Why* are you staring at *the sky?* Unlike his transfiguration, Jesus will not rejoin you when the clouds roll back. But he will *come back* someday. Until he does, remember: you have his orders to carry out!"

The promise to the apostles (and to us) is that *this same Jesus* will return *in the same way* he left: personally, visibly, bodily, unexpectedly, and gloriously. At his trial, Jesus prophesied that his accusers would see him "coming on the clouds of heaven" (Mark 14:62; see also Revelation 1:7). The early Christians lived with a joyous expectation of Jesus' imminent return. This promise encouraged them as they moved out to win as many as possible to his kingdom before he came again. Our expectation of Jesus' coming should do the same for us, for this is certain: with every day that passes we are one day closer to his return.

THE DAY OF PENTECOST (ACTS 2:1-4, 37-47)

Establishing the Groundwork

Acts 1 records that following Jesus' ascension into Heaven, the apostles were guided by the Lord in selecting a replacement for Judas. This man, Matthias, most likely joined the other apostles during the time that they were "continually at the temple, praising God" (Luke 24:53). As the days passed, there must have been tremendous excitement among the apostles. They could hardly wait to share the good news of Jesus' resurrection. Still, they followed their Master's instructions and remained together until they were "clothed with power from on high" (Luke 24:49).

Examining the Text

I. The Spirit Descends (Acts 2:1-4)
A. Wondrous Wind (vv. 1, 2)

¹ When the day of Pentecost came, they were all together in one place.

The Feast of *Pentecost* was one of the three great sacred assemblies of the Jewish faith. (The others were Passover and Tabernacles, as noted in Exodus 23:14-17 and Leviticus 23:4-22.) The word *Pentecost* means "fifty" because the observance of this feast fell fifty days after the Passover Sabbath. This means that Pentecost would have occurred on the first day of the week. The church was born on the day we call Sunday.

Although Luke does not mention it, Pentecost was a harvest feast that celebrated the end of the barley harvest. It was also referred to as the "day of firstfruits" (Numbers 28:26), the "Feast of Harvest" (Exodus 23:16), and the "Feast of Weeks" (Numbers 28:26; Deuteronomy 16:10). The Jews observed it as a kind of thanksgiving day on which the firstfruits of the harvest were offered to God. Out of all the days that God could have chosen to begin his church, he chose a harvest celebration to plant the seed of the gospel and reap his first crop of souls. In addition, it was a harvest that included "Jews from every nation under heaven" (Acts 2:5). In time many of these converts would return to their homes as Christian missionaries.

Luke states that on this special day, *they were all together in one place.* But what group is designated by the pronoun *they?* Some students believe it refers to the 120 disciples mentioned in Acts 1:15. Others propose that it describes only the 12 apostles.

The 120 has been suggested primarily because that group included both men and women. That is significant because, at the beginning of his address to the crowd that gathered, Peter linked the events of Pentecost with the prophecy of Joel, who predicted that the Spirit of God would be poured out on both men and women (Acts 2:16-21; Joel 2:28-32). But this prophecy can also be understood to refer to all the work of the Holy Spirit from that first day (when the church began) until the day when Christ comes again—a period of time when many men and women would be filled with the Spirit. This removes the necessity for identifying the group as one containing men and women.

It is better to understand the word *they* in the verse before us as a reference to the twelve apostles for the following reasons: First, the immediate antecedent of the pronoun—the group named in the previous verse—is the apostles (Acts 1:26). Second, the group consisted only of Galileans (Acts 2:7). And finally, the group is specifically identified twice as Peter and the other eleven apostles (Acts 2:14, 37).

Some have suggested that the *one place* where the apostles were gathered was the upstairs room mentioned in Acts 1:13. If so, they must have left that place as the crowd began to assemble. Otherwise they could not have addressed so large a crowd that three thousand hearers could respond to their message. For that reason, many students believe that the *one place* was somewhere around the temple courts—perhaps near the Court of the Gentiles. Such a place would have been large enough to accommodate the thousands who would soon convene to hear the apostles' preaching. That the place is called a "house" in verse 2 is not a problem, since the temple—or even the tabernacle—is also called a house (Matthew 21:13; Mark 2:26; John 2:16, 17; Acts 7:47).

> *² Suddenly a sound like the blowing of a violent wind came from heaven and filled the whole house where they were sitting.*

Although the apostles had been waiting for the arrival of the Holy Spirit for ten days, they had not been informed exactly when or how he would appear. The suddenness with which he did come must have been startling. The first of a cluster of four events described is a *sound*—a noise that resembled the echoing roar of a *violent wind* (perhaps something akin to a tornado). Note that Luke does not say that an actual wind was present, only the sound that a wind would have made. He may have been using a play on words, for the Greek word that is translated "wind" is also the word that is translated, in other contexts, as "spirit." Like the wind, the Holy Spirit is unseen but not unnoticed; his movement is mysterious and powerful, and the effects of his working are undeniable (John 3:8).

B. Testifying Tongues (vv. 3, 4)

³ They saw what seemed to be tongues of fire that separated and came to rest on each of them.

Here Luke tries to describe the second event, which was something the apostles *saw*. The shape of what they saw resembled a group of *tongues of fire*. Apparently the tongues moved from a central point, then separated until one bright shape came to rest *on each of* the apostles. If there had been any doubt that the sound of the wind signaled that something unusual was about to happen, this visual sign would certainly have put such doubt to rest.

⁴ All of them were filled with the Holy Spirit and began to speak in other tongues as the Spirit enabled them.

The last two events comprised another pair of miracles. The first miracle was that twelve ordinary human beings *were filled with the Holy Spirit*. The second miracle was the result of the Spirit's power; he *enabled* the apostles *to speak in other tongues*, thus providing them with the ability they needed to preach "the wonders of God" (v. 11) to the crowd that soon gathered.

Jesus had promised the apostles that they would be "baptized with the Holy Spirit" (Acts 1:5). Now that moment had arrived. Both expressions, being "baptized" and being "filled" with the Spirit, suggest that the apostles were completely under the control of the Spirit. Verse 6 makes it quite clear that the tongues spoken by the apostles were recognizable languages or dialects that the listeners readily understood without the aid of an interpreter.

Speaking in foreign languages that the apostles had never learned served two purposes. First, it gave clear evidence to the audience that the power of God was upon the apostles. It also allowed the apostles to communicate more effectively with the many foreign visitors in Jerusalem by speaking to each group in its native language (v. 11). Since a most vital message was about to be delivered, it was important that it be understood without obstacles of any kind.

The people who had come to Jerusalem for Pentecost no doubt heard the sound of the "violent wind" and rushed out into the streets and into the temple area to find out what was causing all the commotion. By this time, the apostles had left the place where they were meeting when the Holy Spirit came upon them and they had gone out into a more public area, possibly in the temple court. We do not know if the tongues of fire remained on their heads when they went out among the people; if so, this certainly would have attracted the gathering crowd's attention.

The apostles, with Peter as their primary spokesman, used this unique opportunity to proclaim publicly for the first time that Jesus of Nazareth is the

Lord of glory and the Messiah for whom God's people had waited so long. Central to his message was the fact that, though these people had crucified Jesus, God had raised him from the dead (v. 32). Peter's declaration that God had made Jesus "both Lord and Christ" (v. 36) struck a blow at the people's messianic hopes. They had rejected the very Messiah they had awaited for centuries—what hope was left for them?

II. The Crowd Responds (Acts 2:37-41)
A. Inspired Instructions (vv. 37, 38)

37 When the people heard this, they were cut to the heart and said to Peter and the other apostles, "Brothers, what shall we do?"

Peter's preaching about Jesus *cut to the heart* of the people in the crowd. When they realized what they had done in crucifying the Son of God, they pleaded to *Peter and the other apostles, "Brothers, what shall we do?"* Was there any possible way to escape the destruction they deserved? (Addressing the apostles as *brothers* reflected the common heritage of the Jewish faith that the hearers shared with the apostles.)

38 Peter replied, "Repent and be baptized, every one of you, in the name of Jesus Christ for the forgiveness of your sins. And you will receive the gift of the Holy Spirit.

On one occasion, Jesus had promised to give Peter "the keys of the kingdom of heaven" (Matthew 16:19). Now on this special day, Peter, led by the Holy Spirit, used these keys for the first time to open the gates of the kingdom by declaring the terms of admission. *Peter* responded to the crowd's question with two commands and two promises. The first command was that those who believe in Jesus as the Messiah must *repent*. This theme was also a part of the preaching of John the Baptist and of Jesus (Matthew 3:1, 2; 4:17). Repentance means turning from sin and self-centeredness to obedience to God. Repentance does not mean that we suddenly become perfect, but rather that we start moving in a new direction, daily striving to become more like Jesus.

The second command was that those who believed and repented should be *baptized . . . in the name of Jesus Christ*. Water baptism was designed by God to be a common experience uniting all Christians (Ephesians 4:4-6). To be baptized in the name of Jesus Christ means that the act of baptism is carried out under his authority and by his terms. In baptism we reenact what Jesus did for us: we die (to sin, in repentance), we are buried (in the water), and we are resurrected, or brought forth from the water, into "a new life" (Romans 6:1-4).

The two promises attached to faith in Jesus Christ, expressed in repentance and baptism, are the *forgiveness of . . . sins* and *the gift of the Holy Spirit.* We should not think that God forgives our sins as a "reward" for our faith, repentance, and baptism. We are saved by the grace of what Jesus did for us, not by any goodness of anything that we do for him. The Holy Spirit comes to dwell within us and renew us so that we may grow daily to become more like Christ. As forgiveness removes the condemnation of our sin, so the Holy Spirit breaks our slavery to sin.

B. Warning Words (vv. 39-41)

[39] *"The promise is for you and your children and for all who are far off— for all whom the Lord our God will call."*

God has had one unchangeable plan for man's redemption, and that plan was described by Peter on Pentecost in answer to the crowd's question, "What shall we do?" The "keys to the kingdom," or terms of admission, that he announced and the accompanying *promise* to be received by those who complied with those terms were made available to three groups. The first was the crowd before Peter that day. They represented all of that generation of Jews. The second group comprised the children of those gathered—in other words, the generation that was to come. This indicated that God's promise was not limited simply to the time of the apostles' ministry. The third group included *all who are far off*, which indicated that the promise of the gospel was not to be limited by any national or geographical boundaries. Peter himself later used his "keys" to open the gates of the kingdom to Gentiles by means of the conversion of Cornelius and his household (Acts 10:44-48).

The phrase *all whom the Lord our God will call* brings to mind the concluding words of the prophecy from Joel that Peter had cited earlier (Joel 2:32). It should be noted that this verse also includes the words, "And everyone who calls on the name of the Lord will be saved." Thus God's call does not diminish the need for human responsibility. We answer God's call by calling on his name (Acts 22:16).

It is important to distinguish between the "gift" that was "promised" to the apostles (Acts 1:4) and the *promise* offered here at Pentecost by Peter. What Peter offered on this day was something that every human being needs: forgiveness of sins, for all have sinned (Romans 3:23). The unusual power that enabled the apostles to speak in languages they had not studied was not intended for every human being. Its uniqueness stands out when we realize that only twice is this power mentioned again—once when the gates of the kingdom were opened to the Gentiles by Peter (Acts 10:44-48), and again when Paul discussed its use (and abuse) among the Corinthians (see 1 Corinthians 12–14).

40 With many other words he warned them; and he pleaded with them, "Save yourselves from this corrupt generation."

This clearly indicates that, although many in the crowd were convicted, they were not yet saved. They were part of a *corrupt generation*, the most obvious sign of this being the fact that they had rejected and crucified God's Messiah. They were to *save* themselves by complying with the conditions Peter had stated earlier. No one is saved apart from his or her own volition.

41 Those who accepted his message were baptized, and about three thousand were added to their number that day.

With this verse, Luke summarizes the spiritual harvest that the Lord reaped at the harvest festival of Pentecost. Those in the crowd who believed what Peter had preached about Jesus, who had placed their faith in him as Lord and Christ, and who were willing to turn from their sins in repentance *were baptized*—most likely in some of the many pools in Jerusalem.

To baptize *three thousand* people on *that day* should not be considered impossible. The apostles would not have had to do all the baptizing. If those who had been baptized in turn baptized others, the entire number could have been baptized in a few hours.

III. The Church Grows (Acts 2:42-47)
A. Primary Practices (v. 42)

42 They devoted themselves to the apostles' teaching and to the fellowship, to the breaking of bread and to prayer.

The early Christians were a *devoted* people; they lived faithfully in regard to four essential elements of church life. First, all of them came under the instruction of the *apostles' teaching*, whether in large groups at the temple or in smaller groups in homes (v. 46). Consider that at this point, not a single book of the New Testament had been written. But the church "inherited" the Old Testament from the Jews, and that was taught by the apostles—not as a law to be followed, but as fulfilled by Christ. Quite naturally, the early Christians looked to the apostles for teaching leadership. These men had accompanied Jesus throughout his ministry and had been empowered with the Holy Spirit in a special manner to enable them to remember what they had been taught (John 14:26).

Second, the church in Jerusalem devoted itself to *fellowship*—a commonly shared life. These followers of Jesus created a new and close community within the city as they supported and encouraged each other. The idea of fellowship (the Greek word is *koinonia*) can embrace both a spiritual communion (as in Philippians 2:1) and a material sharing (as in 2 Corinthians 8:4, where the word is translated "sharing"). The Greek text in Acts 2:42 literally says "*the* fellowship," perhaps highlighting the special concern for one another that characterized these followers of Jesus. Such concern is noted in verses 44 and 45 and in Acts 4:32-35.

The third and fourth items to which these believers committed themselves relate more directly to worship. While the term *breaking of bread* can simply mean sharing a meal (as in verse 46), here the presence of the definite article *the* most likely indicates a reference to the Lord's Supper. Finally, *prayer* was vital to the early church—a theme emphasized throughout Acts (Acts 4:24-31; 6:4, 6; 11:4, 5; 12:5; 13:3; 14:23; 16:25; 22:17; 28:8). Here the Greek text uses the definite article and the plural noun: "*the* prayers." Perhaps this term designates regular times of prayer at fixed hours, such as (but not limited to) the Jewish time for prayer that Peter and John were observing in Acts 3:1.

B. Startling Signs (v. 43)

⁴³ Everyone was filled with awe, and many wonders and miraculous signs were done by the apostles.

Wonders and miraculous signs supported the authority of the teaching of the *apostles*, for such demonstrations of God's power indicated that they spoke on his behalf (2 Corinthians 12:12; Hebrews 2:3, 4). Luke gives several examples of such miracles in the rest of his account (Acts 3:1-10; 5:12-16; 8:13; 9:32-42; 14:8-10; 19:11, 12; 20:9-12; 28:7-9).

C. Common Concern (vv. 44-47)

⁴⁴, ⁴⁵ All the believers were together and had everything in common. Selling their possessions and goods, they gave to anyone as he had need.

What Luke describes here is not the establishment of an early Christian commune; it is simply a description of how wealthier *believers* helped their poorer brothers and sisters. Some were *selling their possessions and goods*, then giving the money obtained from these transactions *to anyone as he had need*.

It is important to remember in considering these actions the unique situation that faced the early Christians in Jerusalem. Three thousand people had been baptized; many were Jews who had come to the city from distant places to attend the Feast of Pentecost. Now they were far from home and had doubtless brought just enough money and provisions to last for the days they planned to be away. When they became followers of Jesus, they remained in the city, learning from the apostles' teaching and desiring to become more acquainted with the new life they had chosen to embrace before returning to their homes. Thus there would have been a special need for sharing during this time.

There is no command, either by Jesus or by the apostles, that bound such a practice as this upon churches or Christians in general. That certain families kept their private homes is clear from the following verse. It is true that the example of these early Christians should move us to show compassion toward brothers and sisters in need, but it is not true that our benevolence must be expressed in exactly the same manner as it was within the Jerusalem church.

⁴⁶ Every day they continued to meet together in the temple courts. They broke bread in their homes and ate together with glad and sincere hearts,

It may seem surprising that the early Christians continued to worship *in the temple courts*. However, one should remember that the antagonisms that later affected relations between Jews and Christians had not yet developed. Those Jews who became Christians did not look upon Judaism as something opposed to Christianity. Rather, they saw Christianity as the flowering of their previous Jewish faith. Meeting in the temple area gave them the opportunity to witness of their newfound faith to Jews who came to worship.

In addition, the temple courts at Jerusalem covered several acres and had many porches or porticos where it would be convenient to gather for teaching. The gathering of groups of believers in different areas would not be considered unusual. The daily meetings may have taken place during the regular prayer times and may have included teaching sessions conducted by the apostles. Furthermore, these Christians met together in private *homes* to share their meals and their joy.

⁴⁷ . . . praising God and enjoying the favor of all the people. And the Lord added to their number daily those who were being saved.

Although the early Christians were faithful in *praising God*, the *favor of all the people* was something that the church could not expect to enjoy forever. This "honeymoon period" would soon be replaced by opposition and persecution. But the Lord was able to use both good times and bad to keep adding to the Christians' *number daily those who were being saved* (as he still is). New Christians become a part of the Lord's church at the same moment that they are saved.

AN EXAMPLE OF GENEROSITY IN ACTION (ACTS 4:32-37)

Establishing the Groundwork

As noted in the previous study, the second chapter of Acts concludes with a description of the Jerusalem church as a joyful, worshiping, caring, and growing body of believers. Acts 3 and 4 are largely taken up with the healing of a lame man at a gate of the temple (Acts 3:1-10) and the aftermath of this miracle: Peter's preaching to the crowd that quickly gathered (Acts 3:11-26), resulting in additional converts (Acts 4:4); the arrest of Peter and John (Acts 4:3); their release the following day, with a warning not to speak again in Jesus' name (Acts 4:18-22); and the prayers of the believers for boldness in proclaiming the message of Jesus (Acts 4:23-31). Chapter 4 closes with a summary of the unity of the early Christians and the way they shared their possessions.

Examining the Text

I. A Generous Church (Acts 4:32-35)
A. Believers' Unity (v. 32)

32 All the believers were one in heart and mind. No one claimed that any of his possessions was his own, but they shared everything they had.

Acts 4:31 tells us that after Peter and John and those gathered with them prayed, "the place where they were meeting was shaken" and that "they were all filled with the Holy Spirit and spoke the word of God boldly." The unity described in the verse before us (*one in heart and mind*) was another sign of the Spirit's presence. This oneness manifested itself in a willingness to share their *possessions* with those in need. These followers of Jesus realized that all they had belonged to God; they were merely stewards of his property.

B. Apostles' Testimony (v. 33)

33 With great power the apostles continued to testify to the resurrection of the Lord Jesus, and much grace was upon them all.

The *apostles* had all seen the risen Lord. He had showed himself to them and had given "many convincing proofs that he was alive" (Acts 1:3). Peter and John's words before the Sanhedrin could have been uttered by any of the twelve: "For we cannot help speaking about what we have seen and heard" (Acts 4:20). As the apostles faithfully bore their testimony, *much grace was upon them all*—most likely referring to all the Christians. At this point, they were still "enjoying the favor of all the people" (Acts 2:47). It was because the members of the Sanhedrin feared the reaction of the people that they had dismissed Peter and John with only threats (Acts 4:21).

C. Believers' Actions (vv. 34, 35)

34, 35 *There were no needy persons among them. For from time to time those who owned lands or houses sold them, brought the money from the sales and put it at the apostles' feet, and it was distributed to anyone as he had need.*

As noted earlier in the comments on Acts 2:44, 45, a special situation confronted these early Christians in Jerusalem. Many Jews had come from some distance away to celebrate Pentecost, and were now planning to stay longer than they had intended. They wanted to learn more about Jesus from the apostles and to become better established in their new faith. Each would return to his or her home as a witness of this new faith. Thus it was essential that some provision be made for these people during their stay.

Since we have no record of any commandment given to individuals to sell their *houses* or *lands*, one must assume that this action was voluntary—an exercise of compassion by those who were genuinely concerned for their *needy* brothers and sisters in Christ. This assumption is confirmed in chapter 5. There Peter reminds Ananias that both his land and the money he received in the sale of the land were at his disposal (Acts 5:4). There was no compulsion for him to sell or to give the proceeds to the church.

Responsibility for distributing the money collected naturally fell to the *apostles* at this point, for they were the spiritual leaders. Later, this responsibility became too time-consuming for them, leading to the selection of trustworthy, Spirit-filled men who could oversee this ministry equally as well (Acts 6:1-6).

II. A Generous Individual (Acts 4:36, 37)
A. His Identity (v. 36)

36 *Joseph, a Levite from Cyprus, whom the apostles called Barnabas (which means Son of Encouragement),*

This verse and the following one set before us a specific example of Christian compassion in action. A man whose given name was *Joseph* was given the nickname of *Barnabas* by *the apostles*. Barnabas is an Aramaic name meaning *Son of Encouragement*. The phrase *Son of* is a Hebrew idiom often used to describe a person's character or characteristics. Jesus literally referred to Judas as the "son of destruction" in John 17:12, meaning that Judas was a man characterized by the evil that led to his downfall.

Barnabas's background as a *Levite* meant that he would have been a Jew who was quite knowledgeable of the Mosaic law. The Levites were the descendants of the tribe of Levi from which the priesthood came, specifically from the family of Aaron. The non-Aaronic Levites were those who performed services in the temple apart from the more sacred responsibilities of sacrifice and prayer, which were reserved exclusively for the Aaronic priesthood.

It is also recorded that Barnabas's home was *Cyprus*, a large island located in the eastern Mediterranean Sea, about sixty miles west of Syria and some forty miles south of the southern coast of Turkey. These ingredients in his background helped to prepare Barnabas for the important role he would later play in encouraging and aiding the spread of the gospel throughout new territories, particularly during Paul's first missionary journey (Acts 13:1-3).

B. His Initiative (v. 37)

[37] *. . . sold a field he owned and brought the money and put it at the apostles' feet.*

Barnabas's ownership of land may seem strange, since Levites, according to the law of Moses, were not to be landowners (Numbers 18:20-24; Deuteronomy 10:9). But these regulations may not have applied to Levites in other countries such as Cyprus. Perhaps Barnabas sold land he owned in Cyprus and brought the proceeds to the apostles. Or he may have been married, and the land sold could have been from his wife's property. It is also possible that by this time, the regulations in the law of Moses were no longer recognized or enforced.

The sale of property and the giving of the *money* from the sale to the church was purely voluntary. This is illustrated by the very next incident recorded by Luke, which provides a stark contrast to the generosity of Barnabas: it is the deceit of Ananias and Sapphira (Acts 5:1-11). Peter's words of rebuke to Ananias show that Ananias was not forced to sell his land or share his money after the land was sold: "Didn't it belong to you before it was sold? And after it was sold, wasn't the money at your disposal?" (Acts 5:4).

Christians today should follow the example of the early church's generosity. Paul commended the sacrificial yet cheerful giving of the Macedonians and urged the Corinthians to imitate them (2 Corinthians 8, 9). John writes that anyone who does not share with a brother in need does not really have the love of God in him (1 John 3:17). This is true, even if that brother is halfway around the globe.

How to Say It

AARON. *Air*-un.

AARONIC. Air-*ahn*-ik.

ANANIAS. An-uh-*nye*-us.

ARAMAIC. *Air*-uh-*may*-ik (strong accent on *may*).

BARNABAS. *Bar*-nuh-bus.

CORNELIUS. Cor-*neel*-yus.

CYPRUS. *Sigh*-prus.

GENTILES. *Jen*-tiles.

KOINONIA *(Greek).* koy-no-*nee*-uh.

LEVITE. *Lee*-vite.

MACEDONIANS. Mass-eh-*doe*-nee-unz.

MATTHIAS. Muh-*thigh*-us (*th* as in *thin*).

MEDITERRANEAN. *Med*-uh-tuh-*ray*-nee-un (strong accent on *ray*).

MESSIAH. Meh-*sigh*-uh.

MESSIANIC. Mess-ee-*an*-ick.

MOSAIC. Mo-*zay*-ik.

NAZARETH. *Naz*-uh-reth.

PENTECOST. *Pent*-ih-kost.

SAPPHIRA. Suh-*fye*-ruh.

SYRIA. *Sear*-ee-uh.

THEOPHILUS. Thee-*ahf*-ih-luss (*th* as in *thin*).

Chapter 2

Growth of Persecution and Outreach
Acts 5:27-42; 6:1-7; 7:54-60; 8:26-40; 9:1-6, 10-20

THE APOSTLES BEFORE THE SANHEDRIN (ACTS 5:27-42)

Establishing the Groundwork

As noted during the examination of the previous passage (at the conclusion of chapter 1), the end of Acts 4 and the beginning of Acts 5 provide a study in contrasts: the generosity of Barnabas and the greed of Ananias and Sapphira. After Ananias and Sapphira died because of their deceit, a respectful fear spread through the church (Acts 5:11). Still, the church grew as the apostles preached and healed many people. Their successful evangelistic efforts soon aroused the jealous wrath of the Sanhedrin, who had all the apostles arrested and held overnight for trial.

Near dawn an angel came and released the apostles, telling them to go back to the temple area and resume their preaching. Thus, when the Sanhedrin sent to have the jailed prisoners brought before them, the officers sent found no one there. They ran back to the council to announce that the men were missing. Then, in the middle of their report, another messenger reported that the apostles were back in the temple area—preaching Jesus again! This time the captain of the guard took some men to re-arrest the apostles (quietly, because of the high esteem in which the general public held them) and to return them for trial before the Sanhedrin.

Amazingly, the council seemed uninterested in how the apostles' miraculous escape from jail had occurred. This group was far more concerned with the apostles' stubborn refusal to keep silent about Jesus.

Examining the Text

I. Apostles' Testimony (Acts 5:27-32)
A. Charge of Disobedience (vv. 27, 28)

27 Having brought the apostles, they made them appear before the Sanhedrin to be questioned by the high priest.

On a previous occasion, only Peter and John had faced the *Sanhedrin* (Acts 4:13-15). The same group that tried Jesus was about to put his *apostles* on trial.

The *high priest* was the president of the Sanhedrin and thus began the hearing. Technically Caiaphas was the high priest (Matthew 26:3, 57; John 11:49; 18:24), but Luke calls Annas the high priest in Acts 4:6. Thus it is quite likely that Annas is the high priest in question here. The discrepancy is resolved when one realizes that the Romans had deposed Annas and put his son-in-law Caiaphas in the position instead. But the Jews considered the high priesthood a lifetime position, so even the deposed Annas was regarded by them as the legitimate high priest. Luke refers to the dual "high priesthood of Annas and Caiaphas" (Luke 3:2), and John describes Annas's leading role in the proceedings against Jesus (John 18:13-24), using the title high priest for Annas (v. 19) as well as for Caiaphas (vv. 13, 24).

> [28] *"We gave you strict orders not to teach in this name," he said. "Yet you have filled Jerusalem with your teaching and are determined to make us guilty of this man's blood."*

The high priest brought two charges against the apostles. But first, he called attention to the fact that these men had ignored the Sanhedrin's earlier *strict orders* to Peter and John *not to teach in* the *name* of Jesus Christ (Acts 4:18). What the council had demanded of just two of the apostles was binding on all of them. Notice that the high priest refused even to say the name *Jesus*. He then charged the apostles with having *filled Jerusalem with* their *teaching*. They had made Jesus "the talk of the town." The high priest, however, tried to diminish this accomplishment by claiming that the teaching was theirs, originating with them and not with God.

Second, the high priest accused the apostles of blaming the Sanhedrin for Jesus' death. His reference to making the group *guilty of this man's blood* may reflect what transpired during Jesus' trial before Pilate. After the Roman governor had declared Jesus to be innocent and had publicly washed his hands, he stated that he was "innocent of this man's blood." Then the crowd (spurred on by the religious leaders) shouted back at Pilate that they would accept the responsibility for Jesus' blood (Matthew 27:24, 25). Perhaps these men feared that their words were coming back to haunt them.

B. Defense of Obedience (vv. 29-32)

> [29] *Peter and the other apostles replied: "We must obey God rather than men!*

Peter's defense was quite similar to the one he made to the Sanhedrin the previous time that he and John had appeared before them (Acts 4:19): what *God* says is more important than what *men* say. When the laws of man and God conflict, any and all human orders must be brought into harmony with divine directives; if reconciliation is impossible, human laws must be disregarded.

³⁰ *"The God of our fathers raised Jesus from the dead—whom you had killed by hanging him on a tree.*

Peter then called attention to another contrast between the will of God and the will of the council. God *raised Jesus from the dead* after the council had *killed* him *by hanging him on a tree* (the cross). The law of Moses declared that the body of anyone who was executed for a crime should be hung on a tree for public display and that such a person had God's curse on him (Deuteronomy 21:22, 23). The members of the Sanhedrin had treated Jesus in this manner, intending to humiliate him. They did not realize that in so doing, they were fulfilling the promises made by God to their *fathers*. The curse associated with Jesus' death was not for his own sins; he became a curse for us (Galatians 3:13) by taking the punishment that we rightfully deserved for our sins.

³¹ *"God exalted him to his own right hand as Prince and Savior that he might give repentance and forgiveness of sins to Israel.*

For someone to be *exalted to* the *right hand* of a monarch meant that the ruler had given that individual both honor and authority. This is also clear from the titles of *Prince* and *Savior* that are used of Jesus.

Peter then elaborated on how Jesus carries out his mission as Savior: he is said to *give repentance and forgiveness of sins to Israel*. This does not mean that Jesus forces anyone to repent, but that he provides what is necessary for us to carry out this crucial step of returning to God. Jesus has sent the Holy Spirit to convict us of our sins (John 16:7-11). He has shown us the love of God by giving his life to pay for our sins (1 John 4:9, 10). Because of this, it is now possible for us to turn from our sins and turn back to God. As Peter preached on the Day of Pentecost, repentance and forgiveness are closely linked (Acts 2:38).

³² *"We are witnesses of these things, and so is the Holy Spirit, whom God has given to those who obey him."*

Peter concluded his defense by stating the *witnesses* whose testimony supported his case. This was in keeping with the requirements of the law of Moses (Deuteronomy 17:6). Peter himself, along with the rest of the apostles (*we*), made up one group of witnesses to who Jesus is and what he has done. The second witness was the *Holy Spirit*, who supported the apostles' testimony by empowering them to do miraculous signs (Hebrews 2:3, 4).

Peter then reminded the Sanhedrin that God gives his Spirit only *to those who obey him*. The unrepentant, disobedient world cannot receive the Spirit, nor can the Spirit dwell in the unredeemed (John 14:17; 1 Corinthians 6:19). The apostles were obeying God by continuing to preach Jesus, even when this meant disobeying the Sanhedrin.

II. Gamaliel's Advice (Acts 5:33-39)
A. Learn from the Past (vv. 33-37)

33 When they heard this, they were furious and wanted to put them to death.

The members of the Sanhedrin realized that only *death* could stop the apostles' testimony, and, at that moment, the council was so *furious* that they were poised to execute all 12 of them (as they later did Stephen).

34 But a Pharisee named Gamaliel, a teacher of the law, who was honored by all the people, stood up in the Sanhedrin and ordered that the men be put outside for a little while.

At this crucial moment, the Lord provided a voice of calm and reason. *Gamaliel* was the most respected Jewish *teacher* of his day. The apostle Paul (when he was Saul) studied under Gamaliel before he became a Christian (Acts 22:3). Gamaliel *ordered* that the apostles be removed from the meeting *for a little while* so that he could speak freely about their case.

35 Then he addressed them: "Men of Israel, consider carefully what you intend to do to these men.

Gamaliel began his remarks by suggesting caution and restraint rather than hasty judgment and violent action against the apostles.

36 "Some time ago Theudas appeared, claiming to be somebody, and about four hundred men rallied to him. He was killed, all his followers were dispersed, and it all came to nothing.

In typical rabbinical style, Gamaliel appealed to recent well-known events to remind his hearers of the lessons of history. His first illustration called attention to a man named *Theudas*. The only information we know about this person and his *followers* is what Gamaliel tells us. In 4 BC King Herod the Great died. During the power vacuum that resulted, many insurrectionists rose up trying to seize control. The situation became so bad that the Roman army came in to put down all the uprisings. Theudas may well have been one of these insurgent leaders. His boast to be *somebody* was likely a claim to be a prophet of God or even the Messiah.

Theudas attracted a small following of *four hundred men* (many more than Jesus' 12). However, as soon as Theudas was *killed*, his movement fell apart. Gamaliel suggested that perhaps Jesus' movement would also end up as a similar futile endeavor.

[37] *"After him, Judas the Galilean appeared in the days of the census and led a band of people in revolt. He too was killed, and all his followers were scattered.*

The writings of the Jewish historian Josephus provide information about *Judas the Galilean.* In AD 6 the Roman governor of Syria and Judea, Quirinius (mentioned in Luke 2:2), took a *census* of the territories he controlled in order to determine how much he could raise in taxes from them. (Note that this is a different census from the one mentioned in Luke 2:2.) Judas of Galilee publicly opposed the census and its taxation, claiming that this action was just the first step to enslaving the Jews and causing them to serve another god. He called on all Jews to oppose this taxation—by force if necessary. He attracted a large following to his endeavor. However, once more the might of Rome prevailed and crushed the uprising. Judas *was killed*, and all the people whom he had persuaded to join his cause *were scattered* and returned to their normal lives, except for those injured or killed.

Although Judas of Galilee had been very popular for a time, at this point the only group who followed his anti-Roman philosophy was the group known as the Zealots. Gamaliel seemed to be saying that the Sanhedrin tolerated the Zealot movement, so why not be equally tolerant of these followers of Jesus?

B. Leave These Men Alone (vv. 38, 39)

[38] *"Therefore, in the present case I advise you: Leave these men alone! Let them go! For if their purpose or activity is of human origin, it will fail.*

Gamaliel now stated his position concerning the apostles: *Leave these men alone! Let them go!* If their movement is merely the remains left over from the followers of some dead fanatical leader, it will disappear on its own without help from the Sanhedrin. There was, however, another possibility to consider.

[39] *"But if it is from God, you will not be able to stop these men; you will only find yourselves fighting against God."*

Suppose the apostles' movement was indeed *from God.* If so, Gamaliel asked his fellow council members, did they really think they could successfully fight *against God?* They were supposed to be the religious leaders of the Jews; did they want to appear to be God's enemies? To avoid such an embarrassing position, the council should heed Gamaliel's advice and release the apostles.

III. Trial's Outcome (Acts 5:40-42)
A. Council's Decision (v. 40)

40 His speech persuaded them. They called the apostles in and had them flogged. Then they ordered them not to speak in the name of Jesus, and let them go.

The Sanhedrin agreed with Gamaliel that putting the *apostles* to death would not be wise. At the same time, these men had to be given some kind of punishment for disobeying the explicit instructions of the council. So each apostle was *flogged*, most likely with the standard 39 lashes. The number was carefully counted so that the punishment did not exceed the 40 lashes allowed by the law (Deuteronomy 25:3).

The Sanhedrin then ordered the apostles to do what they had already refused to do: to refrain from speaking *in the name of Jesus.* They *let them go*, no doubt hoping that the sting of the whip would silence these troublemakers. How wrong they were!

B. Apostles' Response (vv. 41, 42)

41 The apostles left the Sanhedrin, rejoicing because they had been counted worthy of suffering disgrace for the Name.

The *apostles'* desire to serve Jesus was not diminished in any way by the beating they received; on the contrary, they *left the Sanhedrin* determined more than ever to proclaim the good news. In spite of their pain, these men were *rejoicing!* They were honored to be dishonored for Jesus, and dignified by their indignity on his behalf.

42 Day after day, in the temple courts and from house to house, they never stopped teaching and proclaiming the good news that Jesus is the Christ.

The apostles made it their practice *day after day* to go right back to the *temple courts* where they had been arrested and continue *teaching and proclaiming the good news that Jesus is the Christ*—the very "crime" for which they had been seized and beaten. In addition, they continued to instruct believers *from house to house.* Thus, whether in public or private settings, regardless of the cost, they *never stopped* telling others about Jesus. Their unconquerable faith and devotion continues to challenge us today.

THE CHOOSING OF THE SEVEN (ACTS 6:1-7)

Establishing the Groundwork

The first five chapters of Acts expand on the promise given by Jesus to the 11 apostles just before he ascended into Heaven: "But you will receive power when the Holy Spirit comes on you; and you will be my witnesses in Jerusalem, and in all Judea and Samaria, and to the ends of the earth" (Acts 1:8). Acts 1–5 is concerned primarily with charting the spread of the gospel throughout Jerusalem and Judea and the increasing numbers of disciples. With such rapid growth, however, came new problems and challenges that the church had to address.

Examining the Text

I. A Sensitive Subject (Acts 6:1-4)
A. The Widows' Complaint (v. 1)

¹ In those days when the number of disciples was increasing, the Grecian Jews among them complained against the Hebraic Jews because their widows were being overlooked in the daily distribution of food.

The phrase *those days* describes a time of growth and opportunity for the church that continued in spite of the threats against the apostles recounted in the previous chapter. Before the Day of Pentecost, 120 disciples had prayed together (Acts 1:15); then on that day 3000 believers declared themselves obedient followers of Jesus as Lord and Christ (Acts 2:41). Daily additions soon brought the number of converts to 5000 men (Acts 2:47; 4:4). To that were added "more and more men and women" (Acts 5:14). And in the verse before us it is noted that *the number of disciples was increasing.*

We do not know how much time had elapsed between the events at Pentecost and the situation described at the beginning of Acts 6. It may have been several weeks or even several months. We do know that at this point in the church's growth, all of the followers of Jesus were Jewish. Most were *Jews* by birth. Others were proselytes (Gentile converts to Judaism). These individuals were Jews, but they were *Grecian* in language and culture. Some of these may have been among the 3000 converted on the Day of Pentecost (note the various lands mentioned in Acts 2:8-11). They may have remained in Jerusalem to become a part of the new fellowship of believers in Jesus (Acts 2:42-47). Not having homes or employment in Jerusalem, some of these—especially the widows—would have been among those who were most dependent on the *daily distribution of food.*

As the church grew in substantial numbers, the task for caring for those in need became increasingly more difficult. (Any church that experiences rapid growth is usually subject to such "growing pains.") Widows were especially likely to be overlooked because they had no husbands to watch out for them. Since they were, in a sense, foreigners, the Grecian widows would have had fewer friends and family to make sure their needs were not ignored.

B. The Apostles' Counsel (vv. 2-4)

² So the Twelve gathered all the disciples together and said, "It would not be right for us to neglect the ministry of the word of God in order to wait on tables.

It appears that *the Twelve* (the apostles) were the ones in charge of the daily distribution of food, so they were the ones who received the complaints of those being overlooked. Instead of simply imposing a solution on their own, they *gathered all the disciples together*. The apostles pointed out that if they increased their attention toward addressing people's physical needs, they would have *to neglect* their divinely assigned work—*the ministry of the word of God*. This ministry involved the proclamation of the gospel message in accordance with Jesus' commission to them (Acts 1:8). The apostles were not suggesting that *to wait on tables* was demeaning or beneath their dignity. They were simply recognizing that God had established certain priorities for them that they dared not ignore.

³ "Brothers, choose seven men from among you who are known to be full of the Spirit and wisdom. We will turn this responsibility over to them

The problem had arisen *among* the people, so it was only right to let the solution be found among them. In addition, by allowing the people to make this choice no one could accuse the apostles of being partial in any selections they made. *Seven men* were chosen, most likely because it was determined that this would be an adequate number to address the problem at hand. To preserve the sacred purpose of the entire enterprise, they must be *full of the Spirit*. To handle this sensitive matter correctly, they also needed to possess *wisdom*.

These seven men are often referred to as the first "deacons" of the early church, a term that is derived from the Greek word *diakonos*. The basis for this seems to be the use of two other words in this passage from the same root as *diakonos*. The word *distribution* in verse 1 is from *diakonia*, and the verb for *wait on tables* in verse 2 is from *diakoneo*. However, the Bible never explicitly refers to the Seven as deacons. While deacons today are often responsible for the more "material" matters of church life, the two best known of the Seven

(Stephen and Philip) were especially noted for their speaking and evangelism (Acts 6:9, 10; 8:5, 26-40; 21:8).

4 ". . . and will give our attention to prayer and the ministry of the word."

By delegating the daily food distribution to the seven men, the apostles would be able to give themselves without interruption to their primary task of providing spiritual leadership through *prayer and ministry of the word* (the Greek word translated *ministry* is *diakonia*).

II. A Successful Solution (Acts 6:5-7)
A. Chosen Group (vv. 5, 6)

5 This proposal pleased the whole group. They chose Stephen, a man full of faith and of the Holy Spirit; also Philip, Procorus, Nicanor, Timon, Parmenas, and Nicolas from Antioch, a convert to Judaism.

We are not told how the seven men were chosen. It must have involved a procedure that was familiar and generally accepted among the believers. All of the seven men had Greek names; thus it appears that the Grecians' complaint was being respected. But we cannot attach too much importance to the names, for two of the apostles (Andrew and another Philip) also had Greek names.

Stephen is named first among the Seven, and he is described most fully. This prepares the reader for the record of his activity that will follow. *Philip*, later referred to as "the evangelist" (Acts 21:8), is named second. The reference to *Nicolas* as a *proselyte* and as being *from Antioch* foreshadows the prominence of Antioch as a city where the gospel was first preached to Jews and Gentiles alike, and where the disciples were first called Christians (Acts 11:26).

6 They presented these men to the apostles, who prayed and laid their hands on them.

The seven *men* were *presented . . . to the apostles, who prayed and laid their hands on them* (similar to the modern practice of "ordination" of certain church leaders). The laying on of the apostles' hands provided special empowering by which Stephen and Philip were able to work miracles (Acts 6:8; 8:5-8, 13-20). Perhaps others of the Seven also performed miracles, but we are not told of this in the Scriptures.

B. Continued Growth (v. 7)

7 So the word of God spread. The number of disciples in Jerusalem increased rapidly, and a large number of priests became obedient to the faith.

Positive results came almost immediately from the wise and effective handling of the Grecians' complaint. *The word of God spread:* the gospel continued to bear fruit, as *the number of disciples in Jerusalem increased rapidly.* An astonishing development in the church's growth is also noted: *a large number of priests* embraced *the faith.* The priests had been among the staunchest opponents of the apostles' preaching (Acts 4:1-3; 5:17, 18). By this notation, Luke provides another illustration of how, in spite of opposition from without and problems within, the gospel was able to continue its remarkable progress.

THE STONING OF STEPHEN (ACTS 7:54-60)

Establishing the Groundwork

Following the incident examined in the previous study, the focus of the record in Acts is directed to one of the Seven, Stephen, where it remains through the account of his message and martyrdom. Acts 6:8 cites the "great wonders and miraculous signs" that he did "among the people." Not everyone, however, was favorably impressed with Stephen. Some Jews, apparently of mixed national backgrounds (Acts 6:9), began to oppose him. When they failed in their efforts to discredit Stephen, they brought charges of blasphemy against him before the Sanhedrin; and he was brought to trial to answer the charges. In response, Stephen traced the course of Jewish history from its beginning to the current hour. He highlighted the continual rejection by God's people of both his message and his messengers. The crowning sin, said Stephen, lay in the Jewish leaders' rejection and crucifixion of Jesus. That accusation brought an immediate and hostile reaction from the council.

It should be noted that prior to Stephen's speech, Christianity was still considered as little more than a Jewish sect. But his speech drew a clear and unmistakable line between Judaism and Christianity, and that is the reason Luke includes this message in its entirety in his record.

Examining the Text

I. The Council's Hatred (Acts 7:54-58)
A. Furious Attitude (v. 54)

54 When they heard this, they were furious and gnashed their teeth at him.

To this point, Stephen's speech had traced the history of God's people and their frequent disobedience of him. Such behavior, Stephen said, was the precedent the current leaders were following, continuing to "resist the Holy Spirit" as their fathers had done. (v. 51). It appears that Stephen's audience interrupted his message, so *furious* were they at his accusations, especially his claim that they had "betrayed and murdered" the "Righteous One" (v. 52), an obvious reference to Jesus. They made no attempt to refute Stephen's accusations against them; they expressed their rage as they *gnashed*, or gritted, *their teeth at him*.

B. Faithful Witness (vv. 55, 56)

55 But Stephen, full of the Holy Spirit, looked up to heaven and saw the glory of God, and Jesus standing at the right hand of God.

Stephen was earlier described as *full of the Holy Spirit* (Acts 6:3, 5) and "full of God's grace and power" (Acts 6:8). The Spirit continued to guide Stephen at this critical moment. Perhaps as Isaiah had seen God's glorious presence when he received his prophetic call (Isaiah 6:1-5), so Stephen now *looked up to heaven and saw the glory of God* in the closing moments of his earthly life. But he also saw something more. In the position of highest honor and authority, *at the right hand of God*, Stephen saw *Jesus*. Jesus had said that he would be seen in glory at the right hand of power (Matthew 26:64; cf. Ephesians 1:20; Colossians 3:1; Hebrews 1:3). What everyone will see at the end of time, Stephen saw at that moment. But Stephen saw still more; he saw Jesus *standing*—perhaps even rising to his feet as though to welcome his faithful witness home in a magnificent gesture of divine approval.

56 "Look," he said. "I see heaven open and the Son of Man standing at the right hand of God."

Stephen's words bring to mind the testimony of Jesus before the Sanhedrin when asked if he were the Christ: "I am," said Jesus. "And you will see *the Son of Man* sitting *at the right hand of* the Mighty One and coming on the clouds of *heaven*" (Mark 14:62). Stephen was now describing Jesus using these same terms. Thus he was opening himself up to the same charges of blasphemy leveled against Jesus.

C. Furious Actions (vv. 57, 58)

57 At this they covered their ears and, yelling at the top of their voices, they all rushed at him,

The Sanhedrin had wanted some semblance of justification for killing Stephen. Earlier they had hired false witnesses to testify against him (Acts 6:11-14). But now they could use Stephen's own words against him, much as they had used Jesus' words to accuse him of blasphemy (Mark 14:63, 64). To make sure they heard no more, they covered their ears. Then, having become an enraged mob rather than a court of law, they rushed at Stephen, united in one mindless purpose—to destroy him.

58 *. . . dragged him out of the city and began to stone him. Meanwhile, the witnesses laid their clothes at the feet of a young man named Saul.*

The law of Moses prescribed death by stoning as the punishment for blasphemy (Leviticus 24:16). Roman law, however, did not allow the Jews to execute anyone. But Pilate, the Roman governor of Judea at this time, usually lived in Caesarea, which was nearly sixty miles from Jerusalem. At this point, what had become an unruly mob was in no mood to go through proper channels. Still, in keeping with the law of Moses (Deuteronomy 17:7), those involved made sure the proper *witnesses* took part in Stephen's execution. Stephen was also taken *out of the city* (Leviticus 24:13, 14; Numbers 15:32-36) to be stoned.

In this verse, we are introduced to *a young man named Saul.* Although there is no indication that he took part in the stoning, at least he approved of Stephen's death. The witnesses *laid their clothes* at Saul's *feet.* This probably involved the heavier outer garments that may have hampered the throwing of stones. Saul (later known as Paul) never forgot this scene: "And when the blood of your martyr Stephen was shed, I stood there giving my approval and guarding the clothes of those who were killing him" (Acts 22:20). What a remarkable introduction to the man who would later become the Lord's apostle to the Gentiles!

II. Stephen's Hope (Acts 7:59, 60)
A. Calling on Jesus (v. 59)

59 *While they were stoning him, Stephen prayed, "Lord Jesus, receive my spirit."*

Even *while* his enemies *were stoning him*, Stephen was continuing his courageous witness for Christ. His prayer echoed Jesus' words from the cross: "Father, into your hands I commit my spirit" (Luke 23:46).

B. Praying for His Enemies (v. 60)

60 *Then he fell on his knees and cried out, "Lord, do not hold this sin against them." When he had said this, he fell asleep.*

Stephen then *fell on his knees,* perhaps from weakness or perhaps deliberately in prayer. The fact that he *cried out* his last words, as his Lord did (Luke

23:46), indicates a clear mind and a desire to let his executioners know that he held no bitterness toward them. Stephen's words of forgiveness were once again similar to those of his Master (Luke 23:34). The reference to death as falling *asleep*—as a rest from labor and suffering—was used by Jesus in reference to Jairus's daughter (Luke 8:52, 53) and to Lazarus (John 11:11-14). The figure is nowhere more appropriate than in reference to Stephen's well-earned rest at the end of a turbulent day and at the end of service rendered courageously in the name of Jesus Christ.

PHILIP AND THE ETHIOPIAN EUNUCH (ACTS 8:26-40)

Establishing the Groundwork

Following the account of Stephen's martyrdom at the conclusion of Acts 7, we read at the beginning of chapter 8 of how "a great persecution broke out against the church at Jerusalem." Saul, whose participation in the death of Stephen is mentioned in Acts 7:58, became the most passionate persecutor of the followers of Jesus (Acts 8:3). Luke records that as the persecution intensified, "all except the apostles were scattered throughout Judea and Samaria" (Acts 8:1). Thus God, who "in all things . . . works for the good of those who love him" (Romans 8:28), used persecution to move the Christians beyond where they had been "staying put" to areas where Jesus had commanded his apostles to go (Acts 1:8).

The eighth chapter of Acts notes in particular the efforts of Philip in taking the gospel into new territory. This was not Philip the apostle, for, according to Acts 8:1, the apostles had remained in Jerusalem. This Philip was, like Stephen, one of the seven men chosen to manage the distribution of food to the needy widows in the Jerusalem church (Acts 6:1-6). Also like Stephen, Philip became an effective witness for Christ, leading many to follow Jesus and producing "great joy" among those Samaritans who did so (Acts 8:8). These efforts earned Philip the title of "evangelist" (Acts 21:8). And like Stephen, Philip had been given the power to do miracles—an ability that soon caught the attention of a sorcerer in Samaria named Simon (Acts 8:9-13). Simon was soundly rebuked by another Simon (Peter) for attempting to purchase such power (Acts 8:20-23). Later Peter, with John, continued preaching the gospel in many of the Samaritan villages on their way back to Jerusalem (Acts 8:25). Philip, however, went off in another direction; for the Lord had another task for him.

Examining the Text

I. Willing Teacher (Acts 8:26-35)
A. An Angel's Direction (v. 26)

26 Now an angel of the Lord said to Philip, "Go south to the road—the desert road—that goes down from Jerusalem to Gaza."

Philip may well have wondered why *an angel of the Lord* would want him to leave the region of Samaria when the work there had been so fruitful. But he accepted the angel's message as God's directive; he knew that his responsibility was to obey. *Gaza* was the southernmost of five ancient Philistine cities and was located near the coast of the Mediterranean Sea. That the road was a *desert road* indicates that it was primarily uninhabited.

B. The Eunuch's Description (vv. 27, 28)

27 So he started out, and on his way he met an Ethiopian eunuch, an important official in charge of all the treasury of Candace, queen of the Ethiopians. This man had gone to Jerusalem to worship,

The narrative wastes no time in moving from Philip's departure—*he started out*—to his encounter with *an Ethiopian eunuch*. Ethiopia was one of the kingdoms of Africa located south of Egypt in the territory that would be modern Sudan. This man served as *an important official* responsible for *the treasury of Candace, queen of the Ethiopians.* (*Candace* was a title of queens in Ethiopia much as *Caesar* was a title of Roman emperors.)

In addition, this man was a *eunuch*, as were many attendants in royal courts. (Eunuchs were believed to be less likely to become involved in questionable behavior with any ladies of the court.) He *had gone to Jerusalem to worship*, perhaps at one of the major national feasts. Whether he was born a Jew or had become a proselyte (a convert to the Jewish faith), we do not know. But being a eunuch, he would not have been permitted to go inside the courts of the temple at Jerusalem (Deuteronomy 23:1).

28 . . . and on his way home was sitting in his chariot reading the book of Isaiah the prophet.

No doubt the journey by *chariot* from Jerusalem to the eunuch's homeland (well over a thousand miles) must have been uncomfortable at times. But we know how he was spending some of the long hours: he was reading his Bible! (There may well have been a servant with him to drive the chariot.) Specifically, the eunuch was *reading the book of Isaiah the prophet.* This would have been a scroll, perhaps in the Greek translation (the Septuagint), which was made approximately three centuries earlier in Egypt.

C. The Spirit's Direction (v. 29)

29 The Spirit told Philip, "Go to that chariot and stay near it."

Note the leading of both the angel of the Lord (v. 26) and *the Spirit* in directing Philip where he should go. Yet when the message of salvation was to be communicated, God used Philip to do this. A human messenger of the gospel has always been God's instrument for the salvation of another human being—even "hand-picked" prospects such as this eunuch and Saul of Tarsus (Acts 9:6).

D. The Eunuch's Dilemma (vv. 30-34)

30 Then Philip ran up to the chariot and heard the man reading Isaiah the prophet. "Do you understand what you are reading?" Philip asked.

Philip got close enough to the *chariot* to hear what the eunuch was *reading* (it was a customary practice in that time to read aloud). He asked a question that was designed to open the door for an opportunity to witness of Jesus to this man.

31 "How can I," he said, "unless someone explains it to me?" So he invited Philip to come up and sit with him.

Far from being offended by Philip's question, the eunuch welcomed it as a possible solution to his problem. There was room in the chariot for another passenger, and Philip was warmly *invited* to *sit* with the eunuch.

32, 33 The eunuch was reading this passage of Scripture:
"He was led like a sheep to the slaughter,
and as a lamb before the shearer is silent,
so he did not open his mouth.
In his humiliation he was deprived of justice.
Who can speak of his descendants?
For his life was taken from the earth."

The eunuch was reading from Isaiah's account of God's suffering servant found in Isaiah 53:7, 8. It compares God's servant with a *sheep* or a *lamb* in regard to that creature's quiet acceptance of the most violent treatment, whether in facing the *slaughter* or the *shearer*. One is led to think of Jesus' steadfast refusal to answer or complain about the slander and *humiliation* to which he was subjected both before and during his crucifixion (1 Peter 2:21-23). In all of this, as Isaiah prophesied, Jesus was *deprived of justice*. He was denied every basic right to a fair trial, either by the Jewish council or by the Roman court. Justice gave way to the angry clamor for his death.

The reference to the servant's *descendants* has been interpreted more than one way. If it refers to Jesus' contemporaries, the question *Who can speak of his descendants?* is asking how one can even speak of a generation so evil as to put him to death. If it refers to Jesus' descendants, the question could be asking how Jesus can have any at all if *his life* is *taken from the earth*. Of course, Jesus has millions of spiritual descendants, people who have been born again through him and have become God's children. In them "he will see his offspring" (Isaiah 53:10).

> *34 The eunuch asked Philip, "Tell me, please, who is the prophet talking about, himself or someone else?"*

Obviously Isaiah was *talking about* someone. Was it *himself or someone else?* Had the eunuch heard controversy concerning this passage while in Jerusalem, some claiming it to be written of the Messiah, and others saying that it applied to Isaiah or some other person?

E. Philip's Direction (v. 35)

> *35 Then Philip began with that very passage of Scripture and told him the good news about Jesus.*

Philip now had the opening he needed for telling this man *the good news about Jesus*. His method was like that of Peter on the Day of Pentecost and Stephen before the Sanhedrin. Each had started with an Old Testament text or texts and had then proceeded to show that these passages pointed to Christ.

II. Willing Learner (Acts 8:36-40)
A. Important Question (v. 36)

> *36 As they traveled along the road, they came to some water and the eunuch said, "Look, here is water. Why shouldn't I be baptized?"*

One wishes he knew all that Philip said to the eunuch, but it is evident that he taught him about baptism. To tell the good news about Jesus (v. 35) is to present the central facts about his death, burial, and resurrection in such a way that the hearer is moved to participate in those same events through being *baptized*—dying to sin, then being buried and raised according to Jesus' command and the teaching of the New Testament (Matthew 28:18-20; Romans 6:1-4; Colossians 2:11, 12).

Even the desert country of Judah is not entirely without springs, streams, and pools. Such a source of *water* seems to have been rare enough to excite the eunuch when he saw one. Note that while the teaching about salvation had to come from Philip, the idea of immediate action came from the eunuch. No pressure or prodding was needed here. This man believed and desired to do as he had been taught.

B. Important Answer (v. 37)

37 (footnote) Philip said, "If you believe with all your heart, you may." The eunuch answered, "I believe that Jesus Christ is the Son of God."

This verse is not found in the oldest known manuscripts of Acts, and so it is left out of many English versions. The verse is quoted in some very early Christian writings, however, so it appears to represent one form of confession that was used in the early church. And even if Luke did not write it, we can be sure Philip did not baptize this man without being assured that he believed that *Jesus Christ is the Son of God*. Perhaps this verse originated as a footnote to inform readers of current church practice, and later someone who was copying the book of Acts wrote it into the text.

C. Important Action (v. 38)

38 And he gave orders to stop the chariot. Then both Philip and the eunuch went down into the water and Philip baptized him.

This scene affords us a most graphic picture of baptism. The Scripture implies that Philip immersed the eunuch when he *baptized him*; otherwise there was no need for them both to go *down into the water*. As noted previously in the comments on verse 36, the act of immersion pictures the death, burial, and resurrection of Jesus.

D. Impressive Result (vv. 39, 40)

39 When they came up out of the water, the Spirit of the Lord suddenly took Philip away, and the eunuch did not see him again, but went on his way rejoicing.

The Spirit of the Lord, who had brought Philip into contact with the eunuch (v. 29), had other work for the evangelist to do in other towns. While we know nothing certain of what became of the eunuch when he returned to Ethiopia, we would like to think that (in keeping with the spirit of the book of Acts) he told others of the Christ he had found through the prophecy of Isaiah and the instruction of a man who was bold enough to ask him if he understood what he was reading. With the eunuch, as with the Samaritans to whom Philip had taken the gospel (Acts 8:8), there was *rejoicing*.

40 Philip, however, appeared at Azotus and traveled about, preaching the gospel in all the towns until he reached Caesarea.

The Spirit led *Philip* to *Azotus* (known as Philistine Ashdod in the Old Testament), but we know nothing of his work there. From there he made his way to *Caesarea,* where Paul and Luke found him approximately a quarter of a century later (Acts 21:8)—the final time this effective witness for Christ is mentioned in the New Testament.

THE CONVERSION OF SAUL (ACTS 9:1-6, 10-20)

Establishing the Groundwork

We have already seen how the book of Acts introduces Saul in connection with the martyrdom of Stephen. As noted in a previous study, Saul took care of the cloaks of those who threw stones at Stephen (Acts 7:58). Acts 8:3 records how Saul "began to destroy the church" by seizing men and women in their homes and putting them in prison. Luke then focuses in chapter 8 on the spread of the gospel that resulted from Christians leaving Jerusalem (because of the persecution) and moving into other areas.

Chapter 9 of Acts begins a new section in the book in which Saul moves to center stage. Most of the remaining chapters of the book cover the activities of him and his associates as they carry the gospel to new territories. In a very real sense, this chapter records one of the great turning points in human history. After Saul's conversion, the world was never the same again.

Examining the Text

I. Jesus Appears to Saul (Acts 9:1-6)
A. The Journey to Damascus (vv. 1, 2)

1, 2 Meanwhile, Saul was still breathing out murderous threats against the Lord's disciples. He went to the high priest and asked him for letters to the synagogues in Damascus, so that if he found any there who belonged to the Way, whether men or women, he might take them as prisoners to Jerusalem.

One should recall how Gamaliel, an honored member of the Sanhedrin, had advised restraint in dealing with the Christian movement (Acts 5:33-39). But *Saul,* who had been a student of Gamaliel (Acts 22:3), would have none of that. Perhaps he felt a growing sense of frustration at the fact that in spite of his fervent efforts to destroy the church (Acts 8:3), it had grown even stronger and had spread to new territories. So Saul determined to extend his campaign against the church to new territories.

In particular, Saul set his sights on the city of *Damascus*, located about 140 miles north and east of *Jerusalem*. Apparently the leaders of the synagogue in Damascus possessed enough influence with the governor of that territory that he could be persuaded to do their bidding. (Note the later efforts to arrest Saul in Damascus after his conversion, as noted in 2 Corinthians 11:32.) The synagogues in turn recognized the authority of *the high priest* in Jerusalem, so Saul obtained the necessary permission from the high priest (most likely Caiaphas) and embarked on his mission to arrest any *who belonged to the Way*.

The term *Way* was used in several settings to designate the Christian movement (Acts 19:9, 23; 22:4; 24:14, 22). It may well echo Jesus' description of himself as "the way" in John 14:6.

B. The Light from Heaven (v. 3)

3 As he neared Damascus on his journey, suddenly a light from heaven flashed around him.

The journey to *Damascus* from Jerusalem normally took about a week. As Saul and those accompanying him *neared* the city, *suddenly a light from heaven flashed around him*. Later, in relating this incident before King Agrippa, Saul (now Paul) stated that even though it was noon at the time, the light was "brighter than the sun" and shone around him and his companions (Acts 26:13).

C. The Voice from Heaven (vv. 4-6)

4 He fell to the ground and heard a voice say to him, "Saul, Saul, why do you persecute me?"

Overwhelmed by such an unexpected occurrence, Saul *fell* prostrate *to the ground*; and so did those traveling with him (Acts 26:14). Then he *heard a voice* call him by name. That must have been as terrifying as the sudden light from Heaven, especially when the voice asked, "*Why do you persecute me?*" The men accompanying Saul heard the voice (v. 7), but they saw no one and they did not understand the words that were spoken (Acts 22:9).

5 "Who are you, Lord?" Saul asked.
"I am Jesus, whom you are persecuting," he replied.

Saul's first response to the voice he heard was, "*Who are you, Lord?*" According to rabbinic tradition, such a voice from Heaven would have been understood as the voice of God himself. (The bright light would have also signaled to Saul that he was in the presence of God.)

Jesus described himself as the one *whom* Saul was *persecuting*. Just as those who either helped or did not help those in need were described by Jesus as either helping or ignoring him (Matthew 25:34-45), so those individuals who persecute Christians are considered as treating Jesus in this manner. Jesus could also be saying that those who persecute his body (the church) are doing the same to the Head (Ephesians 1:22, 23).

Apparently it was at this moment that Saul saw Jesus in person (Acts 9:17, 27; 1 Corinthians 15:8). This was necessary to qualify Saul to become an apostle (Acts 1:21, 22; 1 Corinthians 9:1).

⁶ *"Now get up and go into the city, and you will be told what you must do."*

Saul was told to *get up and go into* Damascus, where he would be *told what* he *must do*. It should be noted that Jesus did not tell Saul what to do to be forgiven and saved from his sin. The previous study from Acts told how an angel sent Philip to the road from Jerusalem to Gaza, and then the Holy Spirit told him to approach a passing chariot. Here Jesus appeared to Saul on the road to Damascus. But neither angel nor Spirit nor Jesus explained the way of salvation. That task has been assigned to Christians, and it remains true that no one is going to do that task for us.

II. Jesus Appears to Ananias (Acts 9:10-16)

When Saul got up from the ground after his terrifying experience, he realized that he was blind (v. 8). His companions led him on to Damascus, where, for three days, he remained in utter darkness, abstaining from any food or drink (v. 9). Saul was also praying (v. 11)—perhaps as passionately as he had ever prayed.

A. Jesus' Command (vv. 10-12)

¹⁰ *In Damascus there was a disciple named Ananias. The Lord called to him in a vision, "Ananias!"*
"Yes, Lord," he answered.

The Scriptures tell us little about *Ananias*. How he had been won to the faith or how long he had been a *disciple* of Jesus we have no way of knowing. But when *the Lord called to him in a vision*, he responded immediately. Verse 17 indicates that this was Jesus who appeared to Ananias.

11 The Lord told him, "Go to the house of Judas on Straight Street and ask for a man from Tarsus named Saul, for he is praying.

Straight Street in Damascus is still identifiable today, running in an east and west direction. Streets in ancient cities were narrow and twisting, anything but straight. The fact that this one was straight would make it well known in the city. We know nothing more about the *Judas* mentioned in this verse. We also know nothing about the content of Saul's prayer at this point, but he may have been *praying* for further insight into what Jesus wanted him to do (v. 6).

12 "In a vision he has seen a man named Ananias come and place his hands on him to restore his sight."

Saul was already being prepared for God's answer to his prayer. When the man whom Saul had seen *in a vision* would do as the vision described, Saul could be assured that when this man gave him further instructions (as Ananias did), Saul could accept his words as coming from God.

B. Ananias's Concern (vv. 13, 14)

13 "Lord," Ananias answered, "I have heard many reports about this man and all the harm he has done to your saints in Jerusalem.

Saul's persecution of the church was well known by this time. People had fled from Jerusalem to escape it (Acts 8:1). It is easy to understand Ananias's misgivings at this point.

It is noteworthy that this is the first time in the New Testament that the word *saints* is applied to Christians. Later in his epistles Paul frequently addressed believers using this term. *Saints* are those who have been set aside for God's holy purposes. The term is not restricted to a few who have attained an elevated level of piety.

14 "And he has come here with authority from the chief priests to arrest all who call on your name."

News of Saul's coming to Damascus and his purpose for coming had arrived before he had. Should Ananias go looking for the man who was looking for people like him with the intention of punishing them?

C. Jesus' Commission (vv. 15, 16)

15 But the Lord said to Ananias, "Go! This man is my chosen instrument to carry my name before the Gentiles and their kings and before the people of Israel.

Incredible as it may have seemed, Jesus' worst persecutor was to become his best preacher. Though he had been a fervently devoted Jew to this point, Saul was to become the Lord's *chosen instrument* to proclaim his good news. Saul's voice, once raised against Jesus and his people, would be raised on their behalf *before the Gentiles and their kings and before the people of Israel.*

[16] ***"I will show him how much he must suffer for my name."***

The persecutor would join the ranks of the persecuted. He who had brought suffering to many followers of Jesus *must suffer for* the Lord's *name.* See 2 Corinthians 11:23-29 for a description of a portion of that suffering.

III. Ananias Approaches Saul (Acts 9:17-20)
A. The Lord's Message (vv. 17, 18a)

[17] *Then Ananias went to the house and entered it. Placing his hands on Saul, he said, "Brother Saul, the Lord—Jesus, who appeared to you on the road as you were coming here—has sent me so that you may see again and be filled with the Holy Spirit."*

Having received assurance from Jesus concerning Saul, Ananias promptly found *the house,* found the man, and delivered his message. That message also included these words, found in Acts 22:16, "And now what are you waiting for? Get up, be baptized and wash your sins away, calling on [the Lord's] name." But the primary purpose of the verse before us is to show that Ananias came to Saul exactly as Saul in his vision had seen him coming (v. 12).

[18a] *Immediately, something like scales fell from Saul's eyes, and he could see again.*

Ananias's touch and words were *immediately* effective. Saul's sight was restored.

B. The Lord's Messenger (vv. 18b-20)

[18b] *He got up and was baptized,*

With Saul's baptism, Ananias's purpose for coming to Saul was completed. He had been sent to Saul so that he could receive his sight and be filled with the Spirit (v. 17). Following the restoration of his sight, Saul *was baptized* and thus received the Holy Spirit, in accordance with the promise given by Peter on the Day of Pentecost (Acts 2:38).

¹⁹ . . . and after taking some food, he regained his strength.
Saul spent several days with the disciples in Damascus.

Saul had abstained from *food* and drink since his experience on the road to *Damascus.* He would need strength to begin this new phase of his life. He remained in Damascus *with the disciples* there, no doubt receiving both physical and spiritual nourishment.

²⁰ At once he began to preach in the synagogues that Jesus is the Son of God.

At once Saul began to display the same passion on behalf of Jesus that he had been demonstrating against him. He *began to preach in the synagogues,* establishing a pattern that he would often follow when arriving at a new town or city to preach the good news. One of Jesus' staunchest enemies was now his fiercest spokesman.

It may have been soon after this that Saul went away to Arabia for a time (Galatians 1:15-17). We do not know how long he stayed in Arabia or what he did there, but we can imagine that he spent many days restudying the Old Testament Scriptures and seeing how perfectly Jesus fulfilled the prophecies of the Messiah. From Arabia Saul returned to Damascus and resumed his teaching in the synagogues. Unbelieving Jews who found themselves unable to respond to Saul's arguments conspired to kill him, but fellow disciples helped him escape (Acts 9:23-25). The former persecutor of the church was beginning to experience "how much he must suffer" for Jesus' sake (Acts 9:16).

How to Say It

AGRIPPA. Uh-*grip*-puh.

ANANIAS. An-uh-*nye*-us.

ANTIOCH. *An*-tee-ock.

ASHDOD. *Ash*-dod.

AZOTUS. Uh-*zo*-tus.

CAESAREA. Sess-uh-*ree*-uh.

CAIAPHAS. *Kay*-uh-fus or *Kye*-uh-fus.

CANDACE. *Can*-duh-see.

DIAKONEO *(Greek)*. *dih*-ah-ko-*neh*-o (strong accent on *neh*).

DIAKONIA *(Greek)*. *dih*-ah-ko-*nee*-uh (strong accent on *nee*).

DIAKONOS *(Greek)*. dee-*ah*-ko-nawss.

EUNUCH. *you*-nick.

GAMALIEL. Guh-*may*-lih-ul or Guh-*may*-lee-al.

GRECIAN. *Gree*-shun.

HEBRAIC. Heh-*bray*-ik.

JAIRUS. *Jye*-rus or *Jay*-ih-rus.

JOSEPHUS. Jo-*see*-fus.

JUDAISM. *Joo*-duh-izz-um or *Joo*-day-izz-um.

LAZARUS. *Laz*-uh-rus.

NICANOR. Nye-*cay*-nor.

NICOLAS. *Nick*-uh-lus.

PARMENAS. *Par*-meh-nas.

PENTECOST. *Pent*-ih-kost.

PHARISEE. *Fair*-ih-see.

PHILISTINE. Fuh-*liss*-teen or *Fill*-us-teen.

PROCORUS. *Prock*-uh-rus.

PROSELYTE. *prahss*-uh-light.

QUIRINIUS. Kwy-*rin*-ee-us.

SANHEDRIN. San-huh-drun or San-*heed*-run.

SAPPHIRA. Suh-*fye*-ruh.

SEPTUAGINT. Sep-*too*-ih-jent.

SYNAGOGUE. *sin*-uh-gog.

THEUDAS. *Thoo*-dus.

TIMON. *Ty*-mon.

ZEALOTS. *Zel*-uts.

Chapter 3

The Church's Expanding Ministry to Gentiles
Acts 11:1-18; 11:19-30; 13:1-3; 14:8-20; 15:1-11, 19-21

CONVERSION OF CORNELIUS (ACTS 11:1-18)

Establishing the Groundwork

Following the account of the conversion of Saul and his initial experiences in Damascus and Jerusalem (Acts 9:1-31), the record in the book of Acts shifts back to the activities of Peter. The last time Peter was mentioned in the book, he and John had returned to Jerusalem after preaching the gospel in Samaritan villages (Acts 8:25). When Peter is mentioned in chapter 9, he was traveling again. This time his travels had taken him to Lydda, where he healed a paralytic named Aeneas (Acts 9:32-35), then to Joppa, where he raised Dorcas from the dead (vv. 36-43). While in Joppa, Peter saw a vision of something resembling a large sheet, containing all kinds of unclean animals in it, being let down from Heaven (Acts 10:9-16).

The purpose of this vision was to prepare Peter for some messengers who had come from Caesarea from the house of Cornelius, a Roman centurion (and an "unclean" Gentile). When Peter accompanied them back to Caesarea, he had to overcome his prejudices as a Jew in order to enter the house of a Gentile such as Cornelius. But having understood the significance of the vision he had received from God, Peter presented to Cornelius and those gathered with him the good news of salvation through Jesus Christ. Cornelius, along with his household, responded to the message and was baptized (Acts 10:24-48). Another significant milestone in carrying out the Great Commission of Jesus had been reached.

When Peter returned to Jerusalem, however, he had to confront the prejudices of other Jewish Christians who questioned his association with Gentiles.

Examining the Text

I. Critics Rebuke Peter (Acts 11:1-3)
A. Origin of the Opposition (vv. 1, 2)

[1] The apostles and the brothers throughout Judea heard that the Gentiles also had received the word of God.

We do not know how long Peter stayed at the house of Cornelius; Acts 10:48 simply states that he was asked to stay "a few days." No doubt it was not long before the Jewish Christians throughout Judea heard what had happened in Caesarea, which was located some thirty miles from Jerusalem. And no doubt there was much discussion about how *the Gentiles also had received the word of God* and obeyed the gospel.

² So when Peter went up to Jerusalem, the circumcised believers criticized him

Peter returned to *Jerusalem* to find some of the *circumcised believers* prepared to criticize his actions in Caesarea. It is to the credit of these Jewish Christians that they took the matter directly to Peter rather than criticize him "behind his back."

B. Objection of the Opposition (v. 3)

³ . . . and said, "You went into the house of uncircumcised men and ate with them."

The law of Moses had declared that the people of Israel were holy and were to remain distinct from pagan influences. This included prohibiting any intermarriage with pagans (Deuteronomy 7:1-6). But the teachings of the rabbis extended that distinction to cover any sort of social contact with Gentiles. Note that the objection to Peter's action was not that he had preached the gospel to Gentiles and baptized them into Christ, but that he had accepted their hospitality and eaten *with them*. To do so risked violating the food laws that were a part of the law of Moses (Leviticus 11 in particular); however, Jesus in his teaching had "declared all foods 'clean'" (Mark 7:19). The traditional prejudice against *uncircumcised* Gentiles was hard to overcome; in fact, Peter himself on a later occasion reverted to it and was confronted by Paul (Galatians 2:11-14).

II. Peter Responds to the Critics (Acts 11:4-17)
A. What Peter Saw (vv. 4-10)

⁴ Peter began and explained everything to them precisely as it had happened:

Instead of trying to argue the rightness or wrongness of what he had done or speaking something hastily that he would later regret (as he sometimes did during Jesus' ministry), Peter simply recounted *everything to them precisely as it had happened*. Then his critics could judge his actions for themselves. What he related was a summary of the events recorded in Acts 10:9-48.

⁵ "I was in the city of Joppa praying, and in a trance I saw a vision. I saw something like a large sheet being let down from heaven by its four corners, and it came down to where I was.

Peter's account began with his being *in the city of Joppa praying*. He had been staying there following the miracle of Dorcas's resurrection from the dead (Acts 9:43). One day about noon, while a meal was being prepared, Peter fell into *a trance* and *saw a vision. Something like a large sheet* was *being let down from heaven* to *where* Peter *was*.

⁶ "I looked into it and saw four-footed animals of the earth, wild beasts, reptiles, and birds of the air.

The sheet contained a variety of *four-footed animals, wild beasts, reptiles, and birds*, none of which would have been allowed as food under the Jewish dietary laws.

⁷, ⁸ "Then I heard a voice telling me, 'Get up, Peter. Kill and eat.'
"I replied, 'Surely not, Lord! Nothing impure or unclean has ever entered my mouth.'

The command to eat the creatures within the sheet was in direct violation of the laws found in Leviticus 11 about clean and unclean animals, and Peter knew this. He recognized that the *voice* speaking to him was that of the *Lord* and expressed his repulsion at the thought of eating anything forbidden by the law—even though at the time the vision occurred he was hungry (Acts 10:10).

⁹ "The voice spoke from heaven a second time, 'Do not call anything impure that God has made clean.'

The same God who had defined the difference between clean and unclean animals had the prerogative to withdraw that distinction when he chose to do so.

¹⁰ "This happened three times, and then it was all pulled up to heaven again.

Sending the same vision three times was meant to impress Peter with the importance of God's instructions.

B. What Peter Did (vv. 11-14)

¹¹ "Right then three men who had been sent to me from Caesarea stopped at the house where I was staying.

God had timed the vision so that it concluded just as the *three men who had been sent* from Cornelius in *Caesarea* arrived *at the house* where Peter was *staying*.

12 "The Spirit told me to have no hesitation about going with them. These six brothers also went with me, and we entered the man's house.

The Spirit instructed Peter to accompany the messengers. They were Gentiles, but he was to have no misgivings *about going with them*. He took *six brothers* with him, perhaps recognizing that he might be the target of the kind of criticism that he was now receiving. The six men could attest to all that transpired, though Peter had made it quite clear to this point that all of his actions had been divinely guided; he had not simply acted on his own initiative.

13, 14 "He told us how he had seen an angel appear in his house and say, 'Send to Joppa for Simon who is called Peter. He will bring you a message through which you and all your household will be saved.'

Two points from these verses are worth noting. First, the *angel* who appeared to Cornelius did not bring the *message* of salvation to him. As we have observed with the conversions of the Ethiopian eunuch and Saul, the Spirit, an angel, and Jesus himself instructed individuals where to encounter certain people who then conveyed the message of salvation to them. God has always used human beings to carry the gospel to others.

Second, it should be noted that, although Cornelius is described as "devout and God-fearing" and as one who "gave generously to those in need and prayed to God regularly" (Acts 10:2), these qualities did not save him. As pious as he was, he still needed to hear the good news of Jesus Christ to be *saved*. The angel's words to Cornelius also referred to his *household*, which may have included servants as well as members of his family. Similar conversions in Acts include the households of Lydia (Acts 16:14, 15) and the jailer in Philippi (Acts 16:33, 34).

C. What Peter Saw the Spirit Do (vv. 15-17)

15 "As I began to speak, the Holy Spirit came on them as he had come on us at the beginning.

Acts 10:34-43 records Peter's words before he was "interrupted" by the coming of the *Holy Spirit*. He expressed his conviction, resulting from the vision he had seen, that God "does not show favoritism" (v. 34). Then he began to present the gospel message to Cornelius and his household. As he did so, the Spirit *came on them as he had come on us at the beginning*. Peter was referring to what occurred on the Day of Pentecost, when he and the other apostles received the baptism of the Holy Spirit. Acts 10:46 records that those upon whom this outpouring of the Holy Spirit came spoke in tongues, as did the apostles on Pentecost (Acts 2:4).

*¹⁶ "Then I remembered what the Lord had said: 'John baptized with water,
but you will be baptized with the Holy Spirit.'*

Just before his ascension, Jesus had contrasted *John* the Baptist's baptism
with water with the baptism of the *Holy Spirit* that would come upon the
apostles (Acts 1:5) and did come on the Day of Pentecost (Acts 2:1-4). Apparently this baptism of the Spirit had not occurred since that day. Peter had to
go back to that event to find a parallel with what happened at Caesarea to the
household of Cornelius.

It should be noted that the Spirit baptism received by the household of
Cornelius did not remove the need for Christian baptism in water. According
to the record in Acts 10, Peter, after witnessing the Spirit being "poured out" on
Cornelius and his household, asked, "Can anyone keep these people from being
baptized with water? They have received the Holy Spirit just as we have" (Acts
10:45-47). They were then "baptized in the name of Jesus Christ" (Acts 10:48)
and received the indwelling of the Spirit promised to every baptized believer,
according to Acts 2:38.

Thus, just as the baptism of the Spirit at Pentecost had preceded the
preaching of the gospel to Jews, here it preceded the preaching of the gospel to
Gentiles. It indicated that the "keys of the kingdom" (Matthew 16:19) were to
be used to allow Gentiles—who had previously been excluded—to enter.

*¹⁷ "So if God gave them the same gift as he gave us, who believed in the
Lord Jesus Christ, who was I to think that I could oppose God?"*

Peter had become fully convinced by an impressive amount of evidence: the
vision at noon, the Spirit's clear message to go with the messengers sent from
Caesarea, and the miraculous manifestation of the Spirit on Cornelius and his
household. He dared not *oppose* the plan of God to admit Gentiles into the fellowship of the church.

III. Critics Rejoice with Peter (Acts 11:18)

*¹⁸ When they heard this, they had no further objections and praised God,
saying, "So then, God has granted even the Gentiles repentance unto life."*

After hearing Peter's report, which was supported by the six witnesses, those
who had questioned Peter's actions *had no further objections.* They *praised God,*
convinced that God had *granted even the Gentiles repentance unto life.* This
phrase should be understood in terms of granting the Gentiles the opportunity
to repent—to turn from their sins and find forgiveness through the gospel. (See
similar comments on Acts 5:31 in chapter 2.)

While those circumcised believers who had questioned Peter were satisfied at this point, there were others who still held reservations about including Gentiles in the fellowship of the church. A group of these began to insist that Gentile Christians be required to be circumcised and keep the law of Moses in order to be saved. The ensuing controversy resulted in the gathering known as the Jerusalem Conference, which is recorded in Acts 15:1-35. That will be the subject to a later study in this volume. (See p. 68.)

THE CHURCH EXPANDS ITS OUTREACH TO GENTILES
(ACTS 11:19-30; 13:1-3)

Establishing the Groundwork

We have previously noted how the death of Stephen and the persecution of the Jerusalem church that followed scattered many of the Christians beyond Jerusalem and into new areas not yet reached with the gospel. Earlier studies highlighted the efforts of Philip among the Samaritans and with a government official from Ethiopia. The last study examined what took place in Caesarea, when Peter shared the good news of Jesus with Cornelius and his household, thus admitting Gentiles into the fellowship of the church. A crucial barrier had been broken, opening the door for predominantly Gentile cities to experience the "great joy" associated with accepting the message of salvation (Acts 8:8). One city that became especially significant as the church expanded was Antioch of Syria.

Examining the Text

I. Planting a Church (Acts 11:19-21)
A. Crossing Barriers (vv. 19, 20)

19 Now those who had been scattered by the persecution in connection with Stephen traveled as far as Phoenicia, Cyprus and Antioch, telling the message only to Jews.

Some of the Christians *who had been scattered by the persecution* that arose after the death of *Stephen* moved into areas such as Samaria, as did Philip (Acts 8:5). Those mentioned in the text before us *traveled* much farther north—*as far as Phoenicia, Cyprus and Antioch.* Phoenicia was located north of Galilee, and included the long fertile plain between the Lebanon mountains and the Mediterranean Sea. It also included the coastal cities of Tyre and Sidon. The record in Acts indicates that churches became established in these important cities

(Acts 21:3, 4; 27:3). Cyprus was the foremost island of the eastern Mediterranean. It was the home of Barnabas (Acts 4:36).

Of greatest significance for the church's growth was the movement of Christians into the city of Antioch. (This was Antioch of Syria, not to be confused with Antioch of Pisidia, mentioned in Acts 13:14.) Antioch was another city on the Mediterranean coast, farther north than Phoenicia and approximately 300 miles from Jerusalem. At this time in history, Antioch was the third largest city in the world (following Rome and Alexandria, Egypt). Eventually, Barnabas and Saul were sent forth from the Antioch church on what would become Paul's first missionary journey (Acts 13:1-3).

Disciples of Jesus would not have reached all of these locations at the same time. Probably the progress recorded in this verse took several years, and during those years Peter brought the gospel to the household of Cornelius, as noted in the previous study. Initially, those who traveled to these northern territories preached the gospel *only to Jews.*

20 Some of them, however, men from Cyprus and Cyrene, went to Antioch and began to speak to Greeks also, telling them the good news about the Lord Jesus.

Cyrene was located in what is today northern Africa. It had a large Jewish population; in fact, Jews from there had been among the many thousands gathered in Jerusalem on the Day of Pentecost when Peter preached the first gospel sermon (Acts 2:10). After becoming followers of Jesus, apparently some had stayed in Jerusalem to be taught by the apostles. Now they, along with believers from *Cyprus,* were fleeing from the persecution that had targeted the church in Jerusalem.

Given the location of Cyprus and Cyrene, the Jews from these places must have lived among Gentiles and had probably done business with them. They were probably not as particular about their contacts with Gentiles as the Jews of Palestine were. When they arrived in Antioch, some came in contact with Gentiles there and freely offered *the good news about the Lord Jesus* to them. At this point, probably Peter had already preached to Cornelius and his household in Caesarea, but we do not know this for certain; and even if he had, we do not know whether or not those who came to Antioch were aware of Peter's actions.

B. Receiving God's Blessing (v. 21)

21 The Lord's hand was with them, and a great number of people believed and turned to the Lord.

The church continued to grow in these new fields that were "ripe for harvest" (John 4:35), *and a great number of people believed and turned to the Lord.*

II. Assisting a Church Spiritually (Acts 11:22-26)
A. Contribution of Barnabas (vv. 22-24)

²² News of this reached the ears of the church at Jerusalem, and they sent Barnabas to Antioch.

If there were certain Jews of a stricter persuasion among those who came to Antioch, perhaps they were somewhat disturbed when they saw the gospel being proclaimed to Gentiles. Possibly they sent a messenger to *Jerusalem* to see what the leadership there (the apostles) would say about this development.

If by this time the events in Caesarea involving the household of Cornelius had occurred, the *church* in Jerusalem would have welcomed the news from Antioch. If not, perhaps the leadership believed that such news required further investigation. Regardless of the sequence of events, the church determined to send *Barnabas to Antioch.* He had already become known as the "Son of Encouragement" (Acts 4:36) and would be just the man needed to assess objectively what was happening in Antioch. In addition, Barnabas, being from Cyprus, had a common bond with the believers from there. He likely possessed a better understanding of Gentile culture than some of the other leaders in the Jerusalem church.

²³ When he arrived and saw the evidence of the grace of God, he was glad and encouraged them all to remain true to the Lord with all their hearts.

True to his reputation, Barnabas *encouraged* the Christians in Antioch *to remain true to the Lord with all their hearts.*

²⁴ He was a good man, full of the Holy Spirit and faith, and a great number of people were brought to the Lord.

Through Barnabas's efforts in Antioch, not only were those who were already believers encouraged, but also *a great number of people were brought to the Lord.* Before long, Barnabas realized that he did not want to return to Jerusalem! Exciting things were happening in Antioch, and he was not content with merely observing them or reporting on them. He also thought of someone else whose abilities made him well suited for serving in Antioch.

B. Contribution of Saul (vv. 25, 26)

²⁵, ²⁶ Then Barnabas went to Tarsus to look for Saul, and when he found him, he brought him to Antioch. So for a whole year Barnabas and Saul met with the church and taught great numbers of people. The disciples were called Christians first at Antioch.

Acts 9:30 notes that Saul had been sent away to *Tarsus* (his hometown) when some in Jerusalem had plotted to kill him. That was where Barnabas *found him*. He *brought* Saul *to Antioch*, recognizing that the church there needed his kind of personality, commitment, and gifts, and that Saul needed a place to serve. The two men worked well together in Antioch; whereas "a great number of people were brought to the Lord" earlier (v. 24), now *great numbers of people* were *taught*.

This verse also notes that *the disciples were called Christians first at Antioch*. The specific origin of this new name has been the subject of much study. Some believe that the pagan residents of Antioch first used the name, perhaps in derision. Others suggest that the name *Christians* was a name given by God to the followers of Jesus. They note that the Greek word translated *called* in this verse is used elsewhere in the New Testament to denote God's calling, warning, or speaking to someone (Matthew 2:12, 22; Luke 2:26; Acts 10:22; Hebrews 8:5; 11:7; 12:25). Many who hold this view see the name *Christians* as the fulfillment of a prophecy in Isaiah 62:2: "The nations will see your righteousness, and all kings your glory; you will be called by a new name that the mouth of the Lord will bestow." The "new name" of *Christians* would have been particularly appropriate for the believers in Antioch, where the gospel had begun to make significant inroads among Gentiles.

III. Assisting a Church Materially (Acts 11:27-30)
A. Prophetic Warning (vv. 27, 28)

²⁷ **During this time some prophets came down from Jerusalem to Antioch.**

The communication between the church at Jerusalem and the church at Antioch continued in the form of *prophets* who traveled *from Jerusalem to Antioch*. As Ephesians 4:11, 12 notes, God gifted some to be prophets for the building up of the church. These prophets were especially important at this time because the New Testament Scriptures were not in any completed written form.

²⁸ **One of them, named Agabus, stood up and through the Spirit predicted that a severe famine would spread over the entire Roman world. (This happened during the reign of Claudius.)**

One of the prophets, *Agabus*, is later mentioned in Acts 21:10, 11, where he warned Paul of his coming arrest in Jerusalem. Here Agabus forewarned the church of a *severe famine* that would encompass *the entire Roman world*. According to the historical records of that time, famines did indeed occur in various parts of the empire during the reign of the emperor *Claudius* (AD 41-54). The Jewish historian Josephus refers to a famine in Judea that occurred in the year AD 46.

B. Genuine Caring (vv. 29, 30)

29 The disciples, each according to his ability, decided to provide help for the brothers living in Judea.

The relatively new *disciples* in Antioch showed that they were genuine followers of Jesus by responding to Agabus's message with immediate action. From *each according to his ability* (a plan similar to that which Paul later recommended to the Corinthians in 1 Corinthians 16:1, 2), they *decided to provide help* for their *brothers* in *Judea.*

The Christians in Judea would have suffered particular hardships from any famine. Many had become impoverished because of the persecution of Christians that followed the martyrdom of Stephen (Acts 8:1). Since the gospel had come to Antioch as a consequence of that persecution (Acts 11:19, 20), the believers in that city felt a special responsibility to assist fellow Christians in Jerusalem and the surrounding area.

30 This they did, sending their gift to the elders by Barnabas and Saul.

This is the first mention of *elders* as part of the New Testament church. Qualifications and duties of these men are given in the epistles (1 Timothy 3:1-7; Titus 1:5-9; 1 Peter 5:1-4). It is the elders, not the apostles (as in Acts 4:34-37), who received the *gift* given to the Jerusalem church. Perhaps the persecution initiated by Saul had necessitated some measure of reorganization.

Barnabas, mentioned first in this verse, appears to have led the delegation from Antioch. That is natural since Barnabas had originally come to Antioch at the bidding of the Jerusalem church. Now he would return with both news of the work in Antioch and a gift for the church in Judea. Involving *Saul* in taking the offering may have been another effort by Barnabas to encourage Saul's acceptance by the Jerusalem church (he had done this shortly after Saul's conversion, as Acts 9:26, 27 notes).

In Acts 12 Luke shifts his focus once again to the Jerusalem church and specifically to a period of persecution orchestrated by King Herod Agrippa I (the grandson of Herod the Great, whose attempt to kill the infant Jesus is recorded in Matthew 2:1-12). James the brother of John was put to death during this time. Peter was imprisoned, but was miraculously set free one night by an angel. The chapter includes a record of Herod's terrible death (vv. 19-23) and then concludes with a brief summary of the church's continued growth (in spite of Herod's vicious actions): "But the word of God continued to increase and spread" (v. 24). The final verse notes the return of Barnabas and Saul to Antioch, "taking with them John, also called Mark" (v. 25). However, the travels of Barnabas and Saul were far from over.

IV. Sending Forth Missionaries (Acts 13:1-3)
A. Leaders Brought Together (v. 1)

¹ In the church at Antioch there were prophets and teachers: Barnabas, Simeon called Niger, Lucius of Cyrene, Manaen (who had been brought up with Herod the tetrarch) and Saul.

Apparently *Barnabas* and *Saul* had been able to do some mentoring with the Antioch church, resulting in the assembling of a leadership team. Like most good teams, this one brought together several different personalities and backgrounds.

Niger, the nickname of *Simeon,* means "black" and suggests that he was a dark-complexioned man. Some think that he was the man known as Simon of Cyrene (a man from northern Africa who may have been dark-complexioned), who carried the cross for Jesus (Matthew 27:32). This is nothing but speculation, of course, and impossible to prove one way or the other. It would be unusual, however, for Matthew to use the man's Greek name (Simon) and Luke to use his Jewish name (Simeon) if this were the same man. We would expect just the opposite.

Lucius, who is identified as being of Cyrene, could have been one of the "men from Cyprus and Cyrene" who first began sharing the gospel with the Gentiles in Antioch (Acts 11:20). *Manaen* is described as having been *brought up with Herod the tetrarch.* The Herod mentioned in this verse would have been Herod Antipas, whose rash oath led to the death of John the Baptist (Matthew 14:1-12). Manaen's involvement in the Antioch church indicates that at least some persons of status and education had been led to Christ.

The task of *prophets* is mentioned often in the New Testament. The term could designate individuals with the ability to foretell the future (as Agabus did in Acts 11:27-29). More often, it described those to whom God revealed special messages to be delivered to others (Romans 12:6; Ephesians 3:4, 5; 4:11). The term *teachers* most likely includes those who received no special revelations from God but were quite effective at communicating what they had learned from prophets and from Scripture. Since Luke does not record who exercised which office in the Antioch church, it is possible that the five men named here functioned in both capacities.

B. Leaders Set Apart (vv. 2, 3)

² While they were worshiping the Lord and fasting, the Holy Spirit said, "Set apart for me Barnabas and Saul for the work to which I have called them."

It is not clear whether *they* refers to the five men named in the previous verse or to the entire church in Antioch, which is also mentioned in the previous verse. Nor are we told exactly how the *Holy Spirit* revealed this message regarding *Barnabas and Saul*. (Perhaps he spoke through one of the five who possessed the gift of prophecy.) What is most important to note is that whereas God had brought these men together for a time, now two of them were to be *set apart* from the rest to begin an important new endeavor in the Lord's *work*. It is evident that these men (and most likely the entire church) had been seeking the Lord's leading for their ministry, not only in Antioch but also to the world.

³ *So after they had fasted and prayed, they placed their hands on them and sent them off.*

Fasting is still an important spiritual discipline for the church and for individual Christians. Fasting can take place when an individual has a reason to repent and to seek God's forgiveness and renewal. It can be done when one is seeking some specific direction from God. And it can be done when a church is setting men and women aside to a special purpose in the business of Christ's kingdom. This is what was taking place in Antioch.

After those involved in this activity (whether a smaller group or the entire church) *had fasted and prayed*, they *placed their hands on Barnabas and Saul*, indicating in this instance the approval and blessing of the church. When their travels were concluded, the two men would return to Antioch to report how God had blessed their efforts (Acts 14:26-28).

PAUL AND BARNABAS IN LYSTRA (ACTS 14:8-20)

Establishing the Groundwork

The setting apart of Barnabas and Saul set in motion what we now call Paul's first missionary journey. Taking along John Mark (Barnabas's cousin, according to Colossians 4:10), the men began their preaching of the good news in Cyprus, Barnabas's home (Acts 13:4, 5). From there they proceeded to Perga, where the account simply reads that "John left them to return to Jerusalem" (v. 13). At this point, an interesting shift in focus occurs in the account as verse 13 records that "Paul and his companions sailed to Perga in Pamphylia." Nothing is said in the text to explain how Saul became known as Paul, but it does appear that he was beginning to take on a more prominent role in the endeavor since his name is mentioned first.

Paul and Barnabas then journeyed about 120 miles north to the city of Antioch, located in the territory called Pisidia (v. 14). Their initial preaching in the synagogue had a significant impact, resulting in an invitation to come and speak again on the following Sabbath. However, some of the Jews in the city became jealous of Paul and Barnabas's success and "talked abusively against what Paul was saying" (v. 45). Paul then declared his intentions to take his message to the Gentiles, which brought further and more intense opposition from the Jews in the city. So he and Barnabas left and traveled about ninety miles farther east to the city of Iconium. When they encountered additional resistance there, they moved south to Lystra and to the neighboring city of Derbe, two cities within the region known as Lycaonia.

Examining the Text

I. Miracle (Acts 14:8-10)
A. The Man's Condition (v. 8)

⁸ In Lystra there sat a man crippled in his feet, who was lame from birth and had never walked.

Earlier in Acts, Luke tells of another man, *lame from birth*, who sat begging by the temple gate in Jerusalem (Acts 3:1-10). Perhaps the lame man in Lystra was a beggar too, or possibly he was sitting in a market booth and selling merchandise. Apparently he was located near a place where Paul was preaching. Paul's practice was to begin his preaching in the synagogue of a city or town, but apparently there was no synagogue in Lystra since none is mentioned.

B. Paul's Command (vv. 9, 10)

⁹ He listened to Paul as he was speaking. Paul looked directly at him, saw that he had faith to be healed

Perhaps during his *speaking*, Paul referred to the miracles of Jesus. Possibly the lame man had heard of some of the "miraculous signs and wonders" that Paul and Barnabas had done in nearby Iconium (Acts 14:3). The man's intense interest in Paul's preaching, the expression on his face, or the straining of his crippled body toward Paul may have alerted Paul to the fact that this man *had faith to be healed*.

¹⁰ . . . and called out, "Stand up on your feet!" At that, the man jumped up and began to walk.

Paul *called out* his command, thus making sure that those who were gathered knew the source of the healing that followed. The healing was instantaneous, leaving no doubt that a miracle had indeed taken place.

II. Misunderstanding (Acts 14:11-13)
A. Pagan Thinking (vv. 11, 12)

11 When the crowd saw what Paul had done, they shouted in the Lycaonian language, "The gods have come down to us in human form!"

The *crowd* in Lystra responded excitedly to *what Paul had done*. As people usually do when they are excited, they spoke in their own language, in this case the *Lycaonian language*. Paul probably had been preaching in Greek, which most of the people would have spoken as a second language. The mythology of that time and culture taught that *the gods* sometimes came down to earth *in human form*; thus, when the crowd saw the miracle of the lame man walking, they assumed that the gods had favored them with a visit and a demonstration of their power.

12 Barnabas they called Zeus, and Paul they called Hermes because he was the chief speaker.

In Greek mythology, *Zeus* was the father of the gods (in Roman mythology he was known as Jupiter). We might assume, since Paul was the leader of the team, that he would have been recognized as Zeus. But the Lycaonians did not reason that way. Since Paul was *the chief speaker* and did most of the preaching, they assumed he was the messenger god *Hermes* (the Romans called this god Mercury). That left Barnabas to be the one for whom Hermes spoke, or Zeus. It is generally supposed that Barnabas was a bigger man physically than Paul; if so, that would have added to the perception that he was the greater of the two.

B. Pagan Actions (v. 13)

13 The priest of Zeus, whose temple was just outside the city, brought bulls and wreaths to the city gates because he and the crowd wanted to offer sacrifices to them.

This *priest of Zeus* may well have been the high priest, who initiated a ceremony of praise to the supposed gods who were in their presence. It was customary to decorate the *bulls* that were being offered as *sacrifices* with *wreaths*, or garlands of flowers, as they were being led to the *temple* to be sacrificed.

III. Message (Acts 14:14-18)
A. Concerning Paul and Barnabas (vv. 14, 15a)

14 But when the apostles Barnabas and Paul heard of this, they tore their clothes and rushed out into the crowd, shouting:

Since *Barnabas and Paul* were not familiar with the Lycaonian language, they may not have immediately understood the intentions of the crowd. But when they became aware of the preparations for the sacrifices, they quickly expressed their disapproval of the proceedings by tearing *their clothes*. Such a gesture was the typical Jewish way of expressing grief or dismay (Genesis 37:29, 34; Matthew 26:65).

It may seem odd to see Barnabas described as one of the *apostles*. In this case, *apostle* should be understood according to its general meaning of "one who is sent." In that sense, Barnabas can be called an apostle; for both the Holy Spirit and the church at Antioch had "sent" him, just as they had sent Paul, on this missionary endeavor (Acts 13:2, 3).

15a *"Men, why are you doing this? We too are only men, human like you.*

Besides the visual demonstration of their objecting to the crowd's actions, Barnabas and Paul voiced their disapproval as well. They were quick to point out that they were *only men, human like* the residents of Lystra.

B. Concerning God (vv. 15b-20)

15b *"We are bringing you good news, telling you to turn from these worthless things to the living God, who made heaven and earth and sea and everything in them.*

Paul and Barnabas told the crowd that they had come to Lystra for the purpose of turning people away *from these worthless things*—a reference to the pagan deities that the people believed had come to them in human form through Paul and Barnabas. To have accepted the worship of the people would have destroyed that purpose and badly compromised their message. They had come to proclaim the true and *living God,* the creator of the universe.

Prior to this occasion, Paul and Barnabas had preached primarily to Jewish or proselyte audiences. They knew that those people already believed in the Old Testament and in the God revealed there. But now they were addressing a pagan audience, steeped in idolatry and in the moral corruption that idolatry produces. Paul had to go back to "square one" in such a setting, teaching the people in Lystra about the true God.

16 *"In the past, he let all nations go their own way.*

Paul did not mean that God approved of how the *nations* chose to live, only that he permitted them for a time to *go their own way* without sending down upon them the divine judgment they deserved. Paul made a similar statement in his message at the Areopagus in Athens (Acts 17:30).

17 "Yet he has not left himself without testimony: He has shown kindness by giving you rain from heaven and crops in their seasons; he provides you with plenty of food and fills your hearts with joy."

While God permitted the nations to walk in their own ways, he did not leave *himself without testimony* in the world he had created. What people often refer to as the "natural world" is really "supernatural" because it provides a witness to all humanity of the *kindness* of God. Paul developed this idea more fully in his letter to the Romans: "For since the creation of the world God's invisible qualities—his eternal power and divine nature—have been clearly seen, being understood from what has been made, so that men are without excuse" (Romans 1:20).

18 Even with these words, they had difficulty keeping the crowd from sacrificing to them.

In spite of Paul's impassioned speech, he and Barnabas *had difficulty keeping the crowd* from making them the objects of their worship. People so thoroughly steeped in pagan thinking are often not quickly persuaded to change their ways.

19 Then some Jews came from Antioch and Iconium and won the crowd over. They stoned Paul and dragged him outside the city, thinking he was dead.

Sadly, Paul and Barnabas encountered the same opposition in Lystra that they had experienced in previous cities when *some Jews came from Antioch and Iconium and won the crowd over.* They were so successful that they were able to convince the crowd that had so recently wanted to worship Paul to participate in the Jewish means of executing him as a blasphemer: stoning.

20 But after the disciples had gathered around him, he got up and went back into the city. The next day he and Barnabas left for Derbe.

Luke's account implies a miraculous recovery. Even if Paul were not raised from the dead, for him to be able to get up and go back into the city after being injured to the point of unconsciousness was indeed miraculous.

While one may presume from this account that Paul and Barnabas's ministry in Lystra was rather fruitless, the further reading of Acts leads to a different conclusion. Near the conclusion of Acts 14, Luke notes that Paul and Barnabas returned to the cities they had visited, including Lystra, "strengthening the disciples and encouraging them to remain true to the faith" (v. 22). They even appointed elders in each church (v. 23).

Later when Paul and Silas returned to Lystra during Paul's second missionary journey, they met a follower of Jesus of whom other Christians were speaking very highly. This young man became one of Paul's most trusted associates. Perhaps he was led to Christ during Paul's first visit and was emboldened to serve Jesus by the example of courage and dedication that Paul had shown during that visit. That young man was Timothy (Acts 16:1-5).

THE JERUSALEM CONFERENCE (ACTS 15:1-11, 19-21)

Establishing the Groundwork

The final verses of Acts 14 record the return of Paul and Barnabas to their sending congregation in Antioch of Syria. There they reported all that had happened during their travels. They also determined to remain in Antioch, and they worked with the church there for "a long time" (v. 28). Then a serious problem arose that demanded immediate attention.

Examining the Text

I. Controversy (Acts 15:1-3)

From the beginning of the church at Antioch, its fellowship with the church in Jerusalem had been cordial. The church in Jerusalem had sent Barnabas, the encourager, to Antioch, and then he had brought Saul to Antioch to assist in the teaching ministry there (Acts 11:19-26). Later the Antioch church had sent famine relief to Judea (Acts 11:27-30). But now some self-appointed teachers came from Judea. They were not encouragers like Barnabas.

A. The Demand (v. 1)

1 Some men came down from Judea to Antioch and were teaching the brothers: "Unless you are circumcised, according to the custom taught by Moses, you cannot be saved."

These *men* who *came down from Judea to Antioch and were teaching the brothers* had no authority to do so. In the letter that was composed as a result of the meeting in Jerusalem, the leadership in Jerusalem noted that "some went out from us without our authorization and disturbed you, troubling your minds by what they said" (Acts 15:24).

These unauthorized visitors to Antioch taught, *"Unless you are circumcised, according to the custom taught by Moses, you cannot be saved."* Of course, there was more to this matter than just circumcision. As Paul explained in his letter to the Galatians, "I declare to every man who lets himself be circumcised that he is obligated to obey the whole law" (Galatians 5:3). In effect, the Gentile Christians in Antioch were being told that, without following the system of Jewish ritual observance, they could not be considered Christians.

B. The Delegation (vv. 2, 3)

² This brought Paul and Barnabas into sharp dispute and debate with them. So Paul and Barnabas were appointed, along with some other believers, to go up to Jerusalem to see the apostles and elders about this question.

One can easily see how a *sharp dispute and debate* arose from this turn of events, especially in light of Paul and Barnabas's recent missionary travels among the Gentiles. They had been preaching and teaching messages such as the one that Paul had delivered in Antioch of Pisidia: "Through [Jesus] everyone who believes is justified from everything you could not be justified from by the law of Moses" (Acts 13:38, 39). To sanction what the other teachers were proposing would have had the effect of negating all that had just been accomplished in places such as Antioch.

Since the two groups disagreed so strongly on such a crucial matter (that is, what was necessary for salvation), they agreed to take the matter to the *apostles* and to those who were *elders* in the well-established church in *Jerusalem*.

³ The church sent them on their way, and as they traveled through Phoenicia and Samaria, they told how the Gentiles had been converted. This news made all the brothers very glad.

Disciples of Jesus who had scattered beyond Jerusalem (following the martyrdom of Stephen) had taken the gospel to places such as *Phoenicia and Samaria* (Acts 8:5; 11:19). Paul and Barnabas and those accompanying them were greeted at these locations as they *traveled* to Jerusalem. They reported *how the Gentiles had been converted* in Antioch and in other cities where they had preached. The disciples who heard such *news* were *very glad* to receive it.

II. Conference (Acts 15:4-11)
A. Report to the Church (v. 4)

⁴ When they came to Jerusalem, they were welcomed by the church and the apostles and elders, to whom they reported everything God had done through them.

Here too the delegation led by Paul and Barnabas told of their endeavors and of their success among the Gentiles. They made it clear that *God had done* this great work *through them*. They were only his instruments.

B. Resistance of the Pharisees (v. 5)

⁵ Then some of the believers who belonged to the party of the Pharisees stood up and said, "The Gentiles must be circumcised and required to obey the law of Moses."

The *Pharisees* mentioned in this verse were clearly Christians; they are described as *believers*. But they had not lost their zeal for the law of Moses. Those teachers who had gone to Antioch were of this same persuasion; perhaps the men who spoke at this point were part of that group.

C. Response of the Leadership (vv. 6-11)

⁶ The apostles and elders met to consider this question.

The apostles and elders were the men in Jerusalem with whom the group from Antioch wished to confer. Apparently this was another public meeting (note the reference to "the whole assembly" in verse 12) following the meeting described in verses 4 and 5, though it may be that what transpired with the apostles and elders in verses 6-11 occurred to one side; then the report was presented to the entire assembly. At some point during the conference (perhaps between the two public meetings), there was a private meeting involving Paul, Barnabas, and Titus on the one hand, and Peter, John, and James the Lord's brother on the other. This meeting is described in Galatians 2:1-10. Paul says that in this meeting he "set before them the gospel that I preach among the Gentiles."

⁷ After much discussion, Peter got up and addressed them: "Brothers, you know that some time ago God made a choice among you that the Gentiles might hear from my lips the message of the gospel and believe.

Much discussion of the matter followed, perhaps similar to that which had taken place in Antioch (v. 2). No doubt each side felt very strongly about its position. Then *Peter got up* and addressed the assembly. He pointed out that he was the one whom God had used to expand the church's outreach to include Gentiles. He reminded the gathering that the fundamental issue they were discussing was a matter that God had already decided *some time ago*. The decision to go to the household of Cornelius was not something that Peter initiated on his own. God had sent Peter a vision (the same one three times) to teach him that "God does not show favoritism" (Acts 10:34).

⁸ "God, who knows the heart, showed that he accepted them by giving the Holy Spirit to them, just as he did to us.

While Peter was talking about Jesus to those gathered in the home of Cornelius, the *Holy Spirit* had come on them in a Pentecost-like manifestation, thus certifying that God did indeed want these people to receive his salvation (Acts 10:44-48).

> [9] *"He made no distinction between us and them, for he purified their hearts by faith.*

Peter had not suggested that the Gentiles in Cornelius's house be circumcised, but baptized, as the expression of their *faith* in Jesus as Lord and Christ (Acts 10:47). This was similar to what Peter had told the Jews gathered on the Day of Pentecost to do when he first proclaimed the gospel to them (Acts 2:38). Thus both Jews and Gentiles had been given the same opportunity to be justified by faith—without circumcision and without a commitment to keeping the law of Moses.

> [10] *"Now then, why do you try to test God by putting on the necks of the disciples a yoke that neither we nor our fathers have been able to bear?*

Peter concluded that the unauthorized teachers from Judea were contending with God, not with Paul and Barnabas, in insisting that the Gentiles come under the *yoke* of the law of Moses. The demands that these teachers were making of Gentile believers were demands that the Jews themselves had never *been able* to meet. The history of the Jewish nation proved this to be true. It seemed absurd, even hypocritical, to force it upon others.

> [11] *"No! We believe it is through the grace of our Lord Jesus that we are saved, just as they are."*

The key to salvation for Jews and Gentiles alike was *the grace of our Lord Jesus*. Those who insisted on forcing Gentiles to keep the law should be thankful that God had accepted the Gentiles by grace because the Jews, having failed to find salvation through keeping the law, could also be *saved* through grace.

III. Conclusions (Acts 15:19-21)

Verses 12-18 record how Barnabas and Paul reported on their work among the Gentiles to the "whole assembly" and how God had done miraculous signs and wonders through them. Then James spoke. This was "the Lord's brother" (Galatians 1:19), or more accurately "half-brother," who had become a believer apparently after Jesus' resurrection (1 Corinthians 15:7; Acts 1:14). By this time, he had become a highly respected leader in the Jerusalem church; and in his remarks he stated the consensus of those who had convened. He quoted from the Old Testament prophet Amos (Amos 9:11, 12) to show that the inclusion of Gentiles in the church was not the idea of Peter, Barnabas, Paul, or any human being. It was the fulfillment of God's great plan.

A. Respecting Gentile Believers (vv. 19, 20)

[19] *"It is my judgment, therefore, that we should not make it difficult for the Gentiles who are turning to God.*

Though James used the words *my judgment*, one can assume that what he was about to say was in harmony with the leading of the Holy Spirit, as were the statements others had already spoken. The Gentile believers had been deeply troubled by the teaching of those who had come from Judea to Antioch. To impose keeping the law of Moses on the *Gentiles* as a condition of salvation was rejected outright. However, there were some areas of concern that the Gentile believers needed to be aware of, and James proceeded to mention those.

[20] *"Instead we should write to them, telling them to abstain from food polluted by idols, from sexual immorality, from the meat of strangled animals and from blood.*

While the decision of the conference rejected any imposition of the law of Moses upon Gentiles, at the same time certain practical admonitions were not ruled out. Even though Gentile Christians had no obligations to the law of Moses as such, they did have an obligation, based on Christian love, to respect the moral sensitivities of their Jewish brothers and sisters.

For the Gentile believers to be told to *abstain from food polluted by idols* and *from sexual immorality* were especially appropriate warnings. The pagan worship in cities where the gospel was making inroads often included a mixture of idol worship and illicit sexual activity. Christians must not be idolaters or fornicators. They cannot worship other gods, and they cannot worship their own fleshly lusts.

The final two items mentioned by James (abstaining *from the meat of strangled animals and from blood*) appear to cover issues that were important in the Jewish law (Genesis 9:4; Leviticus 17:13, 14; Deuteronomy 12:16, 23, 27), but they are never emphasized in any presentation of the gospel. Why should they be imposed on Gentiles?

Some believe that these commands were meant primarily as an aid to fellowship between Jewish and Gentile Christians. An important part of fellowship in such settings was the readiness to understand and appreciate the sensitivities of others in the church. (It still is important.) The idea of eating the meat of strangled animals or of eating blood would have been highly offensive to Jewish believers. For the Gentile believers to respect these areas of conduct would make fellowship between Jews and Gentiles (particularly sharing meals together) much more harmonious.

B. Respecting the Law (v. 21)

[21] *"For Moses has been preached in every city from the earliest times and is read in the synagogues on every Sabbath."*

Scattered across the Roman Empire in *city* after city were *synagogues* where the law of *Moses* continued to be *read. . . on every Sabbath.* For generations Jews had heard and continued to hear week by week its regulations and prohibitions. These were deeply ingrained in their thinking and could not be erased all at once. For this reason, Gentile Christians needed to be especially sensitive to such matters to avoid offending Jewish consciences and damaging the unity of the church.

Paul and Barnabas, along with some others chosen from the gathering that had taken place, took a letter stating the assembly's decision back to Antioch (vv. 22, 23, 30, 31), where it was gladly received. Paul and Silas later delivered its message to other Gentile churches (Acts 16:4). However, the influence of the false teachers was not quickly put to rest. Paul rebuked the Galatians for being led astray by such a perversion of the gospel (Galatians 1:6-9; 3:1-5). He continued to teach that to seek salvation by keeping the law is to nullify the death of Jesus on the cross and to fall from grace (Galatians 2:21; 5:4).

How to Say It

AENEAS. Ee-*nee*-us.

AGABUS. *Ag*-uh-bus.

AGRIPPA. Uh-*grip*-puh.

ANTIOCH. *An*-tee-ock.

ANTIPAS. *An*-tih-pus.

AREOPAGUS. Air-ee-*op*-uh-gus.

BARNABAS. *Bar*-nuh-bus.

CAESAREA. Sess-uh-*ree*-uh.

CLAUDIUS. *Claw*-dee-us.

CORNELIUS. Cor-*neel*-yus.

CYRENE. Sigh-*ree*-nee.

DERBE. *Der*-be.

ETHIOPIAN. E-thee-*o*-pee-un (*th* as in *thin*).

EUNUCH. *you*-nick.

HERMES. *Her*-meez.

HEROD. *Hair*-ud.

ICONIUM. Eye-*ko*-nee-um.

JOPPA. *Jop*-uh.

JOSEPHUS. Jo-*see*-fus.

LUCIUS. *Lew*-shus.

LYCAONIA. *Lik*-uh-*o*-ni-uh (strong accent on *o*).

LYDDA. *Lid*-uh.

LYSTRA. *Liss*-truh.

MANAEN. *Man*-uh-en.

NIGER. *Nye*-jer.

PHILIPPI. Fih-*lip*-pie or *Fil*-ih-pie.

PHOENICIA. Fuh-*nish*-uh.

PISIDIA. Pih-*sid*-ee-uh.

PROSELYTE. *prahss*-uh-light.

SAMARIA. Suh-*mare*-ee-uh.

SIMEON. *Sim*-ee-un.

SYNAGOGUE. *sin*-uh-gog.

TARSUS. *Tar*-sus.

TETRARCH. *Teh*-trark or *Tee*-trark.

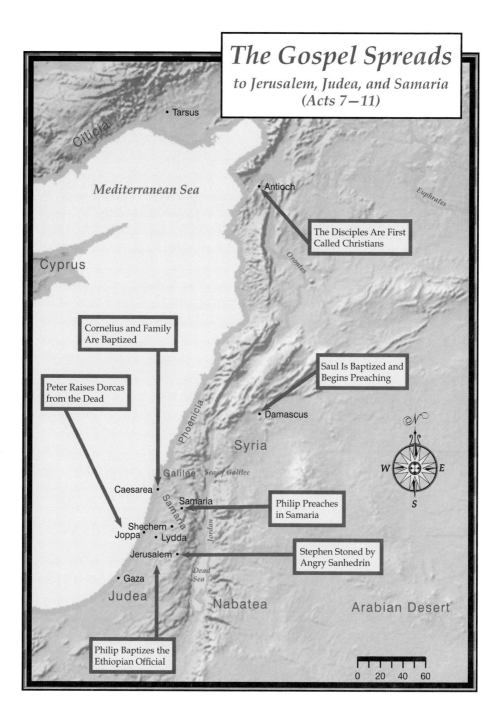

The Gospel Spreads
to Jerusalem, Judea, and Samaria
(Acts 7—11)

Tarsus

Cilicia

Mediterranean Sea

Antioch

Euphrates

The Disciples Are First
Called Christians

Cyprus

Orontes

Cornelius and Family
Are Baptized

Saul Is Baptized and
Begins Preaching

Peter Raises Dorcas
from the Dead

Damascus

Syria

Phoenicia

Galilee *Sea of Galilee*

W E

Caesarea

Samaria

Samaria

Philip Preaches
in Samaria

S

Shechem
Joppa   Lydda

Jordan

Jerusalem

Stephen Stoned by
Angry Sanhedrin

Gaza

Dead Sea

Judea

Nabatea

Arabian Desert

Philip Baptizes the
Ethiopian Official

0   20   40   60

Chapter 4

Paul's Second Missionary Journey

Acts 15:36-41; 16:1-10; 16:25-34; 17:22-34

DISAGREEMENT BETWEEN PAUL AND BARNABAS (ACTS 15:36-41)

Establishing the Groundwork

The previous chapter ended with a study of what is often called the "Jerusalem Conference." This gathering took place in response to some false teachers who claimed Gentile Christians needed to observe the law of Moses in order to be saved. Because this controversy had originated in the Antioch church, Paul and Barnabas, who had been serving there, traveled to Jerusalem and reported on their successful efforts among the Gentiles (Acts 15:12).

After those at this gathering had come to a decision (recorded in Acts 15:19-21), a letter explaining the decision was composed, which Paul, Barnabas, and others from the assembly delivered to the church in Antioch. Those "others" included Judas and Silas, who are described as "prophets" and who "said much to encourage and strengthen the brothers" (Acts 15:32). Eventually these two men returned to Jerusalem, while Paul and Barnabas remained in Antioch, continuing their teaching ministry (v. 35).

The church had thus survived a serious threat from the influence of false doctrine. But as anyone involved in church work can attest, not all problems that a church confronts are doctrinal in nature. Some involve more personal matters—such as the one that appears next in Luke's account.

Examining the Text

I. Disagreement (Acts 15:36-38)

A. Paul's Proposal (v. 36)

36 Some time later Paul said to Barnabas, "Let us go back and visit the brothers in all the towns where we preached the word of the Lord and see how they are doing."

It is hard to know exactly how long *some time later* signifies. Perhaps several months had passed since the Jerusalem Conference had taken place. Some suggest that during this time, the visit of Peter that Paul mentions in

Galatians 2:11-16 occurred. On that occasion, Paul rebuked Peter for withdrawing himself from fellowship with Gentile Christians because of pressure from "the circumcision group" (Galatians 2:12).

Paul wanted to *go back* to the churches that he and Barnabas had planted during their first missionary journey and *see how they* were *doing*. This was a sensible plan, and Barnabas was eager to go along. But the agreement between the two men ended there.

B. Barnabas's Preference (v. 37)

37 Barnabas wanted to take John, also called Mark, with them,

Barnabas wanted to take John, also called Mark, who was his cousin (Colossians 4:10). John Mark had accompanied Paul and Barnabas during a portion of their earlier travels (Acts 12:25; 13:5). He was most likely the author of the Gospel of Mark. Many believe that he was also the young man whose presence in the Garden of Gethsemane is reported only in Mark's Gospel (Mark 14:51, 52).

C. Paul's Protest (v. 38)

38 . . . but Paul did not think it wise to take him, because he had deserted them in Pamphylia and had not continued with them in the work.

Paul objected to Barnabas's idea of taking John Mark along, *because he had deserted them in Pamphylia* during the early stages of their journey. For some unknown reason (Luke gives no clue as to why this happened), John Mark had left Paul and Barnabas at Perga in Pamphylia to return to Jerusalem (Acts 13:13). Evidently Paul feared that whatever had induced the young man to desert them earlier might lead to similar action again. A repetition of those circumstances would not be good for the missionaries, for the Christians they planned to visit, or for John Mark himself.

II. Decision (Acts 15:39-41)
A. Barnabas and John Mark (v. 39)

39 They had such a sharp disagreement that they parted company. Barnabas took Mark and sailed for Cyprus,

Fresh from a successful effort in Jerusalem where they had stood together for including Gentiles in the church, two of the most noteworthy leaders in the early church now *parted company* over an issue of procedure! Paul and Barnabas were great men, but men nonetheless. Sometimes people live under the illusion that the outstanding individuals of the Bible never had disagreements or showed any weaknesses. This text dismisses that notion.

Ever the encourager, Barnabas probably was much more willing to give John Mark a second chance than Paul was. (Perhaps the fact that John Mark was Barnabas's cousin, as noted earlier, played a role in Barnabas's attitude.) *Barnabas took Mark and sailed for Cyprus.* Nothing more is said about this trip, and Barnabas and John Mark are not mentioned again in Acts. They are, however, mentioned in complimentary terms in later letters of Paul (1 Corinthians 9:6; Colossians 4:10; 2 Timothy 4:11; Philemon 24); so there must have been some kind of reconciliation at some point. In fact, in the 2 Timothy 4:11 reference, Paul describes John Mark as "helpful to me in my ministry." Perhaps it was the combination of Paul's toughness and Barnabas's gentleness that developed Mark into the "helpful" servant he eventually became.

B. Paul and Silas (vv. 40, 41)

40 . . . but Paul chose Silas and left, commended by the brothers to the grace of the Lord.

Paul chose Silas and left with him, eventually carrying out the plan he had earlier suggested to Barnabas (v. 36). Silas was one of the men who accompanied Paul and Barnabas to Antioch to deliver the report of the Jerusalem Conference and encourage the believers in Antioch (Acts 15:22). It is noted that these two men were *commended by the brothers* in Antioch *to the grace of the Lord*, though no such action is recorded concerning Barnabas and John Mark.

41 He went through Syria and Cilicia, strengthening the churches.

The letter that recorded the decision of the Jerusalem Conference was to be passed along to the Gentile Christians in *Syria and Cilicia* (Acts 15:23). No doubt Paul did this as he and Silas traveled through these territories. Syria was the area around Antioch. Most likely Christians from Antioch had established churches in this region. Cilicia was northwest of Syria and was the region where Tarsus, Paul's hometown, was located. Perhaps Paul worked to establish churches in this area while he was at Tarsus between the times when he fled Jerusalem (Acts 9:29, 30) and when Barnabas came to Tarsus to take him to Antioch (Acts 11:22-26).

Was it God's intention that Paul and Barnabas part company? Probably not. But God in his grace "works all things for good" in every situation (Romans 8:28), and this incident is no different. Perhaps without this opportunity, Silas would never have become as involved in missionary work as he did. And without Barnabas's continued mentoring, perhaps John Mark would have given up all hope of ever finding his place in the Lord's service.

TIMOTHY JOINS PAUL AND SILAS; THE MACEDONIAN CALL (ACTS 16:1-10)

Establishing the Groundwork

Timothy became one of the most beloved co-workers of the apostle Paul. His name means "one who honors God," and his ministry with Paul lived up to this description. The two were partners during most of Paul's second and third missionary journeys recorded in Acts, and we find additional details of their partnership in the epistles Paul wrote during those two journeys.

The frequency with which Timothy is mentioned in these books illustrates the important role he played in the apostle's life and ministry. During the second journey, while Paul was in Corinth, he wrote two letters to the Thessalonian believers, and Timothy is mentioned in each (1 Thessalonians 1:1; 3:2, 6; 2 Thessalonians 1:1). At some point during this ministry, Paul sent Timothy back to Thessalonica for a brief mission of encouragement (1 Thessalonians 3:2-6). During the third journey, Paul had a lengthy ministry in Ephesus (Acts 19:10; 20:31). During that time Timothy worked with Paul or went to other places on Paul's behalf. Acts 19:22 tells of a trip to Macedonia; 1 Corinthians 4:17 tells of one to Corinth. Later Paul was in Macedonia, from which 2 Corinthians was written. Timothy is mentioned in 2 Corinthians 1:1, so it appears he was with Paul in Macedonia as well. Romans was written at about the same time, either from Macedonia or Corinth. Since Timothy is named in Romans 16:21, it appears Timothy accompanied Paul from Macedonia, into Greece (Corinth), and then back to Macedonia, from where he then accompanied Paul as he started for Jerusalem (Acts 20:1-4).

Timothy was with Paul when he wrote Philippians, Colossians, and Philemon also (as indicated in the opening verse of each). These are called "prison epistles," written from Rome during Paul's first imprisonment there. Ephesians is also one of the prison epistles, but Timothy is not mentioned. What is significant, however, is that Timothy was with Paul during this time, even though he is not mentioned in Acts. And if Hebrews was written by Paul, or at least during Paul's lifetime, it appears Timothy may have been imprisoned with the apostle at some point as well (Hebrews 13:23).

That an intimate friendship developed between Timothy and Paul is obvious from the terminology the apostle uses of his younger companion in those letters addressed to him. Paul describes Timothy as "my true son" in 1 Timothy 1:2 and as "my dear son" in 2 Timothy 1:2. Philippians 2:19-22 includes what may be Paul's finest tribute to Timothy. He says of him, "I have no one else like him, who takes a genuine interest in your welfare" (v. 20). He also writes, "You know that Timothy has proved himself, because as a son with his father he has served with me in the work of the gospel" (v. 22).

The following text records Paul's initial contact with Timothy and the beginning of Timothy's participation in Paul's ministry.

Examining the Text

I. A New Associate (Acts 16:1-5)
A. Introduction to Timothy (vv. 1, 2)

¹ He came to Derbe and then to Lystra, where a disciple named Timothy lived, whose mother was a Jewess and a believer, but whose father was a Greek.

Paul, with Silas as his companion, had embarked on his second missionary journey when he arrived at *Derbe* and *Lystra*. On Paul's previous missionary journey, he and Barnabas had visited these cities. They had established churches in both locations, returning a short time later to Lystra to see that elders were ordained in that church (Acts 14:21-23).

It is possible, as noted in the previous chapter, that *Timothy*, who lived in Lystra, became a *disciple* of Jesus during Paul's earlier visit there. Timothy's *mother*, a *Jewess* whose name was Eunice (2 Timothy 1:5), had married a *Greek*, or Gentile. Such a marriage was not uncommon among Jews living outside of Palestine, though it would have brought criticism from many Jews in Palestine. The fact that Timothy's *father* is not described as a proselyte or "God-fearer" probably means that he had little or no personal interest in promoting the gospel in his family.

² The brothers at Lystra and Iconium spoke well of him.

Timothy's reputation as a young man who was serious about his faith had spread throughout the church at *Lystra* and even to *Iconium* some twenty miles away. Believers in these cities considered his spiritual development to be quite impressive.

B. Invitation from Paul (vv. 3-5)

³ Paul wanted to take him along on the journey, so he circumcised him because of the Jews who lived in that area, for they all knew that his father was a Greek.

So interested was Paul in this promising young man that he *wanted to take him along* as part of the missionary team. But Paul usually began his evangelistic work in any city by going to the synagogue and preaching to the Jews there (Acts 17:1, 2). This posed a potential problem with *the Jews who lived in that area* who *knew* of Timothy's background and upbringing. They were aware of the fact that *his father was a Greek*, and that he apparently refused to have Timothy circumcised as an infant. This could constitute a significant stumbling block in their minds and give them reason to oppose Paul's efforts (no doubt many of them would be quite pleased to have such grounds). In order to keep this from becoming a barrier to his evangelistic work, Paul *circumcised* Timothy in accordance with the Old Testament regulation.

It is important to note the distinction between this situation and that involving Titus, whose situation regarding circumcision is cited in Galatians 2:3-5. There Paul was contending that circumcision should not be imposed on Gentiles as a condition of salvation (Galatians 5:6-12). Timothy's circumcision, however, was not being forced upon him; it was a voluntary act, performed out of a desire to become "all things to all men so that by all possible means" others might be saved (1 Corinthians 9:22; see also vv. 19, 20).

⁴ As they traveled from town to town, they delivered the decisions reached by the apostles and elders in Jerusalem for the people to obey.

The towns covered by Paul, Silas, and their new companion included those locations visited during Paul's first missionary journey. Within these predominantly Gentile churches, the question of whether or not Gentile Christians were required to be circumcised and keep the law of Moses had arisen. *The decisions reached by the apostles and elders* at the *Jerusalem* Conference (Acts 15) were now *delivered* by the missionaries *as they traveled.* Timothy's presence with the group, and how circumcision had been handled in his case, probably helped clarify additional questions that were raised.

⁵ So the churches were strengthened in the faith and grew daily in numbers.

This provides a summary statement of the progress to this point of Paul's second missionary journey. The reference to both spiritual and numerical growth recognizes the importance of each.

II. A New Area (Acts 16:6-10)
A. Closed Doors (vv. 6-8)

6 Paul and his companions traveled throughout the region of Phrygia and Galatia, having been kept by the Holy Spirit from preaching the word in the province of Asia.

The region of Phrygia and Galatia lay northwest of Cilicia, where Paul and Silas had gone at the beginning of their travels together (Acts 15:40, 41). To each church, *Paul and his companions* delivered the message from the Jerusalem Conference (Acts 16:4). The churches they visited in Galatia likely included those in Lystra, Derbe, Iconium, and Pisidian Antioch, which Paul and Barnabas had established during their first journey.

The borders of Phrygia and Galatia varied from time to time. For purposes of government, it seems that the Romans had assigned the territory of Phrygia partly to Asia and partly to Galatia. One should note that the term *Asia* in the New Testament does not signify the continent that we associate with the term today. It was a *province* that included much of what is now western and central Turkey, and was located west of Phrygia and Galatia.

The reason that Paul and his companions were *kept by the Holy Spirit* from moving farther westward into Asia is not given. Eventually Paul would bring the gospel to this territory; as a result of his later ministry in Ephesus, "all the Jews and Greeks who lived in the province of Asia heard the word of the Lord" (Acts 19:10).

7 When they came to the border of Mysia, they tried to enter Bithynia, but the Spirit of Jesus would not allow them to.

Mysia was located in the northwest part of the province of Asia. *Bithynia* was a province east of Mysia, at the southern end of the Black Sea. Again, *the Spirit of Jesus would not allow them to enter* these places. Note that as the "Holy Spirit" could be used interchangeably with "God" (Acts 5:3, 4), so in this passage the "Holy Spirit" is used interchangeably with "the Spirit of Jesus." Just how the Spirit made his desires known is not indicated; we are told only that he closed the door to this opportunity.

8 So they passed by Mysia and went down to Troas.

Troas was situated on the Aegean Sea at the northwestern end of modern Turkey. At some time (perhaps during either Paul's second or third missionary journey) a church was established in Troas, for Paul ministered at Troas at the end of his third journey as he made his way to Jerusalem (Acts 20:5-12).

B. Open Door (vv. 9, 10)

⁹ During the night Paul had a vision of a man of Macedonia standing and begging him, "Come over to Macedonia and help us."

Macedonia was a Roman province located approximately one hundred miles across the Aegean Sea from Troas, north of Greece. It was an area of great significance at this time, astride the main highway from the east to Rome. Here we are provided with details as to how Paul was guided to go to Macedonia: he was summoned *during the night* by *a vision of a man* from Macedonia *begging* Paul to *come* and *help*.

¹⁰ After Paul had seen the vision, we got ready at once to leave for Macedonia, concluding that God had called us to preach the gospel to them.

Paul and his companions immediately concluded that the same Spirit who had forbidden them to preach in both Asia and Bithynia was now directing them through this vision to *preach the gospel* in *Macedonia.* It should be noted that this is the first appearance of the *"we passages"* that one finds in the book of Acts, indicating the presence of Luke, the author. Apparently he joined the missionary team at this point. Luke was a doctor (Colossians 4:14) and perhaps cared for Paul at times when he became ill (Galatians 4:13), experienced trouble with his "thorn in the flesh" (2 Corinthians 12:7), or was severely beaten (2 Corinthians 11:24, 25).

Responding to God's call, the missionary team prepared to take the gospel into what is modern Europe. Their first major stop would be Philippi.

PAUL AND SILAS JAILED IN PHILIPPI (ACTS 16:25-34)

Establishing the Groundwork

Luke, who may have been a native of Philippi, calls it "a Roman colony and the leading city of that district of Macedonia" (Acts 16:12). It commanded a fertile plain, was located on an important highway, and was enriched by the gold mines in the mountains to the north.

Apparently the Jewish population in Philippi was not large enough to warrant building a synagogue. (According to Jewish tradition, ten married men were required to have a synagogue.) So instead of beginning his evangelistic efforts there, as he usually did, Paul found a place by a river where people were gathered to pray on the Sabbath. There he met Lydia, a dealer in purple cloth from the city of Thyatira who is described as "a worshiper of God" (Acts 16:14). Lydia and her household were baptized, after which she invited Paul and his companions to stay at her house.

Soon after this, a young woman possessed of a spirit by which she predicted the future began to follow the missionaries, shouting that they were "servants of the Most High God, who are telling you the way to be saved" (Acts 16:17). Paul commanded the spirit to come out of the girl, and it did. When the men who profited from her fortune-telling discovered what had happened, they were so angry that they had Paul and Silas arrested under false charges. Deprived of any opportunity to defend themselves, the two men were stripped and severely flogged, then thrown into prison in the "inner cell" (the most closely guarded part of the jail) where their feet were fastened in the stocks (Acts 16:24). These men, however, were no ordinary prisoners.

Examining the Text

I. The Jailer's Responsibility (Acts 16:25-28)
A. Songs of Praise (v. 25)

25 About midnight Paul and Silas were praying and singing hymns to God, and the other prisoners were listening to them.

Instead of cursing their surroundings—or God—as many prisoners might have done, *Paul and Silas were praying*. And instead of complaining, they were *singing hymns*. Nor was this a private time of worship, for *the other prisoners were listening to them*. Even a prison can become a sanctuary when God's people are present, and even there one can bear testimony for Christ. The bodies of Paul and Silas may have been in chains, but their spirits were celebrating the freedom that only Jesus can give.

Such activity taking place *about midnight* must have seemed strange to the other prisoners. But what happened next was even stranger.

B. Sudden Earthquake (v. 26)

26 Suddenly there was such a violent earthquake that the foundations of the prison were shaken. At once all the prison doors flew open, and everybody's chains came loose.

Not only were the other prisoners listening to Paul and Silas (as the previous verse states), but God was too! *A violent earthquake* occurred—of such magnitude that *the foundations of the prison were shaken*. The words *suddenly* and *at once* indicate God's power at work. *All the prison doors flew open*, and every prisoner's *chains came loose*. Perhaps the other prisoners recognized a divine hand at work as well (or were simply stunned by the sudden turn of events), since no one took the opportunity to escape.

C. Startled Jailer (v. 27)

27 The jailer woke up, and when he saw the prison doors open, he drew his sword and was about to kill himself because he thought the prisoners had escaped.

The primary responsibility of the *jailer* was to keep his *prisoners* in custody. If they were to escape, it would mean his life for theirs. Assuming that the prisoners had used the earthquake as their opportunity to flee, this jailer was certain that suicide would be less painful or less shameful than the sentence that his superiors would carry out on him.

D. Soothing Words (v. 28)

28 But Paul shouted, "Don't harm yourself! We are all here!"

If the jailer could not see the prisoners, how did Paul know what he was about to do? Was it darker in the "inner cell" so that the prisoners could see the jailer but he could not see them? Did he give a cry of despair, announcing his intentions to kill himself? Did the Holy Spirit reveal to Paul what the jailer was about to do? We do not know the answer for certain, but we do know that *Paul shouted* from the darkness and assured the alarmed jailer that no one had fled.

II. The Jailer's Request (Acts 16:29-32)
A. His Question (vv. 29, 30)

29, 30 The jailer called for lights, rushed in and fell trembling before Paul and Silas. He then brought them out and asked, "Sirs, what must I do to be saved?"

Quickly *the jailer called for lights* (probably a torch or lamp of some kind). He *rushed in* toward the inner cell where *Paul and Silas* had been imprisoned and *fell trembling before* them. Why did he go directly to Paul and Silas rather than the other prisoners? Perhaps the jailer had heard about Paul and Silas or had even heard them preaching prior to their arrest. Possibly the references to God in their messages made him think that they could explain the earthquake that had just happened. He may have recalled that they were preaching a message that had something to do with salvation, and now, deeply distressed over what had just taken place, he turned to Paul and Silas for help.

B. Paul's Answer (vv. 31, 32)

31 They replied, "Believe in the Lord Jesus, and you will be saved—you and your household."

In answering the jailer's question at this point, Paul and Silas did not provide a lengthy or detailed explanation. There would be an opportunity for that later. For now, they simply stated the starting point of salvation for any person: *Believe in the Lord Jesus, and you will be saved.*

32 *Then they spoke the word of the Lord to him and to all the others in his house.*

The jailer's house was probably located not far from the prison (perhaps those in the house had been awakened by the earthquake). The jailer and *all the others in his house* gathered to hear *the word of the Lord* from Paul and Silas. This would have included not only children but also any servants who lived with the jailer. Such a setting provided a more favorable opportunity to explain what believing in Jesus Christ meant.

III. The Jailer's Response (Acts 16:33, 34)
A. Following Jesus (v. 33)

33 *At that hour of the night the jailer took them and washed their wounds; then immediately he and all his family were baptized.*

Less than twenty-four hours earlier, this *jailer* had confined Paul and Silas to the inner cell of his prison and fastened their feet in the stocks. He cared little that they had been severely flogged. Now the same man *took them and washed their wounds*, perhaps using olive oil and/or wine to cleanse the wounds (Luke 10:34). *Then immediately he and all his family* were taken to a place where they could be buried and raised with Christ in baptism. Thus "the word of the Lord" (v. 32) that Paul and Silas had declared to this man and his family included instructions concerning baptism, much as Philip's preaching of the good news about Jesus to the Ethiopian eunuch included such instructions (Acts 8:35-38). Note that baptism was thought of as something so important that it needed to be done at once, even though it came at the end of a long, eventful, and emotionally draining night.

John Chrysostom, one of the outstanding preachers of early church history, wrote of the Philippian jailer: "He washed and was washed. He washed them from their stripes, and he himself was washed from his sins."

B. Filled with Joy (v. 34)

34 *The jailer brought them into his house and set a meal before them; he was filled with joy because he had come to believe in God—he and his whole family.*

Earlier Lydia had shown hospitality toward Paul and his companions by inviting them to stay in her home (Acts 16:15). Here we see a similar spirit of generosity demonstrated by the converted *jailer*. Perhaps it should not be surprising, given such examples of sharing, that after Paul left Philippi, the Philippian church was attentive to his needs and sent him offerings "again and again" to aid him in his evangelistic work in other places (Philippians 4:15, 16).

How different was the jailer's outlook now that he had given his life to Christ! Whereas a few hours earlier he had been filled with despair and was on the verge of taking his own life, now *he was filled with joy because he had come to believe in God*. We have already seen how frequently in the book of Acts gladness and joy are associated with following Jesus (Acts 2:46; 5:41; 8:8, 39; 11:23). We should remember that a decision such as the jailer's causes joy in Heaven as well (Luke 15:7).

PAUL AT THE AREOPAGUS IN ATHENS (ACTS 17:22-34)

Establishing the Groundwork

In the previous study, we observed how the first of the "we passages" in Acts occurs when Paul travels to Macedonia in answer to the "Macedonian call" (Acts 16:9, 10). However, at the end of the chapter when Paul and Silas leave Philippi the text reads, "Then *they* left" (Acts 16:40). It seems that Luke, who (as earlier noted) may have been a native of Philippi, stayed there to provide encouragement and leadership to the new church that had been established there.

Meanwhile Paul and Silas proceeded to Thessalonica, which was approximately 100 miles southwest of Philippi. There Paul experienced initial success among both Jews and Greeks as a result of his preaching in the synagogue (Acts 17:1-4). As was the case in other cities, however, certain Jews stirred up opposition against his efforts; and eventually Paul and Silas were sent away to Berea, about fifty miles southwest of Thessalonica.

In Berea, as in Thessalonica, there was at first a positive response to the gospel from both Jews and Greeks. The Bereans' passion for studying the Scriptures is highlighted (Acts 17:11); sadly, so is the further hostility to Paul's preaching from the Jews who had caused him trouble in Thessalonica (17:13). This time only Paul was sent away, while Silas and Timothy remained at Berea. (This is the first mention of Timothy since Acts 16:3, where Paul wanted to take him along. We assume Timothy had been traveling with Paul ever since, until he and Silas got a special task.) Acts 17:15 says, "The men who escorted

Paul brought him to Athens and then left with instructions for Silas and Timothy to join him as soon as possible." Athens was some 200 miles south of Berea, down the western coast of the Aegean Sea. (Paul may well have traveled much of that distance by boat.)

In Athens, Paul saw a city "full of idols." "Greatly distressed" by this (Acts 17:16), he began to reason with worshipers in the synagogue and with others whom he encountered in the marketplace. Athens was a center of Greek culture, and a favorite gathering place for philosophers who liked to discuss most any topic. Hearing Paul "preaching the good news about Jesus and the resurrection" (Acts 17:18), some of the philosophers realized that he was talking about matters unfamiliar to them. A group of them invited Paul to a meeting place called the Areopagus. In this setting, which was less noisy than the marketplace, Paul was asked to explain the "new teaching" and the "strange ideas" that he had been presenting (vv. 19, 20).

Examining the Text

I. Our Creator God (Acts 17:22-25)
A. Unknown to the Athenians (vv. 22, 23)

²² Paul then stood up in the meeting of the Areopagus and said: "Men of Athens! I see that in every way you are very religious.

The location for Paul's address in Athens was the *Areopagus*, also known as Mars' Hill—an elevated plateau in the middle of the city. (This name originated because, according to legend, the trial of the god Mars for the murder of the son of the god Neptune was held here.) It was the place where the Athenian Supreme Court deliberated, as well as one of several locations in the city where public debates were held.

Paul had been able to *see* something about the religious tendencies of the people of Athens by observing their public idols and temples. It has been estimated that first-century Athens may have had two to three thousand idols on display. This would have been overwhelming to a Christian who was a first-time visitor. No doubt it was the reason Paul, as noted earlier, was "greatly distressed" at such idolatry. Nevertheless, as he began his speech to the Athenians, he referred to them as *in every way . . . very religious*. Perhaps Paul intended this as a mild compliment that was devised to "soften up" his audience so that they would give him a fair hearing. The word for "religious" can also have the connotation of "superstitious," so some have suggested that Paul intended to be ambiguous with the term. By thus making the Athenians wonder whether they had just been complimented or criticized, he would have given them further reason to listen carefully to what else he had to say.

23 "For as I walked around and looked carefully at your objects of worship, I even found an altar with this inscription: TO AN UNKNOWN GOD. Now what you worship as something unknown I am going to proclaim to you.

We do not know the occasion for setting up an anonymous *altar*, but we can imagine how it was used thereafter. The Athenians apparently intended to pay tribute to every god that existed, without slighting even one. This would be a daunting challenge if one did not know for certain how many gods there are. An undesignated altar, however, could serve as a "miscellaneous" object of worship to cover any god that may have been inadvertently missed. One must admire Paul's creativity in using something with which his audience was familiar as a way of introducing them to the true God. His method is similar to Jesus' use of his thirst for water as a way of introducing the Samaritan woman to "living water" (John 4:7-10).

B. Unfathomable to All (vv. 24, 25)

24 "The God who made the world and everything in it is the Lord of heaven and earth and does not live in temples built by hands.

As Paul looked for some common ground with the Athenians from which he could present the gospel, he began with the most fundamental of beliefs: the existence of a divine creator. As Paul explains in Romans 1, human beings have always sensed that someone wise and powerful must be responsible for all that we see (Romans 1:20). All of nature, from living beings to inanimate objects to the heavenly bodies, possesses an intricacy and beauty that testify to an intelligent Designer. Theologians speak of this testimony that creation gives on behalf of its creator as "general revelation."

The Areopagus, where Paul was speaking, was located within view of one of the most significant worship centers of that time—the Parthenon. But Paul asserted that a God of such power and majesty—a God who is *the Lord of heaven and earth*—most certainly cannot be confined to such manmade buildings: he *does not live in temples built by hands.* In some sense, he did promise to meet with Moses at the "ark of the Testimony" or ark of the covenant in the tabernacle (Exodus 25:22); but such a place was never to be considered his primary or permanent dwelling place. Solomon recognized this truth when he dedicated his temple (1 Kings 8:27), and Stephen acknowledged it as well in his defense before the Sanhedrin (Acts 7:48, 49).

[25] *"And he is not served by human hands, as if he needed anything, because he himself gives all men life and breath and everything else."*

In addition, the Lord of heaven and earth does not require the services or gifts of *human hands* in order to maintain his existence. While it is true that we can and must serve God, we do not do so *as if he needed anything*. The church building in which we worship is not erected to meet God's need; it is there to meet our needs and the needs of others who must hear the good news of salvation. Anyone capable of creating a universe is obviously too big to fit inside a building suited for people, and is far too powerful to require assistance from someone as small as a human being.

Such an argument as this would have sounded reasonable to the Greek philosophers whom Paul was addressing. In fact, by the first century many of the educated Greeks and Romans no longer believed the ancient pagan myths, though they retained a belief that there was some kind of divine creator. Paul's description of the creator was meant to appeal to the thinking of the "modern" philosopher of the first century.

II. Our Religious Duty (Acts 17:26-29)
A. To Seek After God (vv. 26-28)

[26] *"From one man he made every nation of men, that they should inhabit the whole earth; and he determined the times set for them and the exact places where they should live.*

Without mentioning the name of Adam, Paul declared that the human race originated *from one man*. Greek philosophy typically did not speak this way; and yet the philosophers could readily grant that humanity had to begin somewhere small, then grow to the size it had become.

As for Paul's description of God's involvement in *every nation of men*, the Old Testament declares that God's plan is "determined for the whole world" and that his hand is "stretched out over all nations" (Isaiah 14:26). To King Nebuchadnezzar of Babylon, Daniel asserted that God "changes times and seasons; he sets up kings and deposes them" (Daniel 2:21).

All of this is in keeping with Paul's statement to the Athenians that God has *determined the times set for* the various nations *and the exact places where they should live*. Exactly how he does all of this is not certain to us, because from our perspective the workings of God in the world are very discreet. Even so, we must pray about social and political issues, confidently believing that God remains actively involved in the affairs of humanity, though we may not always know how.

[27] *"God did this so that men would seek him and perhaps reach out for him and find him, though he is not far from each one of us.*

Once one realizes that a creator exists, he should naturally desire to know more about this creator—who he is, what he is like, and how one can please him. Paul expresses a similar idea in Romans 1 when he explains why God's wrath is directed toward pagans who have seen his general revelation, yet refuse to *seek him*: "what may be known about God is plain to them, because God has made it plain to them. For since the creation of the world God's invisible qualities—his eternal power and divine nature—have been clearly seen, being understood from what has been made, so that men are without excuse. For although they knew God, they neither glorified him as God nor gave thanks to him" (Romans 1:19-21). This is religious duty in its most elementary form, something with which Paul's philosophy-minded listeners could agree.

[28] *"'For in him we live and move and have our being.' As some of your own poets have said, 'We are his offspring.'*

Paul reveals something about his own education by citing two statements from ancient Greek literature. These quotations were meant to highlight man's special relationship to his creator. *For in him we live and move and have our being* was apparently written by a poet from Crete named Epimenides, who lived around 600 BC. *We are his* [God's] *offspring* was first recorded by the third-century BC Greek philosopher Cleanthes in his "Hymn to Zeus," and then later repeated by the poet Aratus (at around 270 BC) in a poem entitled, "Phenomena."

Why would Paul quote material from pagan sources? To do so would enhance his credentials in the eyes of this critical and skeptical audience. By showing that he was well versed in their literature, Paul would appear to them as a learned man worthy of their time and attention. By giving the Greek poets credit for knowing some truth about the God he was describing, Paul would more likely be judged an honest and fair-minded man by the Athenians.

B. To Think of Him Correctly (v. 29)

[29] *"Therefore since we are God's offspring, we should not think that the divine being is like gold or silver or stone—an image made by man's design and skill."*

Having established some intellectual rapport with his audience, Paul could present a more direct criticism of their position. If human beings are the *offspring* of God, how is it possible for anyone to *think that the divine being is like gold or silver or stone* carved into an image *made by man's design and skill?* No work or creation of man's hands can truly represent the living God any more than it can adequately represent a human being.

III. Our Final Judgment (Acts 17:30, 31)
A. God's Desire for Repentance (v. 30)

[30] *"In the past God overlooked such ignorance, but now he commands all people everywhere to repent.*

Even when linked with good intentions, idolatry is always an offense against God. Throughout the Old Testament age, God was gracious enough to restrain his wrath at *such ignorance* and not bring the fury of Hell upon the nations at that time. But whereas he overlooked that disobedience, *now he commands all people everywhere to repent.* "In these last days he has spoken to us by his Son" (Hebrews 1:2). His Son has given his life to atone for the sins of every person. That good news is meant for "all nations" (Matthew 28:19), and Paul was declaring it to those gathered at the Areopagus.

B. God's Day of Judgment (v. 31)

[31] *"For he has set a day when he will judge the world with justice by the man he has appointed. He has given proof of this to all men by raising him from the dead."*

The Athenian philosophers would readily grant that a creator exists. They could concede the logic of Paul's description of man's religious duty to that creator (though they might not have appreciated his criticism regarding idols). And if they were honest, they would have to admit that they had considered the possibility that one day they may have to give an account to this creator regarding how they have treated him. Paul builds upon this natural instinct and declares with certainty: you will be condemned by the creator whom you have offended, if you do not respond to his plan of salvation.

Some readers of Paul's message to the Athenians are troubled that the name of Jesus is not mentioned in this account. But what is provided in the Acts account is obviously a summary of Paul's message. (We assume that he preached longer than the five minutes or so that it takes to read these verses in Acts.) It may be that during the complete message, Paul mentioned Jesus several times. Note that it was Paul's preaching of "Jesus and the resurrection" (v. 18) that led to his being invited to speak at the Areopagus. That Jesus' name is not mentioned in this brief summary should not disturb us.

IV. A Mixed Response (Acts 17:32-34)
A. Doubters and Deliberators (vv. 32, 33)

32, 33 When they heard about the resurrection of the dead, some of them sneered, but others said, "We want to hear you again on this subject." At that, Paul left the Council.

For some of the philosophers, Paul lost his credibility as a logical thinker when he spoke of *the resurrection of the dead*. "Perhaps *he* is the one who is 'too religious,'" they may have thought. Others were interested in hearing more from Paul, but assumed that they had plenty of time to consider and debate this new topic later. We are not told whether or not those who made this proposal followed through with it. Anyone who has been involved in evangelism can relate to Paul's mixed responses; some people are rather hostile to the gospel, while others express varying degrees of interest. One hopes and prays that those who say they want to hear more will put actions to their words.

B. Disciples (v. 34)

34 A few men became followers of Paul and believed. Among them was Dionysius, a member of the Areopagus, also a woman named Damaris, and a number of others.

We know nothing about *Dionysius* or *Damaris*, except what is said in this passage. That Dionysius was *a member of the Areopagus* indicates that he was a prominent and respected man in Athens, perhaps one of the judges who were part of the Athenian Supreme Court.

During the New Testament period, we hear nothing further about the Christians in Athens, and, so far as we know, Paul never returned to the city. Many have wondered why the gospel was not more widely received in Athens. There are no ready answers, but throughout the centuries it seems that the intellectual communities have not always been the most fertile ground for the gospel. Sometimes pride and a sense of self-sufficiency can insulate these individuals from a sense of need for what the gospel offers.

In spite of this, Paul's example is a worthy one to emulate today. He took the unchanging gospel and presented it in a way best suited to challenge the hearts and minds of a different kind of hearer, thereby showing us one illustration of what it means to "become all things to all men, so that by all possible means [we] might save some" (1 Corinthians 9:22).

How to Say It

ANTIOCH. *An*-tee-ock.

ARATUS. *Air*-uh-tus.

AREOPAGUS. Air-ee-*op*-uh-gus.

ATHENIAN. Uh-*thin*-e-un.

BARNABAS. *Bar*-nuh-bus.

BITHYNIA. Bih-*thin*-ee-uh.

CHRYSOSTOM. *Kris*-us-tum or Krih-*sahss*-tum.

CILICIA. Sih-*lish*-i-uh.

CLEANTHES. Clee-*an*-theez (*th* as in *thin*).

DAMARIS. *Dam*-uh-ris.

DERBE. *Der*-be.

DIONYSIUS. Die-oh-*nish*-ih-us.

EPIMENIDES. Ep-ih-*men*-ih-deez.

EUNICE. U-*nye*-see or *U*-nis.

GALATIA. Guh-*lay*-shuh.

GETHSEMANE. Geth-*sem*-uh-nee (G as in *get*).

ICONIUM. Eye-*ko*-nee-um.

LYDIA. *Lid*-ee-uh.

LYSTRA. *Liss*-truh.

MACEDONIA. Mass-eh-*doe*-nee-uh.

MYSIA. *Mish*-ee-uh.

PAMPHYLIA. Pam-*fill*-ee-uh.

PARTHENON. *Par*-thuh-non (*th* as in *thin*).

PERGA. *Per*-gah.

PHILIPPI. Fih-*lip*-pie or *Fil*-ih-pie.

PHRYGIA. *Frij*-e-uh.

PISIDIAN. Pih-*sid*-ee-un.

PROSELYTE. *prahss*-uh-light.

SANHEDRIN. San-huh-drun or San-*heed*-run.

SILAS. *Sigh*-luss.

TARSUS. *Tar*-sus.

THYATIRA. *Thy*-uh-*tie*-ruh (strong accent on *tie*; *th* as in *thin*).

TROAS. *Tro*-az.

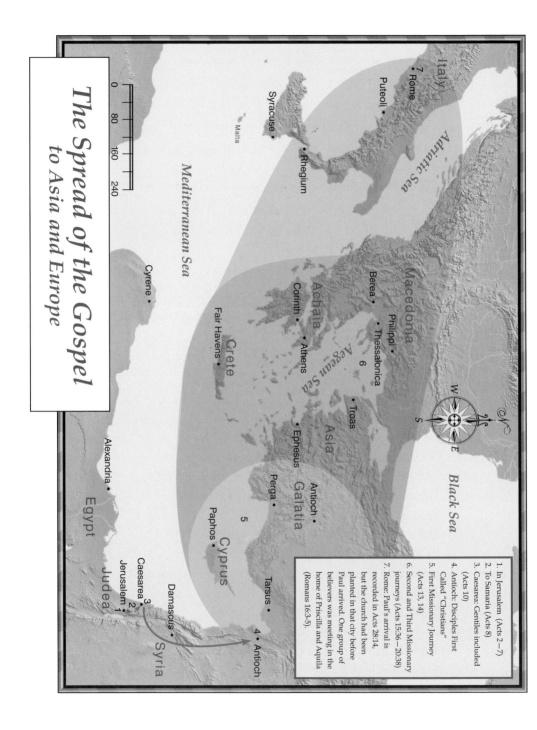

The Spread of the Gospel
to Asia and Europe

1. In Jerusalem (Acts 2—7)
2. To Samaria (Acts 8)
3. Caesarea: Gentiles included (Acts 10)
4. Antioch: Disciples First Called "Christians" (Acts 11)
5. First Missionary Journey (Acts 13, 14)
6. Second and Third Missionary journeys (Acts 15:36 — 20:38)
7. Rome: Paul's arrival is recorded in Acts 28:14, but the church had been planted in that city before Paul arrived. One group of believers was meeting in the home of Priscilla and Aquila (Romans 16:3-5).

Black Sea

Mediterranean Sea

Adriatic Sea

Aegean Sea

Italy
Rome 7
Puteoli
Syracuse
Rhegium
Malta

Macedonia
Berea
Philippi 6
Thessalonica
Achaia
Corinth
Athens
Troas
Crete
Fair Havens
Asia
Ephesus
Perga
Galatia
Antioch
Paphos 5
Cyprus
Tarsus

Cyrene

Alexandria

Egypt

Judea
Jerusalem 1
Caesarea 2 3
Damascus
Syria
Antioch 4

0   80   160   240

Chapter 5

Paul's Further Travels and His Arrival in Rome
Acts 18:24-28; 19:1-6; 20:17-32; 26:19-32; 28:23-31

THE GOSPEL COMES TO EPHESUS (ACTS 18:24-28; 19:1-6)

Establishing the Groundwork

From Athens, Paul continued his second missionary journey by traveling to the city of Corinth, approximately fifty miles west of Athens. Corinth was the capital of the province of Achaia (located in what today would be southern Greece), and was a great commercial center. Corinth was also famed for its temple of the Greek goddess Aphrodite, whose worship fostered prostitution in the name of religion. At one time a thousand "sacred prostitutes" served in her temple, contributing their sordid influence to the city's widespread immorality. So renowned did Corinth become for its immoral activity that the Greek verb "to Corinthianize" was coined, meaning "to practice sexual immorality."

In Corinth Paul became acquainted with a couple, Aquila and Priscilla, who, like him, were tentmakers (Acts 18:1-4). (Since no mention is made of their conversion in Acts, it is usually assumed that they were already Christians when Paul met them.) Paul began to visit the synagogue in Corinth, but when unbelieving Jews started to oppose him, he eventually moved from there to a location next door (vv. 5-7). He continued to preach and teach in Corinth for a year and a half (v. 11). It was during this time (in AD 52) that Paul wrote 1 and 2 Thessalonians.

After this time, Paul left Corinth and traveled to Ephesus, the capital of the province of Asia. He was accompanied by Aquila and Priscilla (Acts 18:18, 19). Paul stayed in Ephesus but briefly, promising to return if God willed (v. 21). He then proceeded to Caesarea and then "went up [in elevation] and greeted the church" in Jerusalem (v. 22). He then returned to Antioch, where he spent "some time" (vv. 22, 23).

Following this respite in Antioch, Paul began what became his third missionary journey. He traveled throughout the territories of Galatia and Phrygia, "strengthening all the disciples" (v. 23). He had left Aquila and Priscilla in Ephesus, and it was during this time (prior to Paul's return to that city) that they helped instruct a man who became a valuable asset to the early church's ministry.

I. Efforts of Aquila and Priscilla (Acts 18:24-28)
A. Apollos Taught (vv. 24-26)

²⁴ Meanwhile a Jew named Apollos, a native of Alexandria, came to Ephesus. He was a learned man, with a thorough knowledge of the Scriptures.

While Aquila and Priscilla were in *Ephesus, a Jew named Apollos, a native of Alexandria, came* there. Alexandria, located in northern Egypt, was a city founded by and named for Alexander the Great in 332 BC. It was a center of learning that rivaled Athens. The scholars of the large Jewish colony in that city had produced the Septuagint (the Greek version of the Old Testament) about 250 years before Christ.

In Alexandria Apollos would have received an education that was second to none. It is no wonder that he is described here as *a learned man, with a thorough knowledge of the Scriptures*. He was a scholar who knew the Old Testament well and knew it with a passion, as the next verse indicates.

²⁵ He had been instructed in the way of the Lord, and he spoke with great fervor and taught about Jesus accurately, though he knew only the baptism of John.

We do not know when, where, or by whom Apollos had been taught about Jesus. Since *he knew only the baptism of John* the Baptist, his information about Jesus (although incomplete) may well have come from disciples of John. These he could have encountered while visiting in Jerusalem during one of the Jewish feasts. How much he knew of Jesus' life and teaching at this point we do not know, but what he said was communicated *accurately* and *with great fervor*.

Thus not only did Apollos know the Old Testament well, but he had proceeded to some degree of knowledge about Jesus. He was not aware that there was still more to know.

²⁶ He began to speak boldly in the synagogue. When Priscilla and Aquila heard him, they invited him to their home and explained to him the way of God more adequately.

Apparently *Priscilla and Aquila*, like Paul, used the *synagogue* as a means of finding new opportunities to present the good news about Jesus. When they heard Apollos, they must have appreciated his depth of knowledge of the Scriptures and his passion. But they also recognized the critical shortcomings in his understanding of *the way of God*. In order to address this deficiency and at the same time encourage this gifted teacher, Priscilla and Aquila did not confront or challenge him publicly. Instead, *they invited him to their home*. There, in a more private, informal setting, this godly couple pointed out to Apollos where his knowledge was incomplete. And to his credit, Apollos was not offended by this effort to "correct" him; he readily accepted the instruction given.

Since Apollos had known only the baptism of John, it may be assumed that Aquila and Priscilla explained to him the meaning and purpose of Christian baptism (Acts 2:38). In this area of his understanding, Apollos resembled those disciples in Ephesus whom Paul later baptized (Acts 19:1-7).

It is interesting to note that Aquila and Priscilla's use of their home as a place of ministry begins and ends this chapter of the book of Acts. Acts 18:3 records how Paul stayed and worked with them after he arrived in Corinth. Other New Testament references show Aquila and Priscilla's home being used in other locations as a gathering place for Christians, including Rome (Romans 16:3-5) and Ephesus (1 Corinthians 16:8, 19).

B. Apollos Encouraged (vv. 27, 28)

27 When Apollos wanted to go to Achaia, the brothers encouraged him and wrote to the disciples there to welcome him. On arriving, he was a great help to those who by grace had believed.

As noted earlier, *Achaia* was the province in which Corinth was located; and it was in that city that Paul had first met Aquila and Priscilla (Acts 18:1-3). In this way, the providential work of God came full circle. Paul instructed Aquila and Priscilla at Corinth, they instructed Apollos at Ephesus, and then Apollos went to Corinth to "water" where Paul had planted (1 Corinthians 3:6).

28 For he vigorously refuted the Jews in public debate, proving from the Scriptures that Jesus was the Christ.

Apollos, whose knowledge of the *Scriptures* was earlier described as "thorough" (v. 24), now possessed a more finely tuned knowledge of them because he was able to prove from them *that Jesus was the Christ*. He could present the various prophecies of the Christ and show how Jesus fulfilled them. He quickly became a passionate spokesman for Christ, *vigorously* defending the faith and refuting *the Jews in public debate*.

So respected a leader did Apollos become that one of the factions that eventually (and regretfully) developed in the Corinthian church claimed to follow him (1 Corinthians 1:12; 3:4), although Apollos himself was surely not to blame for that problem. Other passages that mention his contributions are 1 Corinthians 4:6; 16:12; and Titus 3:13.

II. Efforts of Paul (Acts 19:1-6)
A. Fundamental Questions (vv. 1-3)

[1a] While Apollos was at Corinth, Paul took the road through the interior and arrived at Ephesus.

By the time Paul *arrived at Ephesus*, fulfilling a promise he had made as he concluded his second missionary journey (Acts 18:21), *Apollos was at Corinth*. Later Apollos would come back to Ephesus during Paul's ministry there (see 1 Corinthians 16:12). That Paul had taken *the road through the interior* is what we would expect as he was coming from Galatia and Phrygia (Acts 18:23).

[1b, 2] There he found some disciples and asked them, "Did you receive the Holy Spirit when you believed?"
They answered, "No, we have not even heard that there is a Holy Spirit."

These *disciples* whom Paul encountered in Ephesus had *believed*; therefore, it appears that they were followers of Jesus. However, as was the case with Apollos, their understanding was deficient. Did something about their behavior suggest a deficiency in their faith, or why did Paul ask them about the *Holy Spirit?* In Paul's time some Christians received the Holy Spirit in such a way that they could work miracles, and it is probably that kind of reception of the Spirit that Paul was asking them about. Their answer must have surprised Paul—they had *not even heard that there is a Holy Spirit.*

[3] So Paul asked, "Then what baptism did you receive?"
"John's baptism," they replied.

Since these disciples had not heard of the Holy Spirit, it was evident they had not been baptized as Jesus commanded, "in the name of the Father and of the Son and of the Holy Spirit" (Matthew 28:19). Upon further questioning, Paul learned that the *baptism* these disciples had received was *John's baptism*. Thus they could be considered followers of Jesus, but only indirectly through John the Baptist or some of his followers. Their position was similar to that of Apollos, who "knew only the baptism of John" (Acts 18:25). It is even possible that Apollos, before he left Ephesus, had baptized these men before Aquila and Priscilla had "explained to him the way of God more adequately" (Acts 18:26).

B. Further Teaching (v. 4)

[4] Paul said, "John's baptism was a baptism of repentance. He told the people to believe in the one coming after him, that is, in Jesus."

John's baptism was "*a baptism of repentance* for the forgiveness of sins" (Mark 1:4). Christian baptism is also linked to the remission of sins (Acts 2:38). However, Christian baptism, as Acts 2:38 shows, includes the gift of the Holy Spirit, which John's baptism did not. In addition, John *told the people* who heard him *to believe in the one coming after him*, referring to *Jesus*. Christian baptism looks back at what Jesus did when he came, particularly to his death, burial, and resurrection (Romans 6:1-4).

C. Further Actions (vv. 5, 6)

5 On hearing this, they were baptized into the name of the Lord Jesus.

One should not assume that all of this took place within the span of a few minutes. Perhaps Paul talked with these disciples on a number of occasions, explaining the difference between John's baptism and Christian baptism. Like Apollos, these men were willing to listen to further instruction and to act upon it: *they were baptized into the name of the Lord Jesus.*

6 When Paul placed his hands on them, the Holy Spirit came on them, and they spoke in tongues and prophesied.

When these men in Ephesus were baptized into the name of the Lord Jesus, they would have received the gift of the Holy Spirit, as Peter had promised on the Day of Pentecost (Acts 2:38). Then, *when Paul placed his hands on them*, the *Spirit came* in such a way that they were given miraculous powers; specifically, *they spoke in tongues and prophesied.*

The apostles themselves had received the Spirit with miraculous power without any placing of hands on them (Acts 2:1-4), and so had Cornelius and his household (Acts 10:44-48). But in other cases, miraculous powers were received when the apostles laid their hands on certain Christians. Philip the evangelist worked miracles after the apostles laid their hands on him (Acts 6:1-6; 8:6). However, when Philip won many people in Samaria to Christ, the Spirit gave them no miraculous abilities until two apostles (Peter and John) came and placed their hands on them (Acts 8:4-8, 12-17). This seems to indicate that the special powers and gifts of the Spirit were not conveyed except through the apostles' placing their hands on individuals.

Paul's ministry in Ephesus was quite fruitful. He spent some three years there (Acts 20:31). During that time, according to Acts 19:10, "all the Jews and Greeks who lived in the province of Asia heard the word of the Lord." In addition, Paul wrote his first letter to the Corinthians from Ephesus in AD 56; he mentions his presence there in 1 Corinthians 16:8.

PAUL'S FAREWELL TO THE EPHESIAN ELDERS (ACTS 20:17-32)

Establishing the Groundwork

Eventually Paul had to leave Ephesus when his evangelistic success threatened the local idol makers and caused a near riot (Acts 19:23-41). From there he traveled to Macedonia and then to Corinth, in Greece, where he stayed three months (Acts 20:1-3). It appears that during that time Paul wrote 2 Corinthians in AD 57 from Macedonia (2 Corinthians 2:12, 13 and 7:5, 6 indicate his presence in Macedonia at the time of the letter's composition) and possibly Romans the same year or the next, apparently from Corinth. In Romans 16:23, Paul referred to the hospitality of Gaius, who is probably the same man Paul baptized in Corinth (1 Corinthians 1:14). Paul traveled with another man named Gaius (Acts 19:29; 20:4), but there is no evidence Paul was in Derbe at this time. Probably Paul's letter to the Galatians was written during this time also; however, it is difficult to be certain of this epistle's date.

Paul had done his work well in Ephesus; a healthy church was firmly set in place, and a group of elders had been set apart to guide it. But Paul's hasty departure meant that some of his work had gone undone. As he returned from his third missionary journey, Paul decided to sail past Ephesus in order to reach Jerusalem by the celebration of Pentecost (Acts 20:16).

Still, Paul was quite concerned about the church in Ephesus. When the ship on which he was traveling stopped at Miletus (about 30 miles south of Ephesus), Paul had enough time to send for the elders of the church and meet with them. He reminded these men of what they had been taught before, called their attention to the kind of loving leadership that he had modeled, warned them of threats to their flock, and encouraged them to remain faithful. His words continue to speak powerfully to leaders in Christ's church today.

Examining the Text

I. Paul's Example (Acts 20:17-27)
A. Consistent in Lifestyle (vv. 17, 18)

17 From Miletus, Paul sent to Ephesus for the elders of the church.

As noted above, *Miletus* was approximately thirty miles from *Ephesus*. Vigorous walkers could cover this distance in a day; if the group of *elders* included older men, they may have traveled by some other means.

18 When they arrived, he said to them: "You know how I lived the whole time I was with you, from the first day I came into the province of Asia.

Paul began his remarks to the elders by reminding them of the foundation on which he had built his ministry with them. He had led by an example that began *from the first day* that he had come *into the province of Asia*. The fact that Paul could say *you know* indicates that he had nothing to hide from these men. His conduct gave him no reason to be ashamed; his commitment to Christ had never wavered. This was the kind of leadership that he had modeled for these elders and that he wanted them to demonstrate. Especially during the difficult days that lay ahead (vv. 29, 30), they would need to be men of faith, wisdom, and service.

B. Determined in Service (v. 19)

[19] *"I served the Lord with great humility and with tears, although I was severely tested by the plots of the Jews.*

Paul had a strong emotional attachment to the church in Ephesus, as noted by his reference to *tears* (see also verse 31). No doubt that attachment helped to strengthen his resolve to minister to the Ephesians in spite of the obstacles he faced. Earlier we alluded to the opposition that arose from those who made idols (Acts 19:23-41). Here Paul mentions that there was in Ephesus, as in many other cities, opposition from *the Jews* as well.

C. Faithful in Teaching (vv. 20, 21)

[20] *"You know that I have not hesitated to preach anything that would be helpful to you but have taught you publicly and from house to house.*

Again, Paul emphasized the open and aboveboard nature of his ministry with the words *you know*. He had shared with the Ephesians *anything that would be helpful* to them in their walk with Christ and their witness for him.

The pattern of teaching *publicly and from house to house* is a good one for church leaders in any era to follow. If we are being faithful to Jesus' commission to go, make disciples, baptize, and teach (Matthew 28:19, 20), then teaching opportunities—both in public and private settings—will present themselves regularly.

[21] *"I have declared to both Jews and Greeks that they must turn to God in repentance and have faith in our Lord Jesus.*

The pattern of Paul's evangelistic outreach was "first for the Jew, then for the Gentile" (Romans 1:16). Paul and his companions preached to *Jews* first when they entered a city (often beginning in the synagogue if one was there), then shared with *Greeks* (Gentiles) as other doors opened.

D. Undaunted by Suffering (vv. 22-24)

²² "And now, compelled by the Spirit, I am going to Jerusalem, not knowing what will happen to me there.

Paul was *going to Jerusalem, not knowing what* lay ahead for him. He acknowledged in the next verse that "prison and hardships are facing me." But Paul wanted to bring the financial assistance that various churches had collected to help the poverty-stricken Christians in Jerusalem (1 Corinthians 16:1-4; 2 Corinthians 9:1-5, 12-14). He was *compelled by the Spirit* to complete that task as well as his task of proclaiming the gospel (v. 24).

²³ "I only know that in every city the Holy Spirit warns me that prison and hardships are facing me.

Paul was certain that he would experience *prison and hardships* in Jerusalem—a warning that the *Holy Spirit* had given him *in every city* he had entered as he headed that way. Later this was confirmed through a prophetic message from Agabus (Acts 21:10, 11).

²⁴ "However, I consider my life worth nothing to me, if only I may finish the race and complete the task the Lord Jesus has given me—the task of testifying to the gospel of God's grace.

Most important to Paul—more important to him than his personal welfare or safety—was completing *the task the Lord Jesus* had *given* him. He had been given the responsibility of declaring *the gospel of God's grace* to the Gentiles (Acts 26:15-18). Like a marathon runner, Paul desired to *finish* his *race* in triumph. That he did so is clear from his words in 2 Timothy 4:7, written not long before his death: "I have fought the good fight, I have finished the race, I have kept the faith."

E. Without Regrets (vv. 25-27)

²⁵ "Now I know that none of you among whom I have gone about preaching the kingdom will ever see me again.

Paul's statement that the Ephesian elders would never see him again raises a question, in light of the fact that it appears Paul did return to Ephesus at a later time (see 1 Timothy 1:3). Perhaps Paul was simply stating what he believed to be true at this point; in other instances, he made plans that he then had to change for some reason (2 Corinthians 1:15, 16, 23).

²⁶, ²⁷ "Therefore, I declare to you today that I am innocent of the blood of all men. For I have not hesitated to proclaim to you the whole will of God."

Those in Ephesus and "all the Jews and Greeks who lived in the province of Asia" had "heard the word of the Lord" (Acts 19:10) as a result of Paul's ministry. Anyone who rejected the gospel had only himself to blame; his *blood* would be upon his own head. Paul had done his job.

II. Paul's Exhortation (Acts 20:28-32)
A. A Charge (v. 28)

28 "Keep watch over yourselves and all the flock of which the Holy Spirit has made you overseers. Be shepherds of the church of God, which he bought with his own blood.

This verse provides a helpful definition of what leadership in the Lord's church entails. Leaders must first *keep watch over* themselves. Paul gave similar counsel to Timothy (1 Timothy 4:16). The leader's commitment to his own spiritual development determines how far and how well he will be able to lead others.

Paul also describes elders of the church as *overseers* of the *flock* and as *shepherds of the church of God*. Biblical oversight is not expressed primarily through decision-making or exerting authority in a dictatorial manner. Peter tells elders to "be shepherds of God's flock . . . serving as overseers—not because you must, but because you are willing, . . . not lording it over those entrusted to you, but being examples to the flock" (1 Peter 5:2, 3). Elders hold each other accountable; they meet the needs of their flock; they give responsible oversight to the direction of the church's ministries; they provide spiritual food by seeing that the Word of God is faithfully taught. After all, the church is not the elders'; it is *the church of God*.

Paul then gives an additional reason for taking such special care of God's church: it has been *bought with his own blood*. The Greek phrase can be translated, "the blood of his own," thus referring to the priceless sacrifice that Jesus made to obtain humanity's redemption from sin.

B. A Warning (vv. 29-31)

29 "I know that after I leave, savage wolves will come in among you and will not spare the flock.

Paul's reference to *savage wolves* calls to mind Jesus' warning about wolves "in sheep's clothing" (Matthew 7:15). It may seem hard to imagine that a church could fall prey to the influence of such forces after three years of constant, faithful teaching from an apostle (v. 31). And yet, later portions of the New Testament indicate that this was so. Paul sent 1 Timothy (and perhaps 2 Timothy) to Ephesus, where

Timothy had to confront those who were teaching false doctrine (1 Timothy 1:3, 4). Some have suggested that the epistle of 1 John was sent to the churches of Asia, which would have included Ephesus. There we read of the influence of false teachers who were denying that Jesus came in the flesh (1 John 4:1-3). Finally, Jesus' words to the church in Ephesus (Revelation 2:1-7) indicate that it was being influenced by corrupting and disruptive elements. It is no surprise that Paul counseled these elders to "be on your guard" (v. 31).

> *30 "Even from your own number men will arise and distort the truth in order to draw away disciples after them.*

Paul warned that the influences described in the previous verse would, in some cases, originate *from* within the church. Sadly, it is sometimes true that the church is severely harmed by its *own*—by *men* who are interested in building a following rather than following Jesus.

> *31 "So be on your guard! Remember that for three years I never stopped warning each of you night and day with tears.*

The depth of Paul's commitment to *each of* the believers in Ephesus is clear: he poured both time (*night and day* for *three years*) and emotional involvement (*tears*) into their spiritual maturity. The "wolves" (v. 29) would have only their own selfish interests at heart.

C. A Trust (v. 32)

> *32 "Now I commit you to God and to the word of his grace, which can build you up and give you an inheritance among all those who are sanctified."*

Although Paul was leaving these elders, he was not leaving them alone. He could still *commit* these men *to God and to the word of his grace*. The apostolic instruction they had received would serve them well as a reliable guide in the face of future threats. Today we have these recorded in the New Testament Scriptures. By following them, we too can lay hold of the *inheritance* promised to *all* who faithfully serve Jesus.

PAUL APPEARS BEFORE KING AGRIPPA (ACTS 26:19-32)

Establishing the Groundwork

When Paul finally arrived in Jerusalem, he was received warmly by the Christians there (Acts 21:17). He then met with James (the brother or "half brother" of Jesus, who was one of the leaders in the Jerusalem church) and the elders of the church (v. 18). These men told Paul that many of the Jews in the area had been wrongly informed that he had been encouraging Jews living in predominantly Gentile lands to abandon Jewish teachings and customs (vv. 20, 21).

To counter such misinformation, the leaders in Jerusalem suggested that Paul accompany four men to the temple and join them in a ceremony of purification. They also encouraged him to pay for the sacrifices that would be offered. This would demonstrate in a public setting that Paul himself respected the Jewish customs (vv. 22-24).

However, when Paul came to the temple at the appointed time, some Jews from the province of Asia noticed him there and began raising the false charges earlier noted by the leaders of the Jerusalem church. In addition, they accused him of bringing Greeks into a forbidden section of the temple (v. 27-29). In no time, an angry mob had formed with the intent to kill Paul. Roman troops, however, came to his rescue and took him as a prisoner. Lysias, commander of the troops, took Paul to the Sanhedrin; but the council acted so violently that Lysias took him back to the Roman barracks for his own safety (Acts 22:3–23:10).

After a plot of the Jews to kill Paul was foiled, Lysias decided to send Paul under heavy guard to Caesarea, the headquarters of the Roman governor of Judea. Felix, the governor at the time, took an interest in Paul's case but took no action. He simply kept him in prison, hoping to be offered a bribe for his release; but none was offered. After two years, Felix was replaced by Festus. When Festus traveled to Jerusalem not long after arriving in Judea, the Jewish leaders asked that Paul be brought back to Jerusalem to answer to the Sanhedrin. But Paul refused to go, knowing that the Jews still desired to kill him. Instead, he appealed to the emperor, which as a Roman citizen he had a right to do. This meant that he had to be sent to Rome for a hearing (Acts 23:12–25:12).

This posed a problem for Festus. Paul's case seemed to be a purely Jewish matter. How could he send a prisoner to Rome without some evidence of a crime against Roman law? About that time Agrippa, who was king of Palestine, came to Caesarea to pay his respects to Festus. When Festus discussed Paul's case with him, Agrippa expressed an interest in hearing this unusual prisoner. Festus, eager to find a solution to his dilemma, arranged for this to take place the next day (Acts 25:13-22).

Examining the Text

I. Paul's Obedience (Acts 26:19-23)

Paul's speech before Agrippa begins in Acts 26:2. First, Paul offered words of commendation to Agrippa himself (vv. 2, 3), then he described his life as a

Pharisee, which included doing "all that was possible to oppose the name of Jesus of Nazareth" (v. 9). Next, he proceeded to relate what happened on the day he was journeying to Damascus to carry out another plan to persecute followers of Jesus. He told of the bright light that came from Heaven and of Jesus' words to him that day, including the purpose of his appearance to Paul: "I have appeared to you to appoint you as a servant and as a witness of what you have seen of me and what I will show you" (v. 16). Paul then described his response to this vision.

A. Faithful Preaching (vv. 19, 20)

¹⁹ *"So then, King Agrippa, I was not disobedient to the vision from heaven.*

Even before Paul became a Christian, he was "zealous for God" (Acts 22:3). Whatever else one might say about him, he always obeyed what he thought God wanted him to do. When Paul received his orders from Jesus, he carried them out.

²⁰ *"First to those in Damascus, then to those in Jerusalem and in all Judea, and to the Gentiles also, I preached that they should repent and turn to God and prove their repentance by their deeds.*

Paul then provided a general summary of the territory he had covered in his ministry up to this point. Following his conversion, he "at once" began preaching Jesus in the synagogues in *Damascus* (Acts 9:20). Later he came to *Jerusalem*, "speaking boldly in the name of the Lord" (Acts 9:28). Paul's ministry *to the Gentiles also* describes the general impact of his missionary journeys. Wherever he had gone, his message had been consistent: listeners should *repent and turn to God* (ideas that are virtually synonymous), then should *prove their repentance* by the *deeds* of a transformed life.

B. Fierce Opposition (v. 21)

²¹ *"That is why the Jews seized me in the temple courts and tried to kill me.*

Here Paul refers to the incident described in Acts 21:27-36. (See "Establishing the Groundwork" above.)

C. Fulfilled Scripture (vv. 22, 23)

²² *"But I have had God's help to this very day, and so I stand here and testify to small and great alike. I am saying nothing beyond what the prophets and Moses said would happen—*

Paul acknowledged *God's help to this very day* in protecting him from the plots and attacks of others. He had continued to declare his message in all kinds of settings and to all kinds of people—to those whom society would consider *small* or insignificant and to those who, like King Agrippa, would be considered *great*.

Paul defended his message as being completely consistent with *what the prophets and Moses said would happen*. This was initially a legal defense, since the Jews had accused him of violating Jewish law. But Paul had more in mind than a legal defense. He was actually laying the foundation to preach the resurrection of Jesus, as the next verse indicates.

> [23] *". . . that the Christ would suffer and, as the first to rise from the dead, would proclaim light to his own people and to the Gentiles."*

Because the Jews expected a triumphant Messiah and not one who *would suffer* a humiliating death as Jesus did, the preaching of the cross was a "stumbling block" to them (1 Corinthians 1:23). Of course, others had been raised *from the dead* before Jesus was, including the widow of Nain's son, the daughter of Jairus, and Lazarus. But Jesus was the *first* to do so never to die again. That glorious victory over the grave brought a message of *light* and hope to Jesus' *own people* (the Jews) *and to the Gentiles*. None of this had happened by mere chance; all of this had been foreshadowed by the prophets and Moses (v. 22).

II. Festus's Outburst (Acts 26:24-26)
A. Accusation (v. 24)

> [24] *At this point Festus interrupted Paul's defense. "You are out of your mind, Paul!" he shouted. "Your great learning is driving you insane."*

The idea that Paul seriously believed that Jesus had risen from the dead was something so incredible to *Festus* that he felt anyone making such a claim must be *insane*. Perhaps Festus sensed that Agrippa, his guest, might be offended at what Paul was claiming and felt compelled to stop him. Festus was aware of Paul's *great learning*; perhaps Paul, while imprisoned in Caesarea, had occupied his time by reading scrolls of the prophets and Moses, to whom he had alluded earlier.

B. Answer (vv. 25, 26)

> [25] *"I am not insane, most excellent Festus," Paul replied. "What I am saying is true and reasonable.*

Paul denied Festus's charge of being *insane*. He addressed the governor with respect and dignity—*most excellent Festus*—not as a madman might have done. His words were not those of a madman; they were *true and reasonable*. The resurrection of Jesus is founded on historical facts; it is not a myth or legend.

²⁶ *"The king is familiar with these things, and I can speak freely to him. I am convinced that none of this has escaped his notice, because it was not done in a corner."*

King Agrippa was actually Herod Agrippa II, the son of Herod Agrippa I, during whose reign James the brother of John had been put to death (Acts 12:1, 2). Agrippa I died a painful death, as described in Acts 12:21-23. Given the familiarity of other members of the Herod family with Jesus and with matters relevant to the Christian faith, the Agrippa before whom Paul was making his defense was *familiar with these things*—that is, with the key claims of the Christian message.

Even without such familial ties, however, it was difficult for anyone knowledgeable of recent events to miss the impact of the Christian movement. That *it was not done in a corner* describes the highly public nature of the events surrounding the life and ministry of Jesus and the growth of the church. Paul did not represent a secretive, mysterious cult, but a group whose work was done in the open and whose claims could be investigated by anyone desiring to know more.

III. Agrippa's Observations (Acts 26:27-32)
A. Response to Paul's Statements (vv. 27-29)

²⁷ *"King Agrippa, do you believe the prophets? I know you do."*

Never one to back down from an opportunity to present the gospel, Paul proceeded to question Agrippa as to whether he believed *the prophets*. If he said "Yes," then the next question would be whether he believed the one of whom they spoke. On the other hand, if he answered "No" to Paul's question, then he risked offending devout Jews. Festus's dilemma was now Agrippa's!

²⁸ *Then Agrippa said to Paul, "Do you think that in such a short time you can persuade me to be a Christian?"*

We would probably understand Agrippa's words better if we could hear the tone of his voice and see the expression on his face. The Greek text is somewhat ambiguous, and might literally be rendered, "In a little you persuade me to be a Christian." This leaves us to wonder whether this was a statement or a question. If Agrippa said this as a thoughtful statement, perhaps he was giving serious consideration to what Paul was saying about Jesus. This intent is reflected in the *King James Version:* "Almost thou persuadest me to be a Christian." If the king spoke sarcastically, then his intent would be what is reflected in the question found in our *New International Version*® text.

29 Paul replied, "Short time or long—I pray God that not only you but all who are listening to me today may become what I am, except for these chains."

If Agrippa was sarcastic, Paul was undaunted. He pressed his invitation, not only to Agrippa but to *all who* were *listening* that day. No doubt, Paul expressed this sentiment while gesturing to his *chains*. He certainly did not like being a prisoner (especially for two years), but he wished that, other than that, all in his audience would *become what* he was. It was always Paul's fervent desire that all who listened to him would become Christians.

B. Response to Paul's Status (vv. 30-32)

30 The king rose, and with him the governor and Bernice and those sitting with them.

Apparently Paul's final plea ended the hearing. Those present *rose* and left in order of rank: first *the king*, and *with him the governor*, then *Bernice* (Agrippa's sister, with whom he was living in an incestuous relationship), then *those sitting with them.*

31 They left the room, and while talking with one another, they said, "This man is not doing anything that deserves death or imprisonment."

At this point, those who were present to hear Paul began *talking with one another*. All agreed that Paul had done nothing to deserve *death or imprisonment*. Festus had reached this conclusion already, after hearing Paul earlier (Acts 25:25).

32 Agrippa said to Festus, "This man could have been set free if he had not appealed to Caesar."

Since the accusers had failed to sustain their accusation, justice would have allowed Paul to *have been set free*. But Paul had already *appealed* to Rome and *to Caesar*—a step he had taken to avoid being murdered by the plots of the Jews, and which he had every right to take as a Roman citizen.

PAUL IN ROME (ACTS 28:23-31)

Establishing the Groundwork

At one point during his third missionary journey, Paul had expressed a desire to go to Rome (Acts 19:21). It was not long after that he wrote to the Romans and expressed the same desire to them (Romans 1:10). At that time, he surely did not anticipate going there as a prisoner. But that was his situation at the beginning of Acts 27, as he boarded a ship and prepared to sail to Rome to carry out his appeal to Caesar. It should be noted that in Acts 27, we encounter another of the "we passages" in Acts (beginning in verse 1), indicating the presence of Luke, the author of Acts, on what would be a most eventful journey. Acts 27 describes the furious storm that struck the boat in which Paul was traveling and the eventual shipwreck. There was no loss of life, however, for an angel of the Lord had appeared to Paul and had assured him that all on board the ship would be spared (vv. 21-26).

When the ship broke apart on a beach, the passengers found themselves on an island called Malta. There they stayed for the winter in order to avoid any more inclement weather. When spring came, the journey to Rome resumed. When Paul arrived there, according to Acts 28:16, he "was allowed to live by himself, with a soldier to guard him."

Three days after his arrival, Paul arranged for a meeting with the leaders of the Jews in Rome. Assuming that these men had heard the unfounded rumors about him from Jews elsewhere, Paul explained why he was in Rome and made it quite clear that he had "done nothing against our people or against the customs of our ancestors" (Acts 28:17). He learned, however, that the leaders in Rome had heard nothing negative about Paul. They added, "But we want to hear what your views are, for we know that people everywhere are talking against this sect" (v. 22). Paul was only too happy to speak with these leaders and let them know the truth about this alleged "sect."

Examining the Text

I. Paul's Testimony to the Jews in Rome (Acts 28:23-29)
A. Message Presented (v. 23)

23 They arranged to meet Paul on a certain day, and came in even larger numbers to the place where he was staying. From morning till evening he explained and declared to them the kingdom of God and tried to convince them about Jesus from the Law of Moses and from the Prophets.

They (the Jewish leaders in Rome) *arranged to meet Paul on a certain day* to hear more about the "sect" (v. 22) that he represented. In fact, *even larger numbers* came to meet with him. At this all-day teaching session, Paul *explained and declared to them the kingdom of God.* For centuries the Jews had anticipated the coming of the Messiah and the establishment of his kingdom. However, by the time of Jesus that anticipation had become tainted by selfish and nationalistic ambition. The Jews saw the Messiah as a military leader who would overthrow the hated Romans and restore Israel's greatness to Davidic proportions. Consequently many of the Jews did not recognize Jesus as the Messiah when he came. Paul likely had to spend a portion of this day correcting these misconceptions. But he also used the Scriptures—*the Law of Moses* and *the Prophets*—to make his case for Jesus as the Messiah.

Since this session lasted *from morning till evening,* one assumes that there was time for questions from those gathered and for further discussion of certain points. The discussions probably became quite lively at times!

B. Mixed Response (v. 24)

24 Some were convinced by what he said, but others would not believe.

This was and still is the common response to the message of Jesus. Acts 2:41 tells us that three thousand believed on the Day of Pentecost, but uncounted thousands did not; and among them were the Jewish leaders in Jerusalem. In the previous chapter of studies, we noted that after Paul's speech in Athens, some sneered at his words while others wanted to hear more (Acts 17:32).

C. Prophecy Quoted (vv. 25-27)

25 They disagreed among themselves and began to leave after Paul had made this final statement: "The Holy Spirit spoke the truth to your forefathers when he said through Isaiah the prophet:

Apparently the group of Jews could not reach an agreement concerning Paul and his message concerning Jesus. As the day was ending, Paul made the *final statement,* and it was not in his own words; he quoted *Isaiah the prophet.* Paul and these Jews had the same background; theirs was a common heritage. But Paul may have used the words *your forefathers* in speaking to the unbelieving Jews because they were in danger of committing the same sin for which God's people were condemned by Isaiah—the sin of ignoring or rejecting the word of God.

26, 27 "'Go to this people and say,
"You will be ever hearing but never understanding;
you will be ever seeing but never perceiving."
For this people's heart has become calloused;
they hardly hear with their ears,
and they have closed their eyes.
Otherwise they might see with their eyes, hear with their ears, understand
with their hearts and turn, and I would heal them.'

Isaiah was sent to give God's message to his people approximately 700 years before Jesus came, and he was sent with the warning that most of the hearers would not *understand* and accept the message they would hear. In fact, the sobering warning cited by Paul was given to Isaiah immediately after his vision of the Lord during which he received his prophetic call (Isaiah 6:1-10).

There was nothing wrong with God's message delivered through Isaiah; it was true and understandable. The problem was with the people; they did not want to believe it. They closed their *ears*, *eyes*, and *hearts*; they disregarded Isaiah's call to repentance and went on in their selfish ways until they were taken to captivity in Babylon. Now, some in Paul's audience were doing with the gospel exactly what their forefathers had done—only the stakes were much higher. The result of their rejection would not be seventy years in Babylon, but an eternity in Hell.

D. Preaching Expanded (vv. 28, 29)

28 "Therefore I want you to know that God's salvation has been sent to the Gentiles, and they will listen!"

This too had been foretold by the prophets, but many Jews had overlooked it. Abraham was recognized as the father of the Jewish people, but he was told when God called him, "All peoples on earth will be blessed through you" (Genesis 12:3). James (one of the leaders in the Jerusalem church) had quoted from the prophet Amos during the Jerusalem Conference to show that God desired to include the *Gentiles* among those who would receive his *salvation* (Acts 15:15-18). Here in Rome Paul was following the pattern God had established for presenting the gospel: "first for the Jew, then for the Gentile" (Romans 1:16).

29 (footnote) After he said this, the Jews left, arguing vigorously among themselves.

Many of the ancient manuscripts do not have this verse, and so it is left out of some English versions. Still, we can hardly doubt that what it says describes what happened. The controversy over Paul's teaching likely continued for some time after this meeting.

II. Paul's Testimony to All (Acts 28:30, 31)
A. Welcoming All (v. 30)

30 For two whole years Paul stayed there in his own rented house and welcomed all who came to see him.

Paul had been held prisoner at Caesarea for two years (Acts 24:27), several weeks had passed while on his way to Rome, and now he was in what might be called "protective custody" or "house arrest" for another *two whole years*. He *stayed . . . in his own rented house and welcomed all who came to see him*. For example, Onesimus was led to Christ by Paul during his imprisonment (Philemon 10). Thus Paul enjoyed a certain measure of freedom, though in some of the epistles he wrote during this time he refers to his "chains" (Philippians 1:12-14; Colossians 4:18; Philemon 10). References in his letter to the Philippians indicate that this church in particular helped to supply his needs (Philippians 4:10-18).

It should also be noted that this verse indicates that Luke finished writing his record in Acts at the conclusion of the two years mentioned in this verse. If the record had been written any later, it would have included more, particularly information about the outcome of Paul's trial. This places the writing of Acts in about AD 63.

B. Witnessing to All (v. 31)

³¹ Boldly and without hindrance he preached the kingdom of God and taught about the Lord Jesus Christ.

Thus Paul's preaching and teaching ministry continued *without hindrance*. Not only would this refer to his speaking, but it would also include the four letters that Paul wrote during this imprisonment—the group of letters that are often called "prison epistles." These are Ephesians, Philippians, Colossians, and Philemon. The impact of Paul's ministry was felt all the way into Caesar's household (Philippians 4:22). Paul's confidence, even in these circumstances, encouraged other Christians to preach more *boldly*; indeed, Paul declared that his imprisonment had actually furthered the progress of the gospel (Philippians 1:12-14).

While Acts does not record the outcome of Paul's trial before Caesar, it does appear that he was released. His words in Philippians 1:19 and 25, 26 indicate that he believed that this would take place. Apparently Paul then embarked on additional travels and wrote other letters that are part of the New Testament (1 and 2 Timothy and Titus). More details on those travels will be provided when that portion of the New Testament is covered. For now, suffice it to say that the closing verse of Acts could have made a most appropriate epitaph if a headstone had been erected over Paul's grave. For that matter, these words should describe the passion of every Christian's life.

How to Say It

ABRAHAM. *Ay*-bruh-ham.

ACHAIA. Uh-*kay*-uh.

AGABUS. *Ag*-uh-bus.

AGRIPPA. Uh-*grip*-puh.

ALEXANDRIA. Al-iks-*an*-dree-uh.

APHRODITE. Af-ruh-*dite*-ee.

APOLLOS. Uh-*pahl*-us.

AQUILA. *Ack*-wih-luh.

ATHENS. *Ath*-unz.

BABYLON. *Bab*-uh-lun.

CAESAR. *See*-zur.

CAESAREA. Sess-uh-*ree*-uh.

CORINTH. *Kor*-inth.

CORNELIUS. Kor-*neel*-yus.

DAVIDIC. Duh-*vid*-ick.

EPHESUS. *Ef*-uh-sus.

FELIX. *Fee*-licks.

FESTUS. *Fes*-tus.

GAIUS. *Gay*-us.

GALATIA. Guh-*lay*-shuh.

GALATIANS. Guh-*lay*-shunz.

GENTILES. *Jen*-tiles.

JAIRUS. *Jye*-rus or *Jay*-ih-rus.

LAZARUS. *Laz*-uh-rus.

LYSIAS. *Lis*-ee-us.

MACEDONIA. Mass-eh-*doe*-nee-uh.

MESSIAH. Meh-*sigh*-uh.

MILETUS. My-*lee*-tus.

ONESIMUS. O-*ness*-ih-muss.

PENTECOST. *Pent*-ih-kost.

PHRYGIA. *Frij*-e-uh.

PRISCILLA. Prih-*sil*-uh.

SAMARIA. Suh-*mare*-ee-uh.

SANHEDRIN. *San*-huh-drun or San-*heed*-run.

SEPTUAGINT. Sep-*too*-ih-jent.

SYNAGOGUE. *sin*-uh-gog.

Chapter 6

The Gospel of Grace: Studies in Romans (Part 1)

Romans 1:1-17; 3:19-26; 5:1-11; 6:1-14

UNASHAMED OF THE GOSPEL (ROMANS 1:1-17)

Establishing the Groundwork

With this chapter, our study of the New Testament moves from Luke's record in the book of Acts to the epistles, which comprise twenty-one of the twenty-seven books in the New Testament. Studies from various epistles will make up six of the next seven chapters (the final chapter will cover passages from the book of Revelation).

During Paul's third missionary journey, he spent about three months in Corinth (Acts 20:1-3). It seems best to view this as the time during which he penned the letter to the Romans. In the letter, Paul refers to the hospitality of a man named Gaius (Romans 16:23). This is probably the same man Paul baptized in Corinth (1 Corinthians 1:14). The date would have been AD 58.

In the letter, Paul expressed his desire to conduct a ministry in Spain with a stop in Rome on the way (Romans 15:23, 24). The maturity of the church in Rome was already well known. "Your faith is being reported all over the world," he wrote in Romans 1:8. Paul wanted to meet the Christians there and share in their growth. His desire was to help them, while also benefiting from their faith (Romans 1:11, 12).

While some later church traditions attribute the founding of the church at Rome to Peter, there is no solid historical or Scriptural evidence to support such a tradition. Persons from Rome were among those who heard Peter on the Day of Pentecost (Acts 2:10), and it is very possible that, when they returned to Rome, they carried the gospel with them. At a later time others who had been converted during Paul's missionary journeys made their way to Rome and found fellowship with the Christians already there. This is the reason Paul knew so many people in the Roman church (as is evident from the greetings in chapter 16) even before he had visited the city.

Most students of the Bible consider Paul's letter to the Romans to be his greatest work. It is a profound theological treatise that deals with many aspects of the doctrine of salvation by grace through faith in Christ. But Paul was not just a scholar discussing theology in a remote, "ivory tower" setting. The latter chapters of Romans (especially 12–15) deal with a number of practical issues touching on the daily lives of believers both then and now.

Examining the Text

I. Paul's Greeting (Romans 1:1-5)
A. His Identity (v. 1)

¹ Paul, a servant of Christ Jesus, called to be an apostle and set apart for the gospel of God—

It was a common practice for *Paul* and others of his day to introduce themselves at the beginning of a letter rather than at its close. Paul was well known to some in the Roman church. He had met these believers in other cities during his missionary journeys, and then circumstances such as persecution or unemployment had resulted in their moving to Rome and settling there. A good example is Aquila and Priscilla, whom Paul had first met in Corinth (Acts 18:1-4), but to whom he sent a greeting in Romans 16:3. But other Christians in the church had never met Paul. For them, and as a reminder to his friends, Paul identified himself as *a servant of Christ Jesus*. Literally, this word *servant* means a "bondservant" or "slave." Paul had surrendered himself to Christ so completely that he was a slave. Specifically, he had been *called to be an apostle* to the Gentiles and had been *set apart* to declare the *gospel* to them (Romans 1:13).

B. His Message (vv. 2-4)

² . . . the gospel he promised beforehand through his prophets in the Holy Scriptures

The *gospel* has its roots deep in the *Holy Scriptures*, or what we call the Old Testament. For centuries the Old Testament *prophets* had predicted that God would send a Messiah, a term meaning "anointed one," to save his people. On the Day of Pentecost, Peter boldly announced to his listeners, "God has made this Jesus, whom you crucified, both Lord and Christ" (Acts 2:36). As part of the proclamation of the gospel, Jesus, Paul, and others showed how Jesus fulfilled what the Old Testament prophets *promised* (Luke 24:25-27, 44-47; Acts 2:25-36; 8:32-35; 13:26-41).

³ . . . regarding his Son, who as to his human nature was a descendant of David,

The good news that Paul preached was regarding God's *Son*. The prophets had foretold that the Messiah would be *a descendant of David* as far as *his human nature* was concerned (Isaiah 9:6, 7; Jeremiah 23:5, 6; 33:14-26). God promised David himself that one of his descendants would establish a kingdom that would last forever (2 Samuel 7:12-16). This led to the frequent use of the title "son of David" to describe the Messiah. The New Testament indicates that the promise made to David has been fulfilled in Jesus (Luke 1:30-33; Acts 2:29-31).

> *⁴ . . . and who through the Spirit of holiness was declared with power to be the Son of God by his resurrection from the dead: Jesus Christ our Lord.*

On the human side, Jesus was of the lineage of David. But *through the Spirit of holiness* he is the *Son of God*. Jesus was conceived in the womb of the virgin Mary by the power of the Holy Spirit (Matthew 1:20; Luke 1:34, 35). On numerous occasions during his ministry, Jesus gave dramatic demonstrations of his deity and supported his claims by means of his miracles. The most awe-inspiring way in which Jesus was *declared with power to be* who he claimed to be was *his resurrection from the dead*. Jesus himself made this the primary "sign" that he was who he claimed to be (Matthew 12:38-40). As the one who conquered death and rose never to die again, he is truly *Jesus Christ our Lord*.

C. His Credentials (v. 5)

> *⁵ Through him and for his name's sake, we received grace and apostleship to call people from among all the Gentiles to the obedience that comes from faith.*

The *apostleship* into which Paul was called was not something that he had worked for or earned in any special way. Rather, it came through *grace*; it was a gift from God. Paul's mission was *to call people from among all the Gentiles*. Jesus had given him this charge when he appeared to Paul (Saul) on the road to Damascus (Acts 26:15-18). Paul recognized that Jews were to receive the gospel first (Romans 1:16), but his special ministry was to lead Gentiles to *faith* in Christ and to the *obedience* that ought to follow sincere faith. One should note that Paul mentions this same sequence of faith and obedience at the conclusion of this letter (Romans 16:26).

II. Paul's Readers (Romans 1:6-13)
A. Their Identity (vv. 6, 7a)

> *⁶, ⁷ᵃ And you also are among those who are called to belong to Jesus Christ. To all in Rome who are loved by God and called to be saints:*

Those who are called are those to whom the gospel of Christ has been presented and who have answered the call of Christ to be saved. Paul writes in 1 Timothy 2:3, 4, "God . . . wants all men to be saved and to come to a knowledge of the truth." Thus the call is for all people, but only those who are willing to hear and obey will respond. The reason some respond lies not in God's will to save them, but in their willingness to be saved. Similarly, the phrase *who are loved by God* describes those who have responded to God's love in Christ, although it is clear that God loves all people and sent his Son to die for all of them. The invitation to respond to that love remains open until Christ returns.

Paul also describes the Christians in *Rome* as those *called to be saints*. Many think of a saint as a person who lives on a higher spiritual plane than others. But the Greek word translated "saints" means those who have been set apart and dedicated to God and his service. Thus every Christian is a saint.

B. Paul's Prayer for Them (vv. 7b-10a)

7b Grace and peace to you from God our Father and from the Lord Jesus Christ.

Grace and peace comprise a standard greeting that Paul used in several of his other letters. By using these terms, he combined a Greek greeting (*grace*) with a Jewish greeting (*peace*), showing his ability and desire to transcend ethnic and cultural barriers. He added greater meaning to these common terms by declaring that both grace and peace are gifts *from God our Father and from the Lord Jesus Christ.*

8 First, I thank my God through Jesus Christ for all of you, because your faith is being reported all over the world.

Once he completed his greeting to the Roman Christians, Paul's first thought was a word of thanks to God for them. Specifically, he was thankful for their *faith* and for the fact that it was *being reported all over the world*. (The term *world* likely would have encompassed from Paul's perspective the Roman Empire.) No doubt Paul rejoiced that a vibrant, Christ-honoring church was present in the capital of the political and economic life of that era.

9, 10a God, whom I serve with my whole heart in preaching the gospel of his Son, is my witness how constantly I remember you in my prayers at all times;

What a great prayer life Paul must have had! Not only did he pray for the church at Rome, but for those in Ephesus, Philippi, Colosse, and Thessalonica (Ephesians 1:16; Philippians 1:4; Colossians 1:3; 1 Thessalonians 1:2). He prayed for individuals, including Timothy and Philemon (2 Timothy 1:3;

Philemon 4). To show his sincerity in praying for the Roman Christians, Paul called upon God as his *witness*. (Note similar expressions in 2 Corinthians 1:23; Galatians 1:20; and Philippians 1:8.) Paul's example suggests that we today ought to remember in our *prayers at all times* our brothers and sisters in Christ—both those we know and those in places we have not been.

C. Paul's Desire to Visit Them (vv. 10b-13)

10b . . . and I pray that now at last by God's will the way may be opened for me to come to you.

In verse 8, Paul offered a prayer of thanksgiving for the faith of the Roman Christians. Here his prayer is that he might be able to visit them. Apparently he had harbored this desire for several years (Romans 15:22, 23). His words *now at last* suggest that he was even a bit frustrated that this long-standing desire had not been fulfilled. But Paul's deep faith led him to trust that *by God's will* and in his time such a visit would take place. Eventually God did honor Paul's desire and allow him to *come to* Rome. But he came as a prisoner (Acts 28:16).

11 I long to see you so that I may impart to you some spiritual gift to make you strong—

Paul wanted to see the Roman Christians so that he could *impart* to them *some spiritual gift* that would make them *strong*. The Greek word for gift is *charisma*, which is used in the New Testament to refer to either miraculous or non-miraculous gifts. In this case it probably means the miraculous gifts, such as were bestowed by Paul on the disciples in Ephesus (Acts 19:6) and by Peter and John on the Samaritans (Acts 8:17, 18). There is no record in the New Testament of non-miraculous gifts being given by the laying on of hands; these appear to have been given directly from God.

12 . . . that is, that you and I may be mutually encouraged by each other's faith.

Even as Paul desired to bring a gift to the Romans, he also expected to be blessed himself. This is a most frequent outcome among those who share a common *faith*. When one brings a blessing to other Christians, the giver as well as the recipient is *encouraged*.

13 I do not want you to be unaware, brothers, that I planned many times to come to you (but have been prevented from doing so until now) in order that I might have a harvest among you, just as I have had among the other Gentiles.

Some in Rome may have felt that Paul really wasn't serious or sincere in his desire to visit the church. Here he assured them that he had *planned many times to come to* Rome but had been *prevented from doing so.* We are not told what factors may have kept him from coming. Paul may have been so heavily involved in fruitful evangelistic work elsewhere that he could not leave and go to Rome. The Holy Spirit may have kept him from going (see Acts 16:6, 7). It is also possible that Satan hindered Paul in some way from going (see 1 Thessalonians 2:18).

The *harvest* that Paul expected to reap may refer to converts that he would win to the faith or to spiritual growth that the Roman saints would experience as a result of his teaching. Since Paul was specially called to be Christ's witness to the Gentiles, it was natural that he wanted to visit a church made up predominantly of Gentile believers.

III. Paul's Debt (Romans 1:14-17)
A. His Debt to All (v. 14)

14 I am obligated both to Greeks and non-Greeks, both to the wise and the foolish.

The *Greeks* were an intelligent, educated, and highly civilized people. Sometimes their name was used loosely to mean all the people who had adopted the Greek language and civilization. Those who had not embraced these were considered "barbarians," a word we get from the Greek term translated here *non-Greeks.* The terms *wise* and *foolish* would be a description of the same two groups.

That Paul was *obligated* to both of these groups involved a debt that is different from the debts we sometimes have to pay. Paul had not received anything from the Greeks or the non-Greeks, yet he owed them something. He had received the good news of salvation from the Lord (Galatians 1:11, 12). But it was not given for him alone. It was entrusted to him to be delivered to others, and Paul felt himself to be in debt until it was delivered. Of course, every Christian should feel himself compelled by the same debt.

B. His Eagerness to Pay It (v. 15)

15 That is why I am so eager to preach the gospel also to you who are at Rome.

Every person who has ever lived has a debt to God as Creator. Furthermore, every Christian has a debt to God as Savior. We cannot pay that debt, for salvation is a gift of grace. But since we are saved by grace, we have a debt to others who are yet in need of God's grace; we have an obligation to share the good news with them. Paul had a unique obligation to *preach the gospel* to all Gentiles, and in this case, to those at Rome. It was a debt he was *eager* to pay.

C. His Means of Paying It (vv. 16, 17)

¹⁶ I am not ashamed of the gospel, because it is the power of God for the salvation of everyone who believes: first for the Jew, then for the Gentile.

Paul had committed his life totally to the *gospel*. He was convinced that he would never have a reason to be *ashamed* of this commitment. He had good reason for such confidence: the gospel is *the power of God for the salvation of everyone*. The Greek word translated "power" is the basis for such English words as *dynamic, dynamo,* and even *dynamite*—although Paul obviously did not have anything like exploding dynamite in mind when he wrote this. The power of the gospel was manifested in many ways, including the tearing down of barriers between *Jew* and *Gentile*—a point discussed further by Paul in Ephesians 2:11-22. That power to bring salvation has only one limitation: it comes only to *everyone who believes*.

¹⁷ For in the gospel a righteousness from God is revealed, a righteousness that is by faith from first to last, just as it is written: "The righteous will live by faith."

Why is the *gospel* such a crucial message? Because in it *a righteousness from God is revealed*. The gospel tells sinful people how to become right with God. That is something we can never earn or achieve through our own efforts; Isaiah 64:6 says that "all our righteous acts are like filthy rags" before God. Our only hope is to accept by faith the gift of God's righteousness provided by him through the death of Jesus. As Paul wrote to the Corinthians, "God made him who had no sin to be sin for us, so that in him we might become the righteousness of God" (2 Corinthians 5:21).

It is difficult to know exactly what Paul had in mind with the phrase *faith from first to last*. Perhaps he is indicating that faith must govern our approach to God throughout our walk with him. We never outgrow our need for faith. And God never changes that requirement.

RIGHTEOUSNESS THROUGH FAITH IN CHRIST (ROMANS 3:19-26)

Establishing the Groundwork

In Romans 1:18–2:29, Paul provides support for the "bad news" that every human being is a sinner; no one is exempt. This includes Gentiles, who do not have the benefit of what may be termed the "special revelation" of God's law, and Jews, who do. In the beginning of chapter 3, Paul affirms that the Jews had indeed been favored by God by being entrusted with the revelations of God in the Old Testament. Did this mean that the Jews were better than non-Jews in God's sight? Absolutely not! Paul proceeds in verses 10-18 to marshal an impressive array of Old Testament quotations to make the case that sin is a universal problem. The first one is sufficient to appreciate Paul's argument: "There is no one righteous, not even one; there is no one who understands, no one who seeks God" (Romans 3:10, 11; taken from Ecclesiastes 7:20 and from two Psalms whose language is similar, 14:2, 3 and 53:2, 3).

Thus the picture of humanity painted by Paul to this point is not very attractive at all. We can be thankful, however, that there is more to the picture; there is the grace of God.

Examining the Text

I. The Function of the Law (Romans 3:19, 20)
A. To Declare the World Guilty (v. 19)

¹⁹ Now we know that whatever the law says, it says to those who are under the law, so that every mouth may be silenced and the whole world held accountable to God.

At first glance, one might conclude that Paul is referring specifically to the Mosaic law when he speaks of *the law* in this verse, which would limit its application to the Jews. However, his use of the other Old Testament references mentioned above indicates that he has something more in mind. Many students believe that Paul's condemnation is even more inclusive, taking in the principle of law as well as the specific law of Moses. In the first chapter of Romans, for example, Paul makes a forceful denunciation of the sinfulness of the Gentiles, insisting that they knew enough about God's will (without the use of the written law of God) not to engage in wickedness (Romans 1:19, 20, 32; see also Romans 2:12-15).

With the phrase *so that every mouth may be silenced*, Paul seems to be depicting a court scene in which the evidence against the accused parties is so overwhelming that they have no basis for speaking in their own defense. The court plays no favorites in this judgment; *the whole world* must be *held accountable to God.*

B. To Define Sin (v. 20)

²⁰ Therefore no one will be declared righteous in his sight by observing the law; rather, through the law we become conscious of sin.

In theory, if one could fulfill the requirements of *the law* perfectly, he or she could stand before the divine Judge as justified. Of course, no one can do this and thus earn salvation. One function of the law is to make us conscious of sin—to show us how sinful we are by providing a measuring stick to evaluate our moral status. If this were the end of the story, humanity would have been left in a hopelessly despondent situation. What follows, however, offers hope.

II. The Forgiveness of Sin (Romans 3:21-26)
A. The Foundation of Faith (vv. 21, 22a)

21 But now a righteousness from God, apart from law, has been made known, to which the Law and the Prophets testify.

The word *but* is often found in Scripture at some crucial turning point within a passage. Here is one of them. Once Paul had established that human righteousness is impossible through the works of the *law*, he then turned to the *righteousness* that comes *from God*. Even though God gave his law to humanity, he knew from the beginning that no one would be able to fulfill it perfectly. For that reason, he prepared another way, a way that does not depend on law, for people to be justified. *Now*, that plan *has been made known*, a plan that required God's Son to bear the sins of all humanity on the cross. Precursors of that plan are found in *the Law and the Prophets*. The various sacrifices of the Mosaic system foreshadowed the perfect sacrifice of the Lamb of God, as Hebrews points out (Hebrews 7:26-28; 9:23-28). Some prophecies of the Old Testament give only vague hints about the nature and work of the coming Messiah, while others, especially several in Isaiah, are much more explicit. (Read Isaiah 53 in particular.) Taken together, all of these witnesses provide evidence of God's plan to provide human beings with a way to become right with him.

22a This righteousness from God comes through faith in Jesus Christ to all who believe.

Paul continued to highlight the contrast between *righteousness* through good works and righteousness through God's grace. The first method is doomed to lead to failure. If we violate even one apparently insignificant part of the law, we are guilty of violating the entire law and we stand condemned (James 2:10).

By contrast, the righteousness that God now offers is *through faith in Jesus Christ*. There are no limitations based on race, ethnic background, or language; this righteousness is available *to all who believe*.

B. The Failure of All (vv. 22b, 23)

22b, 23 There is no difference, for all have sinned and fall short of the glory of God,

There is no difference at God's judgment seat between Jew and Gentile or between any categories of human beings. Whatever advantages Jews may have had as custodians of the Scriptures and as ancestors of Jesus Christ, these do not really matter; for *all have sinned*. Because of their sin, all *fall short of the glory of God*.

Students differ as to the precise meaning of the phrase *glory of God*. Some hold that it refers to the glory that Christians will share with God in eternity. Others take the view that all persons come short of the honor or praise that God gives to those who are right with him. Most likely, the term refers to the glory God himself displays because of his absolute holiness. Sin, which is a "falling short" of that mark, separates us from that glory. This is closely linked to the first definition, since we will not be able to live in God's glorious presence for eternity apart from faith in Christ as Savior.

C. The Free Gift of Grace (vv. 24-26)

²⁴ *. . . and are justified freely by his grace through the redemption that came by Christ Jesus.*

This verse sends a brilliant beam of hope into the otherwise desperate scenario described in the previous verse: "All have sinned." There is the opportunity for all to be *justified freely by* God's *grace through the redemption* made possible *by Christ Jesus*. The word *justified* is a legal term that describes the status of an accused person in court. When one is justified, it does not necessarily mean that he or she is innocent. Rather, it means that in the eyes of the court that person will not have to pay the penalty for the crime committed. Christ has already paid the penalty for sin by his death on the cross. This debt has been "paid in full"; the only stipulation required of the condemned is that he or she accept it. This is what *grace* is all about. It is often defined as "unmerited favor," meaning that the recipient does not deserve it and cannot earn it. The only choice is to accept it or reject it.

²⁵ *God presented him as a sacrifice of atonement, through faith in his blood. He did this to demonstrate his justice, because in his forbearance he had left the sins committed beforehand unpunished—*

In the Old Testament, *atonement* was associated with the mercy seat in the Holy of Holies. This mercy seat or "atonement cover" was to be placed on top of the Ark of the Covenant (Exodus 25:17-22). Each year on the Day of Atonement, the high priest entered the Holy of Holies and sprinkled the blood of the sacrificial animal on the mercy seat to atone for the people's sins (Leviticus 16:15-17). In the New Testament, the term atonement takes on a fuller meaning.

Christ is not only the high priest who offers the sacrifice; he is the sacrifice that makes the atonement possible.

It may seem unfair that we, the guilty, go free while Jesus, the innocent, bears the penalty. But this transaction shows us that God is a just Judge who demands an accounting for all sins. In the death of Jesus, the penalty of sin was paid, not only for later sinners but also for earlier sinners, such as Abraham, whose faith "was credited to him as righteousness" (Romans 4:3, 16-25; see also Hebrews 9:15).

> *26 . . . he did it to demonstrate his justice at the present time, so as to be just and the one who justifies those who have faith in Jesus.*

In a sense God was faced with a divine dilemma. As a holy God, he could not tolerate sin. At the same time, he is a loving God who wanted to save everyone. From a human perspective, this is an impossible situation to resolve; but "with God all things are possible" (Matthew 19:26). He resolved the dilemma by offering his Son as the perfect sacrifice for sin. Thus God is both *just*—exacting the fair penalty for sin—and *the one who justifies those who have faith in Jesus.*

JUSTIFIED BY FAITH (ROMANS 5:1-11)

Establishing the Groundwork

Having clearly made his case in the early chapters of Romans for the universal sinfulness of humanity (Romans 1:18–3:20), Paul then began to explain the remedy for this problem: the "righteousness from God" that "comes through faith in Jesus Christ to all who believe" (Romans 3:22). In Romans 4, Paul introduced an example, Abraham, whose faith "was credited to him as righteousness" (Romans 4:3). God's grace was necessary—even for this Old Testament saint. Even he could not have done enough to merit God's favor. He trusted God, and that trust was the reason for his being considered "righteous" in God's sight.

Paul closes the fourth chapter of Romans by building a "bridge" from Abraham to the followers of Jesus. The fact that righteousness "was credited to him" by faith applies not only to Abraham, "but also for us, to whom God will credit righteousness—for us who believe in him who raised Jesus our Lord from the dead" (Romans 4:24). Paul then concludes with a succinct statement of the gospel message: Jesus was "delivered over to death for our sins and was raised to life for our justification" (v. 25).

I. Faith's Provisions (Romans 5:1, 2)
A. Brings Peace (v. 1)

¹ Therefore, since we have been justified through faith, we have peace with God through our Lord Jesus Christ,

Any occurrence of the word *therefore* should encourage the Bible student to ask what it is "there for." In this case, it points back to Paul's use of Abraham as an illustration of grace and *faith* in the previous chapter. That example may have been cited by Paul in an effort to appeal to the Jews to accept the concept of salvation by grace and faith. If the man considered the "father of the Jewish people" was a recipient of grace and was counted righteous by faith, then his descendants should not try to create some other means of coming to God.

Also worth noting is what Paul has already said about the desperate human condition: all have sinned (Romans 3:23); no one is excluded. The finger of God has been pointed at every human being, and our sins have been painted in the dark colors they deserve. The remedy for such a condition is to be *justified through faith*. One often-cited description of what it means to be *justified* is a play on the word: being justified means being treated "just as if I'd" never sinned. God himself has provided the means for bridging the gap between us that was created by our sins (Isaiah 59:2), thereby making *peace*. That means is *our Lord Jesus Christ*, whose death and resurrection Paul highlighted at the conclusion of the previous chapter (Romans 4:25).

B. Accesses Grace (v. 2a)

²ª . . . through whom we have gained access by faith into this grace in which we now stand.

By using the word *grace*, Paul reinforced his central point. There are no works that we can do to gain our justification. Salvation has been provided by God; it is a gift that we must receive. *Faith* in Jesus gives us *access* to God's grace.

To illustrate, consider that to gain an audience with a world leader, the chief executive of a large organization, or anyone with a very full calendar, one must not only make an appointment; he must also be ushered in by someone close to the important person. Jesus (through our trust in him) ushers us into the presence of the God of grace. And Jesus continues to give us access to God and his grace (Hebrews 7:25).

C. Presents Hope (v. 2b)

2b And we rejoice in the hope of the glory of God.

Hope is a frequently misunderstood word. Often people use it to talk about something they desire to have or to see happen, but they don't know whether or not they will get it and see it.

The Bible uses the word *hope* quite differently. In Christ *we rejoice in . . . hope*. The quality of one's hope hinges on the character of the one in whom hope is placed. For one in Christ, there is a confident expectation of receiving all he has promised, including *the glory of God*. By grace we anticipate the time when that glory will be revealed in us (Romans 8:18).

II. Faith's Progress (Romans 5:3-5)
A. From Sufferings to Perseverance (v. 3)

3 Not only so, but we also rejoice in our sufferings, because we know that suffering produces perseverance;

In Christ we have resources for handling the circumstances that come our way, such as *sufferings*. Satan would use such experiences to upset and weaken our faith. But when faith is our guiding principle, what appear to be very bad situations can yield good results. (Read Paul's later affirmation in Romans 8:28.) Those results are not always immediately seen. Think of what happened to Joseph in the Old Testament. But even after all the evil done to him because of his brothers' sin, he could say, "God sent me ahead of you to preserve for you a remnant on earth and to save your lives by a great deliverance" (Genesis 45:7). Thus there is often a need for *perseverance*.

B. From Perseverance to Character (v. 4a)

4a . . . perseverance, character;

Lessons in *perseverance* come from several directions and at various stages of life. Through the patient handling of circumstances, the discovery of solutions, and the discipline of waiting, *character* is developed. And the person of such character can often provide encouragement to someone who needs advice from an individual who's "been there" (2 Corinthians 1:3, 4).

C. From Character to Hope (vv. 4b, 5)

4b . . . and character, hope.

At this point, Paul may appear to be going in circles. As Christians we possess a faith-based *hope*. In living out that hope, we will encounter sufferings.

Those sufferings will teach us perseverance. That perseverance will help develop *character*. And that character in turn will cause us to hope in God. However, let us not think of this as a circle as much as an advancing spiral. With each round of faith-guided living, we gain strength and we become more valuable to the Master.

> [5] *And hope does not disappoint us, because God has poured out his love into our hearts by the Holy Spirit, whom he has given us.*

In times of testing, our *hope* in Christ will *not disappoint us*. Paul emphasizes that all of the attributes he has described in this passage come from God and that God guides the entire process by which they are acquired. He even provides the means for maintaining what he has *given*, namely, *the Holy Spirit*, who gives us *love* and helps us grow in love. When love is clearly visible in the church, it is a sure sign of the Holy Spirit's presence.

III. Christ's Atonement (Romans 5:6-11)
A. His Death for Sinners (vv. 6-8)

> [6] *You see, at just the right time, when we were still powerless, Christ died for the ungodly.*

The right time is God's time! (See Galatians 4:4.) It is remarkable to study the prophecies fulfilled by Jesus, especially those surrounding his death. But the most remarkable aspect of the death of *Christ* is that he *died for the ungodly*. In Romans 1, Paul described in some detail the wicked state into which the human race has fallen. The worst part of man's condition is not his evil but the fact that he is utterly *powerless* to do anything to provide a remedy to his condition.

> [7] *Very rarely will anyone die for a righteous man, though for a good man someone might possibly dare to die.*

What is the difference between a *righteous man* and a *good man*? Some would say that the righteous man describes an especially pious individual who possesses a "holier-than-thou" attitude. He may be highly respected, but he is not the kind of person for whom someone else would be willing to *die*. The good man would be someone whose good deeds make him a much more likable individual, and thus someone for whom others would be more apt *to die*.

Others believe that there is basically no difference between the righteous man and the good man and that Paul is making the same claim in two different ways. The first part of the verse states Paul's claim in a negative way; the second states it in a more positive manner. Either way, the gist of Paul's thought is this: people are not likely to give their lives on behalf of even the best of human beings.

⁸ But God demonstrates his own love for us in this: While we were still sinners, Christ died for us.

Here is the dramatic difference between *God* and human beings. He has shown *his own love for us*, in the form of his crucified Son. And he has done this for *sinners*—not righteous men, not good men, but those who were anything but righteous and good! This is real love—the kind of love that can come only from God.

Not only does God demonstrate such love, but he also commands that Christians demonstrate that love to others (John 13:34, 35; 1 John 4:11), even to our enemies (Matthew 5:44).

B. His Blessings for the Reconciled (vv. 9-11)

⁹ Since we have now been justified by his blood, how much more shall we be saved from God's wrath through him!

Justification is the present possession of the Christian. We can be at peace with God. The work of Christ has been done. We are new creations (2 Corinthians 5:17), we wear a new name, and we have a new destiny that will not be realized until this time in our present world is finished and our time in Heaven has begun. We will be *saved from God's wrath*, from Hell, from the place prepared for those who have trusted in their way rather than God's way. Thus our past, present, and future are all in God's hands.

¹⁰ For if, when we were God's enemies, we were reconciled to him through the death of his Son, how much more, having been reconciled, shall we be saved through his life!

Justification addresses the problem of sin from a legal point of view, while reconciliation approaches it from a personal point of view. In a lawsuit, a court may hand down a decision that meets the requirements of the law for justice. But there is still not reconciliation. Not until the two opponents settle their differences can there be a reconciliation. God has "settled" the hostility between him and sinful humanity *through the death of his Son*. It is up to us to accept his offer of reconciliation (2 Corinthians 5:20).

But even that is not the whole story. *Much more* than this great reconciliation that was effected by Jesus' death is the benefit of his resurrection and continuing *life*. By that, Paul says, we shall *be saved*. Salvation is more than a matter of having our past sins erased by Jesus' atoning death. It is a relationship with a living Lord. And if Christ was willing to die for our sins when we were sinners (and he was willing), how much more will he do for us in this living salvation relationship that we now enjoy with him!

[11] *Not only is this so, but we also rejoice in God through our Lord Jesus Christ, through whom we have now received reconciliation.*

From the study of verse 3, we can see that Paul's phrase *not only is this so* is simply an expression that he uses to say, "There is more." We have been reconciled (reunited) to *God*. We have been saved from sin and death by means of his grace. As a result, we can genuinely *rejoice*. Like hope, joy is more than just a fleeting emotion; it is a constant sense of gratitude and praise for all that God has done and will do. Paul notes that all of what he has just described, including our having *received reconciliation* with God, comes *through our Lord Jesus Christ.*

ALIVE IN CHRIST (ROMANS 6:1-14)

Establishing the Groundwork

In the remaining verses of Romans 5 (vv. 12-21), Paul raises the issue of Adam's sin and its impact versus Christ's death and its impact. Paul's primary emphasis here is that Jesus' death has reversed the effects of Adam's sin. Life, not death, reigns for the followers of Jesus. Near the conclusion of the chapter, Paul writes that "where sin increased, grace increased all the more" (v. 20).

At the beginning of Romans 6, Paul anticipates a question that some may raise (or may have raised in the church in Rome) concerning grace.

Examining the Text

I. Receiving the New Life (Romans 6:1-5)
A. Dead to Sin (vv. 1-3)

[1] *What shall we say, then? Shall we go on sinning so that grace may increase?*

If it is indeed true that "where sin increased, grace increased all the more" (Romans 5:20), isn't the next "logical" step to say, "Let's keep *sinning* all we want, then we'll really give God's *grace* a chance to work"?

True, God is a God of grace. He is able and willing to forgive the most terrible sins. But God wants us to grow toward righteousness, as Paul will later emphasize in this chapter. As someone has put it, "God loves us as we are, but he loves us too much to let us stay that way."

[2] *By no means! We died to sin; how can we live in it any longer?*

Paul's answer to the question raised in verse 1 is unmistakably clear: *By no means!* A vital part of the acceptance of Jesus Christ as Savior and Lord is becoming dead to sin through repentance. The Christian is "under new management," so to speak.

> *3 Or don't you know that all of us who were baptized into Christ Jesus were baptized into his death?*

Baptism is designed to be a defining moment in our relationship with God. Just as *Jesus* was buried in a tomb, the one who accepts Jesus is buried in the "watery grave" of Christian baptism. We are *baptized into his death*; that is, baptism represents our acceptance of Jesus' death as our own. It is a burial of the old self. The penalty for our sin is removed in accepting Jesus' death as the substitute for ours. And sin, as the controlling force in our lives, is dead. Its mastery over us has been broken.

B. Raised with Christ (vv. 4, 5)

> *4 We were therefore buried with him through baptism into death in order that, just as Christ was raised from the dead through the glory of the Father, we too may live a new life.*

Paul continues his explanation of the dynamic image of Christian *baptism*. A candidate is *buried* in water and raised from that water in an act that identifies him or her with the Son of God, who was buried and *raised* for us. God's power and love raised Jesus, and in baptism his power is also at work in those who have chosen to follow Jesus. Paul notes this in Colossians 2:12: "buried with him [Christ] in baptism and raised with him through your faith in the power of God, who raised him from the dead." Paul also calls attention to what is to take place following the act of baptism. This is clear from the phrase *live a new life*. Baptism is a spiritual turning point in one's life; a baptized individual must never live the same as he or she did prior to baptism.

Clearly baptism is much more than just a ritual or a ceremony. It marks the transformation from death to life; it is, spiritually, a matter of life and death.

> *5 If we have been united with him like this in his death, we will certainly also be united with him in his resurrection.*

Jesus was buried and raised for us. And when we have surrendered to Jesus' lordship, after our *death* and burial in baptism, we will *be united with him in his resurrection*. Christian baptism is a demonstration or reenactment of the central facts of the gospel message as defined by Paul in 1 Corinthians 15:1-4 (the death, burial, and *resurrection* of Jesus). Baptism provides a wonderful opportunity to be like Jesus!

II. Living the New Life (Romans 6:6-14)
A. The Old Master (vv. 6-11)

6, 7 For we know that our old self was crucified with him so that the body of sin might be done away with, that we should no longer be slaves to sin—because anyone who has died has been freed from sin.

In the remainder of this chapter and in chapters 7 and 8, Paul will continue to describe the battle in which Christians are engaged—a battle of which we are all keenly aware. As long as we live in this world, the fleshly part of us (the body) will call for attention; and that will be the part of us through which Satan will work the hardest to capture our allegiance and erode our faith.

Here the apostle insists that we do not take orders from *sin* anymore or from its headquarters. He uses the term *our old self* to describe the individual under sin's rule. But now that we are new creations in Christ Jesus (2 Corinthians 5:17), we live under a new master, or by the "new self" (Ephesians 4:24). We are not *slaves to sin*. We serve a new master—Christ. We are not freed from temptation, but we are *freed from sin* as the controlling factor in our lives. God has also given us his Holy Spirit to equip us for the battle, and the Spirit is stronger than Satan (1 John 4:4). Sin will continue to entice, but now it has "met its match." The will to resist temptation operates only in the person in whom the Holy Spirit is at work.

8 Now if we died with Christ, we believe that we will also live with him.

Our symbolic death and burial in baptism illustrates our death to the old way of life—the time when we were living under the power of sin. Now we are dead to that; now we truly *live*, with *Christ* at the helm. Eternal life begins with our relationship with Christ (John 17:3), and it extends into eternity.

9 For we know that since Christ was raised from the dead, he cannot die again; death no longer has mastery over him.

Prior to Jesus, other individuals had been raised from the dead. But these all eventually died again. *Christ was raised from the dead* to die no more. The Christian faces death, knowing that it is a beaten enemy because of Jesus' resurrection. Thus what is true of Jesus is true of the Christian: *death no longer has mastery over him.*

10 The death he died, he died to sin once for all; but the life he lives, he lives to God.

A crucial part of the gospel is that Christ died for our sins (1 Corinthians 15:3). Here Paul writes that Christ *died to sin*, which seems to describe the impact of Jesus' death on sin itself. Perhaps it highlights Jesus' destruction of the power of sin by his death. Christ's victory over the power of sin was decisive. And his death does not need to be repeated; it happened *once for all* (Hebrews 9:24-28). Jesus now *lives to God*, dwelling with the Father as he did before laying aside his glory to come to earth.

¹¹ In the same way, count yourselves dead to sin but alive to God in Christ Jesus.

As Christians we are *dead to sin*. Paul has already made that clear. But that is more than just a point of doctrine; we are to live like that—*alive to God*, alive in the presence of God, alive for God and his eternal purposes.

B. The New Master (vv. 12-14)

¹² Therefore do not let sin reign in your mortal body so that you obey its evil desires.

"Live according to who (and whose) you are," the apostle writes. You have been set free, so live as a free individual. You have become a child of God. You have an alternative to the path of *sin*. Sin no longer has to *reign* over you; through Christ you can reign over it.

¹³ Do not offer the parts of your body to sin, as instruments of wickedness, but rather offer yourselves to God, as those who have been brought from death to life; and offer the parts of your body to him as instruments of righteousness.

Christians live in the era between the moment that *God* dealt *sin* a death-blow through Jesus' death and resurrection and the final victory that will occur at Jesus' return. During this interval, we are to live under God's authority, reflecting the *righteousness* that he requires of his people (Ephesians 4:24).

Here Paul tells us that the *parts* of our *body* are not Satan's possession now; they are God's *instruments*. We are to use our eyes, our hands, our feet, our minds, and our mouths in a way that shows we are people *who have been brought from death to life*. That does not simply mean avoiding wicked uses of those features; it also means putting them to work to serve, to bless, and to draw others to God.

¹⁴ For sin shall not be your master, because you are not under law, but under grace.

This may be considered a summary of Paul's answer to the question raised in verse 1. We must not keep sinning, because *sin* is our former *master*. Although Paul has not mentioned *law* yet in this section, it is part of the reason for sin's mastery. The term *law* should not be limited to the law of Moses. Any system of law points out our sin but cannot provide an answer to sin's mastery; it cannot free us from the guilt sin produces. Only God's *grace* can supply what we need and solve our dilemma. By grace, death has been destroyed, sin's hold has been broken, and we are free to serve a new master. As Paul goes on to say in this chapter, "You have been set free from sin and have become slaves to God" (Romans 6:22).

How to Say It

ABRAHAM. *Ay*-bruh-ham.

AQUILA. *Ack*-wih-luh.

ATONEMENT. uh-*tone*-ment.

CHARISMA *(Greek).* kah-*riss*-mah.

COLOSSE. Ko-*lahss*-ee.

EPHESUS. *Ef*-uh-sus.

GAIUS. *Gay*-us.

MACEDONIA. Mass-eh-*doe*-nee-uh.

MESSIAH. Meh-*sigh*-uh.

MOSAIC. Mo-*zay*-ik.

PENTECOST. *Pent*-ih-kost.

PHILEMON. Fih-*lee*-mun or Fye-*lee*-mun.

PHILIPPI. Fih-*lip*-pie or *Fil*-ih-pie.

PRISCILLA. Prih-*sil*-uh.

SAMARITANS. Suh-*mare*-uh-tunz.

THESSALONICA. *Thess*-uh-lo-*nye*-kuh (strong accent on *nye*; *th* as in *thin*).

Events in the Life of Paul

Event	Date	Event in Paul's Life
	30	Pentecost (Acts 2)
	32	Stoning of Stephen in Jerusalem
	34	Paul's Conversion (Acts 9:1-19)
Aretas, authority in Damascus	37	Paul returns from Arabia; first visit to Jerusalem (Acts 9:26-30; Galatians 1:18-20)
Death of Herod Agrippa I	44	
	46	Second visit to Jerusalem (Acts 11:30; 12:25)
	47–49	First Missionary Journey
	51	Third visit to Jerusalem; Jerusalem Conference (Acts 15; Galatians 2)
	52–54	Second Missionary Journey
Gallio, proconsul of Achaia	52	1 & 2 Thessalonians written from Corinth
	54–58	Third Missionary Journey
	54–57	Lengthy ministry in Ephesus (Acts 19:10; 20:31)
	56	1 Corinthians written from Ephesus
	57	2 Corinthians written from Macedonia
	57/58	Galatians written from Macedonia
	58	Romans written in anticipation of a visit to Rome
	58	Paul arrested in Jerusalem (Acts 21)
	58–60	Imprisonment in Caesarea (Acts 24:27)
Festus, governor of Judea	60	
	61	Trip to Rome (Acts 27, 28)
	61–63	First Roman imprisonment (Acts 28)
	63	Prison Epistles (Ephesians, Philippians, Colossians, Philemon) written from Rome
	63	Hebrews written (by Paul?)
Burning of Rome	64	
	65	1 Timothy written from Macedonia
	65/66	Titus written from Macedonia
	67/68	Second Roman imprisonment
	67	2 Timothy written in anticipation of death
	67/68	Paul executed in Rome
Death of Nero	68	

© 1992, Lewis Foster. Used by permission. See the author's similar work in *The Expositor's Bible Commentary*, vol. 1 (© 1988, Zondervan).

Chapter 7

The Gospel of Grace: Studies in Romans (Part 2)

Romans 8:1-11; 8:28-39; 10:5-17; 12:1, 2, 9-21; 13:1-7

LIFE IN THE SPIRIT (ROMANS 8:1-11)

Establishing the Groundwork

In the remainder of Romans 6 (vv. 15-23) and in all of Romans 7, Paul continues to contrast the old life under sin and the law with the new life in Christ. In particular, he focuses on the ongoing tension between those two paths that he experiences (and that all of us experience).

A brief word is in order concerning Paul's teaching in Romans 7, especially verses 7-25. Is Paul relating his experience before or after becoming a Christian? It is probably best to see these verses as a description of Paul's (and the Christian's) continual struggle with sin following conversion. That struggle—the issue of whether sin or righteousness should "reign" in our lives—is introduced in Romans 6:12. At the end of chapter 7, Paul expresses the intensity of the struggle in these words: "What a wretched man I am! Who will rescue me from this body of death? Thanks be to God—through Jesus Christ our Lord! So then, I myself in my mind am a slave to God's law, but in the sinful nature a slave to the law of sin" (Romans 7:24, 25). In Romans 8, Paul elaborates on the "rescue" provided in Christ.

Examining the Text

I. Way to Freedom and Life (Romans 8:1-8)
A. In Christ Jesus (vv. 1, 2)

¹ Therefore, there is now no condemnation for those who are in Christ Jesus,

God has solved a dilemma that we could not solve. God has paid a price that we could never pay. His Son took the penalty that we deserved because of our sin. Even though our past is marked with frequent inconsistencies and failures, even though our present practice is imperfect, and even though we can count on facing Satan's "fiery darts" in the future, *there is now no condemnation*—because we *are in Christ Jesus*.

To be in Christ, however, involves more than just a position or standing. To accept Christ as Savior marks the beginning of a process of growth.

*² . . . because through Christ Jesus the law of the Spirit of life set me free
from the law of sin and death.*

A new *law* is at work in the Christian. This law is not loaded with restrictions, prescriptions, accusations, or condemnations. It offers *life,* not death—including possibilities, opportunities, freedom from *sin and death,* and help through God's *Spirit.*

B. Not in Law (vv. 3-8)

*³ For what the law was powerless to do in that it was weakened by the
sinful nature, God did by sending his own Son in the likeness of sinful man
to be a sin offering. And so he condemned sin in sinful man,*

The law called people to obedience. It pointed out failures, but it provided no forgiveness for those failures and no power to do better. The law itself was good; in fact, Paul calls it "holy" in Romans 7:12. But it was *weakened by the sinful nature* (the term *sinful nature* is literally *flesh* in the Greek text). Humanity has not been able to keep the standards set forth in the law. The flesh always pulls us in the opposite direction from that established by God's law.

God addressed the law's failure by *sending his own Son in the likeness of sinful man.* "The Word became flesh" (John 1:14) but came only in the *likeness of sinful man.* Jesus had a human body, but Jesus controlled that body and did not allow the flesh to become the starting point for sin (as we have done). His perfection qualified him to become the sacrifice on the cross for those who had sinned (all humanity). Thus God *condemned* our *sin* in the flesh (the body) of Jesus. Then God brought Jesus' body back to life. Sin, death, and the flesh were defeated.

*⁴ . . . in order that the righteous requirements of the law might be fully met
in us, who do not live according to the sinful nature but according to the
Spirit.*

On our own, we could never fulfill *the righteous requirements of the law.* Jesus did so—first, by keeping the law perfectly, and, second, by suffering the punishment of death that the law required of lawbreakers (again, describing all human beings). Those who accept Christ as Savior accept his death on their behalf and are thereby viewed as righteous by God. "God made him who had no sin to be sin for us, so that in him we might become the righteousness of God" (2 Corinthians 5:21). But as noted earlier, to be in Christ is more than a position. Here Paul encourages those in Christ not to *live according to the sinful nature but according to the Spirit.*

⁵ Those who live according to the sinful nature have their minds set on what that nature desires; but those who live in accordance with the Spirit have their minds set on what the Spirit desires.

To *have* one's mind *set on what* the *sinful nature* (or the flesh) . . . *desires* is to follow the standard of conduct described so clearly by the apostle John: "For everything in the world—the cravings of sinful man, the lust of his eyes and the boasting of what he has and does—comes not from the Father but from the world" (1 John 2:16). The flesh conveys a signal, and if we are committed only to this world and to the moment, we rush to obey that signal. But when the *Spirit* of God is actively working in us, we are receiving a different signal from a higher source. And we must listen to that which is higher and permanent, not that which is lower and temporary.

⁶ The mind of sinful man is death, but the mind controlled by the Spirit is life and peace;

It is important that we know the consequences of having a sinful *mind.* If we take orders from the flesh, *death* will be the unavoidable result. Death is primarily separation from God; therefore it includes not only physical death but also spiritual death in sin. But if we are *controlled by the Spirit,* we will share the quality and quantity of *life* in the Spirit.

⁷ . . . the sinful mind is hostile to God. It does not submit to God's law, nor can it do so.

All we have to do is read again the Ten Commandments that God gave his people through Moses to see the contrast between *the sinful mind* and *God's law.* When one submits to the flesh, he or she is not subject to God but is God's enemy.

The warning against being driven by the flesh does not mean that all of our physical requirements or interests are evil. God created us. And he made life to be enjoyed. But he gave us appetites and desires to be used under control, not to be in control over us. It is clear that even good appetites or desires can be abused by someone who does not honor God and his law. And alongside the abuse of healthy appetites have grown-up appetites that are clearly in opposition to the will of God.

⁸ Those controlled by the sinful nature cannot please God.

Later in this letter, Paul writes the following: "Therefore, I urge you, brothers, in view of God's mercy, to offer your bodies as living sacrifices, holy and pleasing to God—this is your spiritual act of worship" (Romans 12:1).

We *please God* when we present our bodies for his use, not when we let fleshly desires control how we use our bodies.

II. Walk of Freedom and Life (Romans 8:9-11)
A. Spiritual Life (vv. 9, 10)

⁹ You, however, are controlled not by the sinful nature but by the Spirit, if the Spirit of God lives in you. And if anyone does not have the Spirit of Christ, he does not belong to Christ.

Again, Paul highlights the contrast between being *controlled* by *the sinful nature* and *by the Spirit*. Christians, by virtue of their relationship with *Christ* and of the "new life" that they have been given (Romans 6:4), are not flesh-guided people. "You have the *Spirit of God* in you," says Paul. So we must take our cues from the Spirit, not the flesh.

Also worth noting is the word *you*. This word is a second person plural in the Greek text. The business of the Christian walk, of living with Christ in us, is carried out in a fellowship of believers. In fact, in the first Corinthian letter Paul writes, "Don't you know that you yourselves are God's temple and that God's Spirit lives in you?" (1 Corinthians 3:16). There too the word *you* is in the plural each time. The Spirit of God energizes the individual believer, and the Spirit of God energizes the church.

One should also consider how Paul refers to the Holy Spirit as the Spirit of life, the Spirit of God, the Spirit of Christ, and later as the Spirit of sonship (v. 15). A person should not be stymied by these different names. With each one Paul refers to the holy presence whom God gives to each Christian. The same divine person is described each time.

¹⁰ But if Christ is in you, your body is dead because of sin, yet your spirit is alive because of righteousness.

Here the apostle makes the same point in a slightly different way. The Christian's *body is dead because of sin*. Not only is it destined to die, but it suffers the consequences of the death resulting from sin (illness, aging, etc.). But because of God's grace and because the *righteousness* of Christ has covered our sins, the result is that the Christian's *spirit is alive*.

B. Physical Life (v. 11)

¹¹ And if the Spirit of him who raised Jesus from the dead is living in you, he who raised Christ from the dead will also give life to your mortal bodies through his Spirit, who lives in you.

The death of the body, mentioned in the previous verse, is not the last word on the subject. The same Holy *Spirit* who lives in us and empowers us spiritually will also *give life* to our *bodies*. The Spirit's presence in us now is considered a "deposit," assuring us of greater blessings to come (2 Corinthians 1:21, 22; Ephesians 1:13, 14).

MORE THAN CONQUERORS (ROMANS 8:28-39)

Establishing the Groundwork

As Paul continues to describe life in the Spirit in Romans 8, he raises the issue of sufferings in verse 17. There he refers to Christians as "heirs of God and co-heirs with Christ" and notes that sharing in Christ's future glory means sharing in present sufferings for him. And yet any sufferings we may undergo "are not worth comparing with the glory that will be revealed in us" (v. 18). A few verses later Paul highlights again the Spirit's ministry on behalf of Christians by noting that he "intercedes for us with groans that words cannot express" (v. 26). Further assurance is provided in the remainder of chapter 8, which includes what many students of the Bible consider some of the most treasured portions of God's Word.

Examining the Text

I. God's Provision (Romans 8:28-34)
A. In the Past (vv. 28-30)

²⁸ And we know that in all things God works for the good of those who love him, who have been called according to his purpose.

Many Christians quote this verse as one of their favorite portions of Scripture, and rightly so. Properly understood, this verse offers hope for the Christian in all kinds of situations. God is the absolute Sovereign of the universe and nothing can occur that lies outside his will. As a part of his permissive will, he has granted humanity a measure of freedom. We have used this freedom in many tragic ways, choosing to reject and disobey our Creator rather than respect and obey him. Our acts of rebellion often lead to suffering. Sometimes even good people make bad decisions that lead to suffering. God could prevent this pain, but to do so he would have to deny human freedom.

Even so, God can use the most arrogant acts of rebellion or the most tragic mistakes to achieve his ultimately *good* purposes. Joseph in the Old Testament recognized this when he told his brothers, who had sold him into slavery, "You intended to harm me, but God intended it for good to accomplish what is now being done, the saving of many lives" (Genesis 50:20). The prime example of this principle at work is the cross of Christ, where God used a heinous act of murder to provide salvation for lost humanity.

Across the centuries, Christians have suffered persecution and even martyrdom. But their suffering has led to the growth of Christianity and the preservation of the faith for modern believers. Only if we understand this verse in terms of God's ultimate purposes for us can we find comfort in it during our own trials. *Good* must be understood in spiritual more than material terms. This is what the ensuing verses teach.

Who are the ones *who have been called according to* God's *purpose*? They are the ones Paul has just mentioned as those who *love him*. They have answered God's call in Christ. This is in accordance with God's divine purpose—to save, bless, and keep all who would accept and receive the gift of his love offered through his Son. It is not that only those were to be called to be saved whom God purposed, but that he purposed to save all who would heed his call to be saved.

> ²⁹ **For those God foreknew he also predestined to be conformed to the likeness of his Son, that he might be the firstborn among many brothers.**

As stated previously, when God created man, he gave him the freedom of choice. Being sovereign, God *foreknew* that some people would respond to his offer of salvation in Christ with love and obedience and some would not. Those who responded in obedience *he . . . predestined to be conformed to the likeness of his Son*. This is not saying that God predestined the choice of these individuals; rather, he determined that all who made the choice to accept Christ would be conformed to his likeness. This is the "purpose" (v. 28) to which he has called all Christians.

Paul goes on to describe Jesus as *the firstborn among many brothers*. In ancient times the firstborn son received a place of honor and a greater inheritance than any of the other children in the family. The term as applied to Jesus means that he has that place of honor as the "one and only Son" of God (John 3:16, 18; 1 John 4:9). However, as Paul has already stated in this eighth chapter of Romans, we can be "God's children" and "co-heirs with Christ" and thus share in the glory that awaits (vv. 16-18).

> ³⁰ **And those he predestined, he also called; those he called, he also justified; those he justified, he also glorified.**

As noted under verse 28, the *called* are not all of those to whom God's call is given; the called are considered those who respond to his call through the gospel and become Christians. Neither predestination nor calling (as the Bible defines them) overrules a person's will or takes away his ability to choose.

Those who respond to God's call are *justified*, or declared "not guilty," by virtue of accepting Christ's death in their place. Their sins are forgiven, and they are made righteous (2 Corinthians 5:21). God declares them righteous, but he does not do so without their cooperation.

The term *glorified* is stated in the past tense, even though it describes something (glory) that awaits the Christian. This is because the Christian's glorification was determined long ago as part of God's "purpose." It "will be revealed in us" (Romans 8:18), but even here on earth we can say, with Paul, that "our citizenship is in heaven" (Philippians 3:20).

B. In the Present (vv. 31-34)

31 What, then, shall we say in response to this? If God is for us, who can be against us?

The word *if* does not express uncertainty. This verse would be better understood if it were translated "since God is for us." Since God is indeed *for us, who can be against us?* Of course, there are many persons and forces that oppose Christianity. But this opposition cannot succeed. Paul's question may be paraphrased, "Who, with any hope of success, can be against us?" The obvious answer is, "No one!"

32 He who did not spare his own Son, but gave him up for us all—how will he not also, along with him, graciously give us all things?

God has already shown that he will stop at nothing—not even the death of *his own Son*—to save us. We can be assured that he will *graciously* continue to *give us all things* we need for maintaining our walk with him.

33 Who will bring any charge against those whom God has chosen? It is God who justifies.

Verse 33 repeats the concept of verse 31 using the image of a courtroom scene. The enemies of the cross have often brought charges against Christians. Of course, our primary accuser is Satan, who is described as "the accuser of our brothers, who accuses them before our God day and night" (Revelation 12:10). But *it is God who justifies*; and since he, the "Supreme Court," as it were, has rendered a "not guilty" verdict, what lower court can *bring any charge*?

34 Who is he that condemns? Christ Jesus, who died—more than that, who was raised to life—is at the right hand of God and is also interceding for us.

The eighth chapter of Romans began with the declaration, "Therefore, there is now no condemnation for those who are in Christ Jesus" (Romans 8:1). Here Paul reaffirms that proposition, based on the fact that God is the one who justifies and *Christ Jesus* is the one who is *interceding for us.* We are immune from condemnation, not by our own goodness, but through Christ *who died* and *was raised to life.* He is now *at the right hand of God,* "always . . . to intercede" for his people (Hebrews 7:25).

II. God's Love (Romans 8:35-39)
A. Greater Than Circumstances (vv. 35-37)

³⁵ Who shall separate us from the love of Christ? Shall trouble or hardship or persecution or famine or nakedness or danger or sword?

The circumstances that Paul mentions in this verse can *separate* us from much that blesses and benefits our lives. *Hardship* or *persecution* can sever us from family ties and even from our home and our country. *Famine* can cut off normal nutrition and affect our health. *Nakedness* would remove our dignity or respectability, as well as leave us unprotected from the elements. The *sword* would likely represent death at the hands of an executioner. Yet none of these situations can *separate us from the love of Christ.* His love remains true, though our circumstances may seem to tell us otherwise.

³⁶ As it is written:
"For your sake we face death all day long;
we are considered as sheep to be slaughtered."

Here Paul quotes Psalm 44:22. The idea of faithful persons facing *death* for the Lord's *sake* was an issue that troubled the psalmist. By quoting this passage, Paul shows that suffering has always been a part of the experience of God's people. In the eyes of the ungodly, the righteous have at times been regarded as so many *sheep to be slaughtered.*

³⁷ No, in all these things we are more than conquerors through him who loved us.

No answers the question raised in verse 35. No, none of the circumstances named there can separate us from the love of Christ. Paul does not claim, as he knew very well from his own experience, that God delivers us from all of these situations. But it is in the midst of them that we are made *more than conquerors,* not by our own strength or virtue, but *through him who loved us.* These circumstances take nothing of eternal value from us. By God's grace we can actually gain from them, since the testing of our faith makes us stronger (James 1:2-4).

B. Greater Than Anything (vv. 38, 39)

38, 39 For I am convinced that neither death nor life, neither angels nor demons, neither the present nor the future, nor any powers, neither height nor depth, nor anything else in all creation, will be able to separate us from the love of God that is in Christ Jesus our Lord.

I am convinced. Paul concludes his answer to the question of verse 35 with a ringing affirmation of his own faith, a faith that allowed him to face persecution and even *death* without flinching. He lists a variety of situations that singly or together may be used by the Christian's enemies (and Satan in particular) to *separate us from the love of God.* Yet none of these has the power to do so.

Paul invites us to share with him in such a determined, unwavering faith. It is vital that we do so! It is still true that no external power or entity can separate us from God's love. But *we* can choose to walk away from that love and to sever our relationship with the Father. The warnings concerning this are among the most ominous in Scripture. (See Hebrews 6:4-6; 10:19-39.)

PROCLAIMING THE MESSAGE OF SALVATION (ROMANS 10:5-17)

Establishing the Groundwork

In the ninth chapter of Romans, Paul introduces a new theme in his letter—the place of the Jews in God's redemptive plan. His discussion springs from his personal passion for his people (he calls the Jews his "brothers" and "those of [his] own race" in verse 3) and his desire that they know the Christ who has done so much for him (Romans 9:1–5). That concern continues in chapter 10, which begins with, "Brothers, my heart's desire and prayer to God for the Israelites is that they may be saved" (v. 1). The apostle describes them as zealous, yet lacking knowledge. Their desire to follow the law of Moses and thus pursue righteousness that is "their own" (v. 3) is ill founded, now that "Christ is the end of the law so that there may be righteousness for everyone who believes" (v. 4). A new way, the way of salvation by grace through faith, is now open for all to accept, but, sadly, many of Paul's kinsmen have rejected it.

Paul proceeds to contrast the righteousness based on keeping the law with the righteousness available through faith. He shows that the way of faith in Christ is the way by which both Jew and Gentile must come to God. He also challenges Christians to accept the responsibility for making that message known so that others may call on the name of the Lord and be saved.

I. Keeping the Law (Romans 10:5-7)
A. Moses' Words on Law (v. 5)

⁵ Moses describes in this way the righteousness that is by the law: "The man who does these things will live by them."

There are only two potential ways to obtain *righteousness,* or a right standing with God: law-keeping and grace through faith. *Moses* is recognized as Israel's lawgiver. So it is fitting to cite him as an authority on law-keeping.

The passage Paul quotes in this verse is from Leviticus 18:5: "the man who obeys [God's decrees and laws] will live by them." In other words, with the principle of righteousness by law-keeping the responsibility is squarely ours. If one should obey every aspect of the law, then he or she would be right with God. But that *if* is huge! In fact, Paul has shown earlier that no one can be justified through keeping the law (Romans 3:20).

B. Moses' Words on Faith (vv. 6, 7)

⁶, ⁷ But the righteousness that is by faith says: "Do not say in your heart, 'Who will ascend into heaven?'" (that is, to bring Christ down) "or 'Who will descend into the deep?'" (that is, to bring Christ up from the dead).

Here Paul describes *the righteousness that is by faith.* In so doing he quotes from Deuteronomy 30:12–14 (which is included in verses 6-8). He pictures someone trying to *ascend into heaven* in order to *bring Christ down* from above or making an attempt to *descend into the deep* in order to *bring Christ up.* It should be noted that Paul's citation varies somewhat from the words in Deuteronomy, which speak of going "beyond the sea" rather than *into the deep* to bring someone back from the dead. Paul should be seen as giving an inspired interpretation of Moses' words and applying them to a New Covenant setting. His desire is to show that the righteousness obtained by faith is not based on our deeds. Even if we could perform heroic deeds such as those described in these verses, that would not be enough to gain right standing with God.

Some have commented on the significance of Paul's use of the book of Deuteronomy to make his case for righteousness by faith. Moses spoke the words of Deuteronomy when the Israelites were on the brink of entering the promised land. He wanted to impress upon the people the covenant that God had made with them. Here in Romans, Paul desires to impress upon his Jewish readers the New Covenant that God has established. Just as God brought his word to Israel through Moses (see Deuteronomy 30:11-14), God now has brought his living Word through Jesus Christ, whom Paul has already declared to be "the end of the law" (Romans 10:4).

Thus it is not by human good works or devoted efforts that righteousness with God is obtained. Salvation is not the result of our perfection or hard work. Salvation is the result of Christ's perfection and God's work through him on our behalf. Indeed, we do not have to *bring Christ down;* he has already come. Nor do we have to *bring Christ up* from the grave; God has done that (Romans 8:11).

II. Living by Faith (Romans 10:8-13)
A. An Affirming Faith (vv. 8-10)

⁸ But what does it say? "The word is near you; it is in your mouth and in your heart," that is, the word of faith we are proclaiming:

Here is the difference between the way of law-keeping (works) and the way of *faith.* We do not have to travel to a distant realm and accomplish daring feats in order to impress God. *The word is near you; it is in your mouth and in your heart.* The message is close to us and ready to be accepted—if we respond in faith. Salvation is not a matter of trying through our own efforts to reach God; it is accepting God's love that is offered to us. Righteousness is received, not achieved.

⁹ That if you confess with your mouth, "Jesus is Lord," and believe in your heart that God raised him from the dead, you will be saved.

This verse calls to mind what Jesus said about the importance of confessing, or acknowledging, him before others (Matthew 10:32, 33). On the basis of this emphasis, many churches ask those who desire to accept Christ to express a "confession" of Jesus as Lord. In some cases, a person is asked to repeat a statement of faith in Jesus; in others, people are asked to express their faith in their own words. The declaration *Jesus is Lord* was a pivotal part of Christian confession and belief early in the history of the church. Notice the requirement of both an external response (confessing the Lord Jesus) and an internal one (believing in one's *heart*).

¹⁰ For it is with your heart that you believe and are justified, and it is with your mouth that you confess and are saved.

A verse such as this one should not be considered to be the entirety of God's plan of salvation. The previous chapter of studies included Paul's teaching about baptism in Romans 6. And just because this verse says nothing about repentance does not mean that Paul considers it insignificant or unnecessary. In the context of Romans 10, Paul has been focusing in particular on the *heart* and the *mouth* (mentioned in verses 6-8 in the reference from Deuteronomy). He wants to show that becoming right with God does not require the kind of efforts described in verses 6 and 7; it requires simple obedient faith.

B. An Available Faith (vv. 11-13)

11 As the Scripture says, "Anyone who trusts in him will never be put to shame."

Paul cites another Old Testament passage—Isaiah 28:16 in this instance. It reinforces the point he made earlier in Romans 10:4, that "Christ is the end of the law so that there may be righteousness for everyone who believes."

12 For there is no difference between Jew and Gentile—the same Lord is Lord of all and richly blesses all who call on him,

Jews and Gentiles enter into God's promise on the same basis—through faith in Christ: *there is no difference!* Paul's language is reminiscent of what he stated earlier about the sin problem that Jews and Gentiles have in common. "There is no difference, for all have sinned and fall short of the glory of God" (Romans 3:22, 23). What a refreshing change from bad news to good news! *The same Lord* whose righteous standard we have failed to meet offers his riches to *all who call on him.*

13 . . . for, "Everyone who calls on the name of the Lord will be saved."

Here Paul cites Joel 2:32, as Peter did on the Day of Pentecost when preaching the first gospel sermon (Acts 2:21). Again, we should mention the importance of taking all that the Scriptures say about what is necessary to be *saved.* Calling *on the name of the Lord* is in line with Paul's emphasis in this passage that "it is with [the] mouth that [we] confess and are saved" (vv. 9, 10).

III. Spreading the Faith (Romans 10:14-17)
A. Helping People Call (v. 14)

14 How, then, can they call on the one they have not believed in? And how can they believe in the one of whom they have not heard? And how can they hear without someone preaching to them?

Paul follows his statement of the responsibility of all people to call on the Lord with a challenge to those who have called on him and are saved to do all they can so that others will know of that responsibility. *How* will people be made aware of whom they need to *call on* to be saved? How will they know how to accept God's gracious gift of salvation?

Calling on the name of the Lord and receiving God's salvation happens only when one believes. And one can't *believe* until he or she has *heard*. And one can't hear unless there is someone—a preacher—who is willing to tell the story. The Greek word translated *someone preaching* describes a herald or an announcer who runs ahead of a king and proclaims what the king wishes others to know. Certainly the task of preaching can be done by any Christian who tells the good news to someone else. At the same time, there must be those who will give their lives to preaching and teaching in the setting of the local church. The church has always needed those willing to answer such a calling. And those who are ready to do so need to be supported and sent, as the next verse indicates.

B. Helping Messengers Go (v. 15)

15 And how can they preach unless they are sent? As it is written, "How beautiful are the feet of those who bring good news!"

Ultimately, Jesus sends us to go and carry his message to the world; we call his words the "Great Commission." But the church also plays a vital part in sending, as illustrated by Barnabas and Saul, who were *sent* by the church in Antioch on their first missionary journey (Acts 13:1–3). Once again, Paul cites an Old Testament reference (Isaiah 52:7) to make his point. In their original context, Isaiah's words described the *good news* of the deliverance of God's people from captivity in Babylon. Paul uses these words to refer to the good news of deliverance from sin through the gospel.

Those who bear such good news are pictured as having *beautiful . . . feet*. Usually the heralds who traveled many miles to convey a message arrived at their destination with dusty, dirty feet. The appearance of their feet was anything but beautiful; the beauty was to be found in the contents of the message delivered. Later Paul will describe the Christian's armor as including "fitted with the readiness that comes from the gospel of peace" (Ephesians 6:15).

C. Helping Sinners Listen (vv. 16, 17)

16 But not all the Israelites accepted the good news. For Isaiah says, "Lord, who has believed our message?"

Here is a harsh reality that can dampen the enthusiasm of confessing, preaching, and sending. Not *all* to whom we tell *the good news* will receive it gladly. In the context, Paul is lamenting the fact that so many Jews, "those of [his] own race" (Romans 9:3) have neither *believed* nor *accepted* the gospel. Again, the words of *Isaiah* are cited. This verse, from Isaiah 53:1, comes in the context of one of the most powerful messianic prophecies in the Old Testament.

¹⁷ Consequently, faith comes from hearing the message, and the message is heard through the word of Christ.

It is up to the church, the body of Christ, to see that everyone hears about Jesus. That means missionaries, sent and supported. That means teachers, trained and developed within the body. That means preachers, called, prepared, and supported both prayerfully and financially. There are many "parachurch" organizations that can accomplish these important tasks, but the local church remains God's primary appointed vehicle for making it possible for men and women to hear *the word of Christ*.

LIVING SACRIFICES (ROMANS 12:1, 2, 9-21)

Establishing the Groundwork

In the remainder of Romans 10 and through chapter 11, Paul continues his examination of the place of the Jews in God's plan of redemption. He concludes chapter 11 with a doxology praising God for the "depth of the riches of the wisdom and knowledge of God!" (v. 33).

Romans 12 begins a new direction in Paul's train of thought. Chapters 1-11 have been primarily doctrinal in their focus. With chapter 12 the apostle begins to examine some of the practical issues that relate to living for Christ in both the church and the world—among Christians and non-Christians. However, this "new" section is very clearly linked with what has preceded through Paul's use of the word *therefore* in verse 1. Paul's purpose in doing this should be clear: doctrine is practical as well as theological. What we believe must affect how we live. If it doesn't, then the world has every right to question the value of what we believe. For if our faith in Christ is making no real difference in our lives, why should others embrace it?

Examining the Text

I. Reason for Goodness (Romans 12:1, 2)
A. God's Mercy (v. 1)

¹ Therefore, I urge you, brothers, in view of God's mercy, to offer your bodies as living sacrifices, holy and pleasing to God—this is your spiritual act of worship.

Apparently some of those in the church in Rome had not fully grasped the necessity of combining Christian faith with godly living. Perhaps their pagan background made it especially challenging to sever ties with the past and die to sin (Romans 6:2). Paul encourages Christians to understand that it is our *spiritual act of worship* to live in this manner. Worship is not something that is meant to occur on Sundays only but daily, through the holy lives we lead.

Why is this lifestyle *spiritual?* Paul says *in view of,* or because of, *God's mercy.* The word *therefore* links this phrase to what Paul has written previously—not only in the immediately preceding verses, but also in the entire epistle to this point. Everything that Paul has discussed in the letter thus far, particularly concerning God's grace as demonstrated in Jesus Christ, could be summarized by *God's mercy.* God in mercy gave his one and only Son to die as a sacrifice to cover our sins. Therefore, it follows that we should live *holy* lives in service to one who provided such a sacrifice. The concept of *living sacrifices* contrasts the Christian's sacrifice with the slain sacrifices of the Old Testament system.

B. Renewed Mind (v. 2)

² Do not conform any longer to the pattern of this world, but be transformed by the renewing of your mind. Then you will be able to test and approve what God's will is—his good, pleasing and perfect will.

Conformed or *transformed?* That is the question Paul challenges us to ask. To be transformed must start from the inside, *by the renewing of your mind.* Wicked thoughts precede wicked deeds (Matthew 15:18-20); godly thoughts produce godly deeds. When our minds are renewed, we are ready to practice the *good, pleasing, and perfect* qualities that Paul will mention later in this chapter.

II. Showing Goodness to God's People (Romans 12:9-13)
A. Loving (v. 9)

⁹ Love must be sincere. Hate what is evil; cling to what is good.

In the remainder of Romans 12, Paul elaborates on what being a living sacrifice entails. In the portion of the chapter not included in our printed text (verses 3-8), Paul highlights the importance of using our various gifts in the Lord's service. Verse 9 begins a section of short, specific commands concerning the attitudes and actions that should characterize every Christian.

Love is the starting point. This is in keeping with what Paul writes elsewhere in his epistles, most notably in 1 Corinthians 13. This kind of love can be defined as "wanting the best for another"; and, although feelings are a part of it, it is primarily a matter of the will. That love *must be sincere* means that love must be genuine, without hypocrisy. In addition, Paul tells us to *hate what is evil* and to *cling to what is good*. There is room for hatred in the Christian life, but it is not a hatred of people. This describes a loathing of sin and a sense of disgust at the destruction it causes to individuals and to the fabric of society.

B. Honoring (v. 10)

10 Be devoted to one another in brotherly love. Honor one another above yourselves.

These words run counter to the "me first" mentality of the modern world. They twice include the words *one another*—words found in other New Testament passages that remind us that we do not live the Christian life in a vacuum.

C. Serving (v. 11)

11 Never be lacking in zeal, but keep your spiritual fervor, serving the Lord.

Paul writes almost in the style of the old Hebrew couplet, as he uses both a negative and positive expression to say very much the same thing. Our service to the Lord should be marked by *zeal,* or *fervor,* a boiling or burning within us that energizes our ministries. Our fire can burn even through difficult times, because it is fed by the presence of the Holy Spirit.

D. Rejoicing (v. 12)

12 Be joyful in hope, patient in affliction, faithful in prayer.

We noted before that biblical *hope* is confident assurance. It rests in God's promises through Christ. Those who possess it have every reason to rejoice because they know that, in the end, Christ and his people will triumph. So we can be *patient in affliction,* calm in the face of any storm. The last phrase in this verse describes a key ingredient to developing the attitudes and actions found in this verse and in this passage: a life that is *faithful in prayer.*

E. Sharing (v. 13)

13 Share with God's people who are in need. Practice hospitality.

Just as God makes the sun to shine and the rain to fall on the just and the unjust (Matthew 5:45), his children are called to assist any who have needs. But Scripture emphasizes our singular responsibility for our brothers and sisters in Christ (see also Galatians 6:10). *Hospitality* is one of the characteristics of those who serve as elders (also called overseers, 1 Timothy 3:2). But it should also be a trademark of all Christians.

III. Showing Goodness to the World (Romans 12:14-19)
A. Acting, Not Reacting (v. 14)

¹⁴ Bless those who persecute you; bless and do not curse.

Here we confront the more challenging part of Paul's exhortations—the ones requiring a higher measure of Christian maturity. It's one thing to help "God's people" (v. 13); it's quite another to show kindness to the "ungodly." Yet, as Jesus pointed out in the Sermon on the Mount, if we love only those who love us, we are no different from the pagans (Matthew 5:46, 47).

B. Empathizing (v. 15)

¹⁵ Rejoice with those who rejoice; mourn with those who mourn.

Generally speaking, it is easier to *mourn with those who mourn* than it is to *rejoice with those who rejoice*. Most of us can offer examples of weeping with those who have gone through situations such as a critical illness, a death in the family, a job loss, or some other crisis. (Or we can recall times when others have mourned with us.) On the other hand, when someone else receives a promotion that we thought we had earned or is able to purchase a special possession that we had hoped for, it can be a bit harder to rejoice at that person's success. In truth, however, both the hardships and the blessings that others experience can be a gauge of whether or not we have learned to be Christlike in our attitudes.

C. Showing No Favoritism (v. 16)

¹⁶ Live in harmony with one another. Do not be proud, but be willing to associate with people of low position. Do not be conceited.

To treat others in the body of Christ as equals—despite clothes, checkbooks, education, or heritage—is to treat them the way the Head of the church would. Jesus was not ashamed to be seen with those of low position, and neither should we be. Nor should we worry about what others will think of us. Jesus' opinion is the only one that matters.

D. Promoting Peace (vv. 17-19)

¹⁷ Do not repay anyone evil for evil. Be careful to do what is right in the eyes of everybody.

This reinforces some of Paul's earlier teaching. Revenge and dishonesty are never acceptable for the Christian. Paul's emphasis on *everybody* shows that his words apply to our conduct in the world as well as in the church.

¹⁸ *If it is possible, as far as it depends on you, live at peace with everyone.*

Here, too, is a challenge concerning everyone—not just fellow Christians. It is important that we wage *peace*, not war, even among those who are not peaceful themselves. At the same time, Paul realizes that peace does not lie completely with us and that some will resist our well-intentioned efforts. "Do all that you can," he says.

¹⁹ *Do not take revenge, my friends, but leave room for God's wrath, for it is written: "It is mine to avenge; I will repay," says the Lord.*

Concerning those individuals who remain stubbornly hostile to our initiatives on behalf of peace, or who oppose us in any way, Paul tells us not to *take revenge* on others. When he writes *leave room for God's wrath,* Paul is saying, "Don't let your anger lead you to take upon yourself something that is God's prerogative. You are not God. He will take care of administering vengeance." The Old Testament reference cited is from Deuteronomy 32:35.

IV. Showing Goodness to an Enemy (Romans 12:20, 21)
A. Person (v. 20)

²⁰ *On the contrary:*
"If your enemy is hungry, feed him;
if he is thirsty, give him something to drink.
In doing this, you will heap burning coals on his head."

It is one thing to offer food and drink to brothers and sisters in Christ. Here Paul describes the "second mile" attitude that should characterize those who walk with Jesus. We should be prepared to help even an *enemy.*

The meaning of heaping *burning coals on* someone's *head* has been subject to much discussion. The reference itself is found in Proverbs 25:21, 22. One suggestion is that it pictures the sense of shame or remorse that "burns" within a person when treated with kindness by someone whom the person deliberately tried to hurt in some way. Possibly such a gesture of kindness will serve as a witness to the offending person of the difference that our faith in Christ has made in the life of the nonvengeful Christian.

B. Principle (v. 21)

²¹ *Do not be overcome by evil, but overcome evil with good.*

Simply put, the world should not be influencing the Christian; the Christian should be influencing the world. Christians should take the initiative on behalf of what is *good* and act, not react.

OBEYING CIVIC AUTHORITIES (ROMANS 13:1-7)

Establishing the Groundwork

In Romans 13, Paul considers a topic of special interest to Christians, whether living in the first or the twenty-first centuries: the duty of Christians regarding civic authorities. We do not know if this was an issue with which the Roman Christians in particular were wrestling. Perhaps Paul decided to include this discussion in his letter because he assumed that Christians living in the capital of the Roman Empire would have a great interest in this. Whatever their concerns may have been, we know that subsequent generations of Christians have struggled with the question of what is the proper way to relate to a secular government, especially when that government is hostile to Christian convictions.

Examining the Text

I. The Principle (Romans 13:1)
A. God's Mercy (v. 1)

¹ Everyone must submit himself to the governing authorities, for there is no authority except that which God has established. The authorities that exist have been established by God.

The Christian's primary duty to civic laws and officials is to *submit*, or be obedient. But could Paul really be saying that even oppressive dictators and regimes that persecute Christians *have been established by God?* Perhaps he is best understood as saying that God has ordained the *principle* of civic government. The heart of man is so sinful that he will repeatedly take advantage of his neighbor if he thinks he can get away with it. That is the reason that it is in the best interest of all of us to have some kind of civic authority over us, to keep us in check when we consider hurting one another. No one form of government has been established in God's Word as the ideal, but the legitimacy of governing authority is clear.

None of this should be thought to imply that God condones the wrong actions of an evil government. The prophet Daniel, for example, informed kings such as Nebuchadnezzar and Belshazzar that God would hold them responsible for the misuse of their God-given authority (Daniel 4:19-28; 5:18-23). Whether the individual is good or bad, we remain obligated to submit to legitimate authority, even if the person exercising that authority is as bad as the infamous Nero—the ruler of the Roman Empire when Paul penned these words.

II. The Purpose (Romans 13:2-7)
A. To Please God (v. 2)

² Consequently, he who rebels against the authority is rebelling against what God has instituted, and those who do so will bring judgment on themselves.

To rebel against a civic *authority* is an implicit rebellion *against* the God who gives authorization to all rulers. It is quite likely that someone defying an earthly power would not intend to oppose God. Regardless of what we intend, however, we will be judged on the basis of what God perceives. Respect for authority, even bad authority, is necessary simply because it is what God expects of us.

B. To Avoid Punishment (vv. 3, 4)

³ For rulers hold no terror for those who do right, but for those who do wrong. Do you want to be free from fear of the one in authority? Then do what is right and he will commend you.

Rulers hold no terror for those who do right. An honest citizen has nothing to *fear* from government officials. After all, if their job is to punish lawbreakers, then we who are not lawbreakers do not need to be apprehensive when we see them or when they drive through our neighborhoods.

⁴ For he is God's servant to do you good. But if you do wrong, be afraid, for he does not bear the sword for nothing. He is God's servant, an agent of wrath to bring punishment on the wrongdoer.

We are accustomed to thinking of the term *God's servant* as describing someone involved in Christian service, such as a preacher or youth minister. Government officials, however, are considered as God's servants because they are the human instruments he uses to effect justice on earth.

Paul also notes that the civic authority is *an agent of wrath to bring punishment on the wrongdoer.* In Romans 12:17-19 Paul teaches that individuals are not to repay anyone "evil for evil." We as individuals have no authority, from the state or from God, to take vengeance on someone who has done us great harm. "'It is mine to avenge; I will repay,' says the Lord." However, God's plan is not always to wait until Judgment Day to administer judgment. Just six verses after Paul's declaration of God's vengeance in Romans 12:19, we are told that even on this earth he will avenge some of the wrong done to us. His agent of justice is government. Criminal penalties by human courts comprise a God-appointed means for getting some relief from the injustices we suffer from criminal activity. Paul himself was not averse to using the legal system of his day to avoid being mistreated (Acts 16:35-39; 22:22-29).

C. To Maintain a Good Conscience (v. 5)

⁵ Therefore, it is necessary to submit to the authorities, not only because of possible punishment but also because of conscience.

Whenever we violate or take lightly the rules of those who have authority over us, we know deep within ourselves that we are wrong. If we want to have good feelings about ourselves, if we want to avoid a guilty *conscience*, then we need to do what is right. Of course, our primary reason for doing right, as Paul has already stated, is because God commands it.

D. To Show Respect (vv. 6, 7)

⁶ This is also why you pay taxes, for the authorities are God's servants, who give their full time to governing.

If we are to be obedient to our governing authorities, we must do so even when we must *pay taxes* to them. Few of us enjoy parting with our money, especially when we have reason to believe that it may not be used wisely. But we cannot justify resisting authority at any point, including the payment of taxes. Jesus himself spoke clearly to this issue when he said, "Give to Caesar what is Caesar's, and to God what is God's" (Matthew 22:21).

Though Christians have a duty to pay whatever taxes are demanded, we may find it necessary in some cases to challenge the amount of taxes required and the way our tax money is used. As noted previously, it is helpful to consider the occasions during Paul's ministry when he protested questionable acts of the civic authorities. In a representative form of government, in which there are legitimate means for citizens to express their views, Christians should feel free to offer their perspective, though always through proper means and always in a Christlike spirit.

⁷ Give everyone what you owe him: If you owe taxes, pay taxes; if revenue, then revenue; if respect, then respect; if honor, then honor.

Here is a helpful summary of our responsibility toward our civic leaders. There is some repetition of concepts here for the sake of emphasis. For instance, the words *taxes* and *revenue* describe virtually the same item. The same is true of the words *respect* and *honor*. Both of them describe the attitude that God wants Christians to demonstrate toward the legitimate authority that someone has by virtue of the office he or she holds. This is a part of our being "salt" and "light" to the world around us (Matthew 5:13-16).

How to Say It

BELSHAZZAR. Bel-*shazz*-er.

CAESAR. *See*-zur.

NEBUCHADNEZZAR. *Neb*-yuh-kud-*nez*-er (strong accent on *nez*).

NERO. *Nee*-roe.

PENTECOST. *Pent*-ih-kost.

Chapter 8

Counsel to a Church in Crisis: Studies in 1 Corinthians

1 Corinthians 1:10-17; 2:1-13; 11:20-34; 12:31–13:13; 15:51-58

DIVISIONS IN THE CHURCH (1 CORINTHIANS 1:10-17)

Establishing the Groundwork

The city of Corinth was one of the great commercial centers of the first-century world. It was located on a very narrow strip of land connecting the two landmasses of Greece. The city had harbors on two seas, the Aegean to the east and the Adriatic to the west. Rather than go around the great stretch of southern Greece (called the Peloponnesus), ships unloaded in one harbor, carried their goods overland, and reloaded on another ship in the other harbor. This gave Corinth many opportunities for employment and for the accumulation of wealth through the taxation of any items that passed through its harbors.

Like many seaport cities Corinth was also the center of frequent immorality. Two temples in particular dominated the city: that of Apollo (the sun god) and that of Aphrodite (the goddess of love and beauty). The latter housed more than a thousand temple prostitutes. Corinth's reputation for immorality was so widespread that it became a byword for vice: the verb "to Corinthianize" was coined to mean "to engage in sexual immorality." It is easy to see why Corinth was an especially challenging place to start a church, and why it appeared to present more problems for Paul than any other church with which he was associated.

Paul came to Corinth from Athens during his second missionary journey. Acts 18:1-18 records his initial visit there. Aquila and Priscilla were among his first contacts in Corinth. A close bond developed since, like Paul, Aquila and Priscilla were tentmakers.

Paul stayed in Corinth for about eighteen months (Acts 18:11). Eventually his success became so great that he encountered serious opposition. Jewish leaders brought him before Gallio, an official of the province of Achaia (where Corinth was located), but Gallio refused to hear the case.

Paul then traveled to Ephesus, where he made a brief stop, then proceeded on to Jerusalem. He returned to Ephesus on his third missionary journey and stayed there for three years (Acts 20:31). It was from Ephesus that he wrote 1 Corinthians, in approximately AD 56. (Paul mentions being in Ephesus in 1 Corinthians 16:8.)

I. Plea for Agreement (1 Corinthians 1:10-12)
A. Paul's Appeal (v. 10)

¹⁰ I appeal to you, brothers, in the name of our Lord Jesus Christ, that all of you agree with one another so that there may be no divisions among you and that you may be perfectly united in mind and thought.

Paul urged that *all* of the Corinthians *agree with one another*. This does not mean that he expected every individual to have exactly the same viewpoint on every issue. There was—and remains—room for private opinions. However, Paul wanted all believers to work for the common good of the church as a whole (Romans 15:6; Ephesians 4:29). He was urging a unity of purpose in Christ.

Paul's challenge to be *perfectly united in mind and thought* may seem to present an unattainable standard. However, the word *perfectly* means "completely." As Christians we do not have to agree on everything, but our disagreements must not be allowed to divide the church. We should all seek to have the mind of Christ, which means "being like-minded, having the same love, being one in spirit and purpose" (Philippians 2:2).

B. Chloe's Report (v. 11)

¹¹ My brothers, some from Chloe's household have informed me that there are quarrels among you.

We do not know who *Chloe* was, or what members of her *household* went to see Paul in Ephesus with the news about the *quarrels* or dissension within the Corinthian church. They were a credible source, however, and Paul took their allegations seriously.

C. Divided Loyalties (v. 12)

¹² What I mean is this: One of you says, "I follow Paul"; another, "I follow Apollos"; another, "I follow Cephas"; still another, "I follow Christ."

People in the Corinthian church had become closely attached to different leaders. This was the primary expression of the friction that had developed within the church.

Apollos had come to Ephesus, apparently after Paul's first visit (Acts 18:24–19:1), and had then proceeded to Corinth. *Cephas* was the Aramaic name for the apostle Peter. The specific factors leading to the formation of these groups are not mentioned. Perhaps some included Jewish Christians (particularly

Peter's group), while the others (such as the followers of Apollos) tended to draw Gentile Christians. Those claiming loyalty to *Christ* may have claimed to belong to Christ in some exclusive sense, or perhaps took some measure of pride in refusing to be labeled by the names of human leaders. As admirable as wearing only the name of Christ seems to be, to do so in a sectarian manner is no better than aligning oneself with a sect called by the name of a human leader.

II. Persuasive Argument (1 Corinthians 1:13-17)
A. Three Important Questions (v. 13)

13 Is Christ divided? Was Paul crucified for you? Were you baptized into the name of Paul?

The sin of division is highlighted in Paul's question, *is Christ divided?* Just as Christ had only one physical body, so the church is to be his one spiritual body (1 Corinthians 12:12; Ephesians 4:4). The obvious answer to Paul's question is "no."

Next, Paul asked a question with an equally evident answer: *Was Paul crucified for you?* Clearly not—Christians must hold allegiance to only one person, and that is the person who gave his life for them at the cross. No human preacher or teacher, however brilliant or prominent, could ever do for us what Jesus did.

The third question raised by Paul was, *were you baptized into the name of Paul?* This raises the issue of the one by whose name or authority baptism takes place. Baptism is an act commanded by Christ (Matthew 28:18, 19; Mark 16:16) and brings a person "into Christ" (Romans 6:3; Galatians 3:27). Baptism joins a person only to Christ, not to Peter, Paul, Apollos, or whoever does the baptizing.

These were three powerful arguments intended to persuade the Christians at Corinth to think seriously about the divisions they had created. They had become sidetracked from the doctrines that really mattered.

B. Paul's Recollection (vv. 14-16)

14-16 I am thankful that I did not baptize any of you except Crispus and Gaius, so no one can say that you were baptized into my name. (Yes, I also baptized the household of Stephanas; beyond that, I don't remember if I baptized anyone else.)

The mention of baptism in the previous verse led to Paul's further consideration of this topic. He kept no records of people whom he had *baptized*; he depended on his memory. *Crispus* was the ruler of the synagogue at Corinth (Acts 18:8). *Gaius* may have been the same man mentioned in Romans 16:23 as Paul's host when he wrote the letter to the Romans. *The household of Stephanas* is described as Paul's "first converts in Achaia" (1 Corinthians 16:15).

Paul was not diminishing the importance of baptism. He was simply expressing his gratitude that others had done most of the baptizing, in view of the divisions that had developed over individuals. Perhaps some in Corinth were aligning with different groups depending on who had baptized them.

C. Paul's Commission (v. 17)

17 For Christ did not send me to baptize, but to preach the gospel—not with words of human wisdom, lest the cross of Christ be emptied of its power.

Again, Paul's intent was not to disparage baptism; if anything, these words and those of verse 16 show how important baptism is. Baptism is meant to be the common experience of all Christians and, thus, a point of unity for them. To focus on who does the baptizing draws attention away from baptism's real significance. When one considers how much Paul had to say about baptism in his letters (Romans 6:3-6; 1 Corinthians 12:13; Galatians 3:27; Ephesians 4:5; Colossians 2:12; Titus 3:5), it is clear that he did not consider it an unimportant topic nor an insignificant act.

In most cases, it seems that Paul's primary concern in his evangelistic efforts was to *preach the gospel*, while others baptized the converts. If we consider that Paul likely suffered poor health (apparently alluded to in 1 Corinthians 2:3; 2 Corinthians 12:7-10; Galatians 4:13), we can see why others might have done the physical work of baptizing whenever possible. In addition, knowing the way that some people can become attached to certain personalities, we can see the wisdom of having someone other than Paul doing the actual baptizing. With the Corinthians, Paul could use the argument that he had baptized very few people to make his case for unity in Christ, not division based on loyalty to human teachers.

WISDOM FROM THE SPIRIT (1 CORINTHIANS 2:1-13)

Establishing the Groundwork

As noted in the "Groundwork" section of the previous study, Paul came to Corinth from Athens during his second missionary journey. Some students believe that Paul left Athens with a sense of having failed there. Pointing to 1 Corinthians 2:2 ("I resolved to know nothing while I was with you except

Jesus Christ and him crucified"), they suggest Paul thought he had tried too hard to appeal to the philosophical thinking of his audience in Athens, at the expense of diminishing the power of the gospel. This verse, they say, signals a change in Paul's method. Other students think such a conclusion reads too much into this verse. They believe Paul's words should be seen in contrast to the Corinthians' own overemphasis on human wisdom rather than in contrast to an earlier method tried by Paul.

Whatever we conclude about Paul's evaluation of his work at Athens, there is no mistaking the determination he expresses in the following lesson text. Every Christian would do well to cultivate this same passion for making Christ known to others.

Examining the Text

I. Paul's Testimony (1 Corinthians 2:1-5)
A. The Method (v. 1)

¹ When I came to you, brothers, I did not come with eloquence or superior wisdom as I proclaimed to you the testimony about God.

Eloquence and *superior wisdom* were highly respected qualities in Paul's time. They can also be powerful tools for those who seek a following for themselves. Paul, however, was seeking a following for the Lord. Thus he was determined to focus his hearers' attention on the *testimony about God*—that is, what God did, through Jesus, at the cross.

B. The Message (v. 2)

² For I resolved to know nothing while I was with you except Jesus Christ and him crucified.

Paul had already emphasized the centrality of *Jesus Christ and him crucified* to the Christian message (1:17-24). He did so knowing that many would be offended by such preaching (1:18, 23). The Greeks at Corinth could not imagine a deity who died for men. They thought that only criminals died on crosses. But Paul refused to tailor his message to suit the sensitivities or prejudices of his audience. Too much was at stake!

C. The Messenger (v. 3)

³ I came to you in weakness and fear, and with much trembling.

Paul's verbal self-portrait in this passage is not a flattering one. His *weakness and fear, and . . . trembling* are attributed by some to his supposed failure in Athens (see "Establishing the Groundwork" above). They say he was afraid he would fail a second time with a Greek audience and thus came unsure of himself. But this explanation is not necessary. His weakness may be attributed to physical issues (as in Galatia; Galatians 4:13). His explanation that "when I am weak, then I am strong" in 2 Corinthians 12:10 is in harmony with what he says here. He felt quite inadequate to proclaim properly so great a message as the gospel, but he had full confidence in the power of the gospel itself.

D. The Motive (vv. 4, 5)

4 My message and my preaching were not with wise and persuasive words, but with a demonstration of the Spirit's power,

We have various words to describe speakers who use *wise and persuasive words* to appeal to people, including demagogue, rabble-rouser, and propagandist. These individuals usually employ deception or distortion rather than truth to get their message across. Paul believed that the truth of the gospel could stand on its own merit without being promoted by such devious means. To use such tactics smothers the *demonstration of the Spirit's power* that is central to the gospel (Romans 1:16; 1 Thessalonians 1:5).

5 . . . so that your faith might not rest on men's wisdom, but on God's power.

Here is the reason Paul refused to use "eloquence or superior wisdom" (v. 1) or "wise and persuasive words" (v. 4) in presenting the gospel to the Corinthians. He did not want their *faith* to *rest* in the method of presentation, which was based on *men's wisdom*, but in the content of the gospel, which magnifies *God's power* to save lost sinners through his Son's death on the cross. This verse is a helpful warning to us to examine whatever methods we use in presenting the gospel, lest those methods draw attention away from the crucified Christ.

II. True Wisdom (1 Corinthians 2:6-13)
A. Not of This World (v. 6)

6 We do, however, speak a message of wisdom among the mature, but not the wisdom of this age or of the rulers of this age, who are coming to nothing.

Paul had already noted the futility of *the wisdom of this age* in attempting to know God (1 Corinthians 1:18-21). Often the *rulers of this age* are governed by such wisdom, and find themselves frustrated that their policies and laws fail to accomplish their desired ends. Those who are *mature* in Christ should turn away from such false wisdom and embrace the higher, spiritual wisdom that comes from heaven (James 3:17).

B. Ordained of God (v. 7)

⁷ No, we speak of God's secret wisdom, a wisdom that has been hidden and that God destined for our glory before time began.

The Greek word translated here as *secret* is the source of our word *mystery.* Today we use the terms *secret* and *mystery* much differently from how they are used in the New Testament. Usually we are talking about something that is unknown or something deliberately kept hidden. Pagan religions in the Greek world were often referred to as "mystery religions" because they claimed to offer their adherents knowledge and insights available from no other source. New converts were initiated by means of secret ceremonies.

In the New Testament, however, these terms describe something that once was *hidden* from man's understanding but has now been revealed by God. *God's secret wisdom* (his plan to save the world through the crucified Christ) was something he *destined*, or determined, *before time began.* (See 1 Peter 1:18-20.) But until God chose to reveal it, it remained a secret, a mystery. Though parts of this plan were outlined in the Old Testament, the full revelation of his plan did not occur until the New Testament era.

C. Unknown by Rulers (v. 8)

⁸ None of the rulers of this age understood it, for if they had, they would not have crucified the Lord of glory.

Earthly rulers are called, as in verse 6, *rulers of this age.* The reference to those who *crucified the Lord of glory* indicates that they include Pilate, Herod, and the religious leaders in Jerusalem whose efforts resulted in Jesus' death. These men failed to recognize the wisdom that Jesus represented and that guided God's plan concerning him. This did not exonerate them, of course. (See Romans 3:5-8.) They had many opportunities to learn of that wisdom, but they rejected those opportunities.

D. Beyond Man's Thinking (v. 9)

⁹ However, as it is written:
"No eye has seen,
no ear has heard,
no mind has conceived
what God has prepared for those who love him"—

Isaiah 64:4, from which this quotation is taken, does not include the line *no mind has conceived*. Apparently Paul was paraphrasing this text, yet providing, under the inspiration of the Holy Spirit, a correct understanding of its meaning. Given the context, *what God has prepared* comprises the mystery of the gospel. It is not something invented by natural means, something the *eye* could observe or the *ear* could hear. It was not *conceived* in the *mind* of man, but was, instead, revealed by God's Spirit (v. 10).

Christians through the years have also seen this promise as a reference to future blessings and to Heaven in particular. That application is justified—though with some limitation. Just as no one in Isaiah's day could have imagined the grandeur of the Christian religion, so no one in our day can imagine the grandeur of Heaven. God has revealed something of that glory to us, but the images are sketchy and the details few. We know it will be a great and marvelous experience to be with the Lord in Heaven, but we cannot imagine just how awesome it will be.

E. Taught by God's Spirit (vv. 10-13)

10, 11 . . . but God has revealed it to us by his Spirit.
The Spirit searches all things, even the deep things of God. For who among men knows the thoughts of a man except the man's spirit within him? In the same way no one knows the thoughts of God except the Spirit of God.

The word *searches* does not mean that the *Spirit* has difficulty finding out *the deep things of God*. It describes his access, as part of what we often call the Trinity (2 Corinthians 13:14), to these deep truths. The Spirit comprehends these truths and is thus able to reveal them to us.

When Paul says that God *has revealed* these matters to us, he is linking the preceding verse about eye and ear and heart to the truths we now know. No man could have discovered these truths by his own effort or through the use of the five senses. The initiative had to come from God. If he had not revealed these truths, they would have remained unknown.

In verse 11 Paul uses the illustration of the human *spirit* to give us insight into the mind of God. No other human can know what a person is thinking; that person must reveal the content of his thoughts. In the same way, only the *Spirit of God* has insight into *the thoughts of God*. They cannot be known by human beings except through revelation. This is the reason the Holy Spirit was given to the apostles (John 14:26; 16:13).

12 We have not received the spirit of the world but the Spirit who is from God, that we may understand what God has freely given us.

Paul's use of the word *we* suggests he is talking about the apostles, not about Christians in general. (Earlier he uses "you" and "your" when speaking of all believers, as in verses 1-5.) The apostles certainly received a measure of the *Spirit* that far exceeds that of any other human being, then or now. Paul observed to the Corinthians that he could speak in tongues "more than all of you" (1 Corinthians 14:18). The apostles' ability to impart gifts by the laying on of hands was so extraordinary that Simon the sorcerer tried in vain to purchase it (Acts 8:14-19).

In the phrase *the spirit of the world*, the *world* may refer to those influences in our surroundings that lure us from God. Perhaps Paul is thinking of one of the "spirits" of whom Christians are warned in 1 John 4:1-3. Whatever the phrase may mean, it is undoubtedly linked to "the wisdom of this age" mentioned in verse 6. The greater emphasis should be on the word *world*. The Spirit who inspired Paul was not of the world, but *from God*.

> [13] *This is what we speak, not in words taught us by human wisdom but in words taught by the Spirit, expressing spiritual truths in spiritual words.*

Paul insisted that the content of his message was not to be found in *human wisdom*, just as he contended in the previous verse that the power behind the message was not of this world. Paul's message was not the product of human creativity or skill. It consisted of words from God himself—*taught by the Spirit*.

The only way we humans can understand anything is by means of words, so it was necessary that the divine revelation be given to Paul in words and that those words be taught by the Holy Spirit. This is in keeping with Jesus' promise of what the Spirit would do for the apostles (John 14:26; 16:13). To know this should bolster our confidence in the words of Scripture. While the personalities of the biblical writers and their purposes in writing come through in their choice of words, we can affirm without hesitation that God governed their words so that they were prevented from error.

The verse ends with a difficult phrase to interpret: *expressing spiritual truths in spiritual words*. The Greek text simply reads "comparing spiritual with spiritual," so it is hard to know what nouns should be added to accompany each adjective. In addition, the verb rendered "expressing" can also mean "interpret," "combine," "compare," or "explain." The translation found in our text here goes well with the thought of the previous verse. Others suggest reading the phrase, "interpreting spiritual truths to spiritual men," which would link this verse with the content of the next two. There Paul refers to the "spiritual man"—a term which, in this context, describes an apostle, but can also be applied to the Christian who is instructed by the inspired apostles' writings in Scripture.

INSTRUCTIONS CONCERNING THE LORD'S SUPPER
(1 CORINTHIANS 11:20-34)

Establishing the Groundwork

As noted previously, the city of Corinth was infamous for its immorality, much of it linked to the worship of the goddess Aphrodite. The contents of 1 Corinthians indicate that many in Corinth who became Christians struggled to overcome their former pagan lifestyles (to which Paul alludes in 6:9-11).

Judging from the subject matter covered in 1 Corinthians, the church had corresponded with Paul and had raised a number of issues for which they wanted Paul's insight. Starting with 1 Corinthians 7:1, which begins, "Now for the matters you wrote about," Paul begins to address those issues. The others are usually introduced with the words, "Now about . . ." or something similar (see 1 Corinthians 8:1; 12:1; 16:1).

Paul's discussion of the Lord's Supper in 1 Corinthians 11 is not introduced with such a phrase. In fact, his introduction to the issue suggests it is a matter that has been reported to him by another source. He is, however, addressing an area of church life in which certain abuses were taking place. At stake was the unity of the church, for which Paul had expressed his deep concern at the beginning of the letter (1 Corinthians 1:10-17).

Examining the Text

I. Worshiping as One (1 Corinthians 11:20-22)
A. Acting as One Body (vv. 20, 21)

²⁰ *When you come together, it is not the Lord's Supper you eat,*

The church at Corinth regularly gathered *together* for corporate worship. According to 1 Corinthians 16:2, this took place on "the first day of every week," or, every Sunday (see also Acts 20:7).

Paul claimed that what the Corinthians were doing during their worship service was *not the Lord's Supper.* This is evidence that the Lord's Supper was a regular weekly feature in New Testament worship. Had eating the Lord's Supper not been expected when they would *come together,* the fact that they didn't would have warranted no comment from Paul. The obvious implication is that observing the Lord's Supper was expected each week when they came together—that they were, in fact, going through the motions of observing it with the bread and the juice—but they were doing it in such a way that their observance did not deserve to be called "the Lord's Supper."

21 . . . for as you eat, each of you goes ahead without waiting for anybody else. One remains hungry, another gets drunk.

The church at Corinth apparently had a practice of eating the Lord's Supper in conjunction with a church fellowship meal, which some have indentified as the *agape*, or "love feast." After all, it would be difficult to imagine why Paul would speak of some going *hungry* and some being *drunk* with just the small portions used during the Lord's Supper.

Probably the practice of having a larger meal with the Lord's Supper was followed to imitate the original institution of the ceremony by Jesus during his final Passover supper in the upper room. The problem with the Corinthians' meal is implied in verse 21, but more precisely stated in verse 18. The church was divided into groups or cliques that would not fellowship with each other. Thus, in the eating of church meals, believers would share their food only with their friends. As a result, some were overlooked while others overindulged. The unity for which Jesus prayed (John 17:20, 21) was shattered!

B. Loving Each Other (v. 22)

22 Don't you have homes to eat and drink in? Or do you despise the church of God and humiliate those who have nothing? What shall I say to you? Shall I praise you for this? Certainly not!

When Paul asked, *Don't you have homes to eat and drink in?* he was not condemning the practice of serving the Lord's Supper with a meal, but the uncaring manner in which the Corinthians ate their meal. He questioned whether the Corinthians intended to *despise the church of God* and *humiliate* each other. The attitude he was condemning was the very opposite of the love he would define in chapter 13. Love would not be so rude and inconsiderate, nor would it hurt and offend.

II. Focusing on Christ (1 Corinthians 11:23-26)
A. His Broken Body (vv. 23, 24)

23 For I received from the Lord what I also passed on to you: The Lord Jesus, on the night he was betrayed, took bread,

Paul could not give firsthand testimony regarding the institution of the Lord's Supper because he had not been one of the apostles present in the upper room. His information had been given to him by revelation *from the Lord*, perhaps during the three-year period that he spent by himself in Arabia in preparation for his ministry (Galatians 1:15-18).

24 . . . and when he had given thanks, he broke it and said, "This is my body, which is for you; do this in remembrance of me."

At some point during the Passover supper, Jesus paused and *broke* a piece of bread. We know it would have been bread made without yeast because it was required that there be no yeast anywhere in a Jewish house during the whole week leading up to the Passover celebration. Most churches today have chosen to use unleavened bread for the Lord's Supper, not only because that is what Jesus would have used, but because of the appropriateness of the symbolism. Since leaven is often used in Scripture to represent sin (Luke 12:1; 1 Corinthians 5:6-8), unleavened bread is a good reminder of what we want our lives to be in Christ.

The purpose for the broken piece of bread is that it serves as a *remembrance* of how Jesus' body was "broken" on the cross of Calvary. That is the reason some churches prefer to serve a larger loaf for Communion. Each worshiper breaks off a piece of bread in order to participate personally in the symbolism. However, even the use of precut wafers can carry the symbolism when we remember that each little piece was "broken" from a larger portion.

B. His Shed Blood (v. 25)

25 In the same way, after supper he took the cup, saying, "This cup is the new covenant in my blood; do this, whenever you drink it, in remembrance of me."

During the institution of the Lord's Supper, the bread and the juice were not given to the disciples at the same time. The bread was broken during the meal, but the cup was presented *after supper*. (For a discussion of the significance of this cup as part of the traditional Passover service, see the comments on Matthew 26:27 in chapter 12 of Volume I.)

The message of the cup is much the same as that of the bread. The broken body of Jesus produced *blood*—the blood that ushered in a *new covenant* (Hebrews 9:11-14), by which sins can be forgiven and forgotten (Hebrews 8:12). Just as many churches prefer to use unleavened bread for the observance of the Lord's Supper, they prefer unfermented grape juice.

C. His Redemptive Death (v. 26)

26 For whenever you eat this bread and drink this cup, you proclaim the Lord's death until he comes.

The simple ceremony that Jesus instituted in the upper room was intended to be observed by his disciples *until he comes* to take us home. It is meant to insure that every Lord's Day when we gather for worship, we will give at least a few minutes to remembering Christ's death—the most important event in history, the key to our salvation, and the reason we are gathered as a church.

III. Examining Our Hearts (1 Corinthians 11:27-34)
A. To Remove Unworthy Motives (vv. 27-32)

27 Therefore, whoever eats the bread or drinks the cup of the Lord in an unworthy manner will be guilty of sinning against the body and blood of the Lord.

Paul raises an issue that has puzzled many readers and even troubled the consciences of some. What is an *unworthy manner* of partaking of the *bread* and the *cup*? The immediate context is focused upon one problem in particular. The church at Corinth was in a state of division, yet had the gall to take part in a ceremony that symbolizes the unity of the body of Christ!

While the primary focus of the Lord's Supper is upon Calvary, Paul also notes a secondary imagery in 1 Corinthians 10:17: "Because there is one loaf, we, who are many, are one body, for we all partake of the one loaf." My individual piece of bread was broken from a larger, single loaf, just as yours was. I may partake of the Lord's Supper in a quiet meditation of my own, but the small piece should remind me that I am a member of a larger fellowship. To participate in a sacred ceremony that symbolizes unity, while willfully being at odds with my Christian brother or sister, is an act of hypocrisy.

Some people wonder if they should stay away from the Lord's Supper while they are wrestling with sinful issues in their lives, lest they be guilty of partaking *in an unworthy manner.* It was not Paul's intention here to keep people away from the Lord's Supper. Believers with a genuine concern for the sin in their lives benefit from being at the Lord's Supper and seeing afresh the sacrifice that has removed their sins entirely. The Lord's Supper does not push sinners away; it draws repentant sinners to it so that their thinking can be challenged and their lives renewed.

28 A man ought to examine himself before he eats of the bread and drinks of the cup.

Rather than abstinence, Paul urges examination. Every time we prepare to partake of the Lord's Supper, we should first *examine* ourselves and ask whether there is any fellow believer from whom we are estranged, or toward whom we have bitterness, or against whom we hold a grudge. If such is the case, we must immediately release that bitterness and repent of it. Some would even suggest that we should not partake until we have first made an effort at reconciliation. (Jesus' counsel in Matthew 5:23, 24 is often cited as a parallel.) But if that is the point, then it is imperative to make reconciliation at once, not simply refrain from partaking of the Lord's Supper while holding on to the grudge.

29 For anyone who eats and drinks without recognizing the body of the Lord eats and drinks judgment on himself.

It is a sin to partake of the Lord's Supper when we are at odds with a Christian brother or sister. To do so will make us "guilty" (v. 27) before God and liable for divine *judgment.* This understanding helps us to grasp what Paul means when he speaks of partaking *without recognizing the body of the Lord.* The *body* refers to the church. To "recognize the Lord's body" means to envision the unity of all believers and to realize that our alienated brother or sister is still a partner with us in Christ's church. We are under obligation to do our part to reestablish unity where we have allowed it to lapse.

30 That is why many among you are weak and sick, and a number of you have fallen asleep.

Here Paul mentions additional consequences of disregarding the unity of the body of Christ. His reference to becoming *weak and sick* and to falling *asleep* could describe a weakening of our moral character. But it is also possible that Paul is referring to physical ailments that may be used in our lives as disciplinary measures to break down our complacency and lead to repentance. This would be consistent with verse 32, which refers to the Lord disciplining us. He wants to see us reform our sinful attitudes before it is too late and we receive the eternal condemnation that he has planned for the rest of the world.

31, 32 But if we judged ourselves, we would not come under judgment. When we are judged by the Lord, we are being disciplined so that we will not be condemned with the world.

How can we avoid being *judged* by God and receiving the accompanying penalties, spiritual and otherwise? We must judge *ourselves* (recall the exhortation in v. 28) and then seek reconciliation where we find it is needed.

B. To Practice Consideration (vv. 33, 34)

33, 34 So then, my brothers, when you come together to eat, wait for each other. If anyone is hungry, he should eat at home, so that when you meet

together it may not result in judgment.
And when I come I will give further directions.

From now on, when the Christians at Corinth *come together,* for a fellowship meal or any other purpose, they are advised to show consideration *for each other.* Anyone present at a fellowship meal who thinks he is too *hungry* to *wait* for others to arrive should have eaten something *at home.*

To build a strong church, the members must learn to exercise love and patience *for each other.* This was practical advice for a church whose thinking was not only foolish, but sinful. The Corinthians now knew what they had to do to address this particular problem; if other matters remained unresolved, Paul promised to *give further directions* when he returned to Corinth.

CHRISTIAN LOVE (1 CORINTHIANS 12:31–13:13)

Establishing the Groundwork

In 1 Corinthians 12–14, Paul discusses the sensitive issue of spiritual gifts. Apparently this had become a problematic area for the Corinthian church. The church was blessed with a variety of spiritual gifts, but pride and selfishness had led some of the members to abuse these gifts so that they had become a source of division rather than the harmony that God intended.

It is in the midst of Paul's counsel concerning spiritual gifts that the portion of Scripture known as the "love chapter" (1 Corinthians 13) is found. Instead of becoming jealous and divisive over spiritual gifts, Paul pointed the Corinthians to "the most excellent way"—the way of love. This chapter is one of the most cherished portions of Scripture in the entire Bible. In it Paul gives us a description of what Christian love is and challenges us to live by its standards.

Examining the Text

I. Priority of Love (1 Corinthians 12:31–13:3)
A. Eloquence Without Love (12:31–13:1)

³¹ But eagerly desire the greater gifts.
And now I will show you the most excellent way.

But eagerly desire the greater gifts. As Paul's statement reads, it is a command; however, the Greek construction of this statement can also be understood as a description of what the people were actually doing ("you are earnestly desiring"). *The greater gifts* were those gifts that the Corinthians had thought most important—perhaps the gifts that Paul cites in 1 Corinthians 13:1 and 2. There

Paul will emphasize the supremacy of love over the gifts: love is the *most excellent way.* Love is not a spiritual gift; it is a fruit of the Spirit (Galatians 5:22) that must govern how gifts are used. If the Corinthians are to desire anything, it should be to love one another. This leads to Paul's timeless description of love.

> *¹ If I speak in the tongues of men and of angels, but have not love, I am only a resounding gong or a clanging cymbal.*

Since Paul uses the personal pronoun in verses 1-3, some commentators think that these verses are autobiographical, with Paul describing some of his own gifts. However, it seems more likely that he was presenting hypothetical situations and making himself the subject of them out of consideration for the feelings of the Corinthians.

Since the gift of *tongues* was particularly controversial in Corinth, it was appropriate for Paul to mention it here in order to draw attention to the importance of *love.* The phrase *a resounding gong or a clanging cymbal* suggests discordant notes that are little more than noise. That, says Paul, is what speaking in tongues amounts to unless it is done with a discerning love for the members of the congregation.

B. Gifts Without Love (v. 2)

> *² If I have the gift of prophecy and can fathom all mysteries and all knowledge, and if I have a faith that can move mountains, but have not love, I am nothing.*

Paul now calls attention to three of the spiritual gifts that he had mentioned in the previous chapter. While he esteemed the gift of *prophecy* quite highly (as 1 Corinthians 14:1 indicates), if it was practiced without *love* it was *nothing.* The gift of *knowledge* apparently gave one the power to understand some of the *mysteries* of God's dealings with man—an understanding that not everyone possessed.

The power to *move mountains* may have included the ability to work miracles in the realm of nature. Jesus mentioned moving mountains on occasion (Matthew 17:20; 21:21; Mark 11:23), although he may have used this expression as a hyperbole (an extreme exaggeration for emphasis). In any case, the point of Paul's proposition is obvious. One might perform the most astounding miracle imaginable, but if it is done without love, it is *nothing.*

C. Giving Without Love (v. 3)

> *³ If I give all I possess to the poor and surrender my body to the flames, but have not love, I gain nothing.*

People have been known to give part of what they *possess* to benefit others, but it is often for the wrong motives. Jesus criticized those who gave to *the poor* when they did so in order to receive the plaudits of men (Matthew 6:1-4). Paul's hypothetical example goes far beyond giving just a part of one's goods; here, the donor gives *all* he possesses *to the poor*.

Then Paul goes a step further, supposing that the person gives not merely all his possessions but himself—his *body to the flames* in an act of martyrdom. Such extreme examples of giving highlight the importance of *love*; as impressive as they may seem, they are totally meaningless if one does not do them out of love.

II. Practice of Love (1 Corinthians 13:4-7)
A. Proper Attitudes (v. 4)

⁴ Love is patient, love is kind. It does not envy, it does not boast, it is not proud.

Having identified several actions that are meaningless without love, Paul turns to love's positive side. Some of these attributes were conspicuously absent from the Corinthian congregation.

A very important part of love is humility. *Love is patient;* that is, love leads one to work patiently with others, even those who may be considered "difficult." The loving person is willing to labor in the shadow of others, allowing them to receive credit for what he may have done. Love is also *kind.* It is not merely passive in its longsuffering; it actively pursues what is in the best interests of another.

It does not envy. It is clear that some people in the Corinthian church had become envious of the gifts that others had received. Envy, however, is not a mark of true love. *It does not boast, it is not proud.* One who lives a life controlled by love is not proud or arrogant. Yet how subtly Satan tempts us in this respect. We want to be "number one." We want to "keep up with the Joneses." Such pride blinds us to the source of our possessions and our talents. They all come from God.

B. Proper Actions (vv. 5, 6)

⁵ It is not rude, it is not self-seeking, it is not easily angered, it keeps no record of wrongs.

Love *is not rude.* Rude behavior is any conduct that brings reproach to Christ or his church. The word here speaks of more than a mere social transgression, as we sometimes define rudeness. It speaks of indecency. Many of us are shocked by the growing rudeness and shameless behavior we see in the society around us. Often this stems from ignorance; children have not been taught simple politeness such as saying "please" and "thank you." But in other cases rudeness is the product of the selfish spirit that seems to be the trademark of our times.

Love *is not easily angered.* Some people are like prickly cactuses. It is painful to approach them from any direction. Nearly every office and every church probably has at least one person who is irritable and hard to get along with. Whatever reasons one may have for this attitude, the underlying problem is that such a person lacks love and consideration for others.

Love *keeps no record of wrongs*; it does not dwell on wrongs done, trying to devise ways of "getting even." Love forgives and forgets.

⁶ Love does not delight in evil but rejoices with the truth.

Today we are immersed in a sea of *evil.* Radio, movies, television, and now various electronic media intrude into our homes with offensive words and images. We have to be alert every minute to keep our minds pure. Living by God's *truth* can help us attain that purity because it helps us determine right from wrong.

C. Proper Relationships (v. 7)

⁷ It always protects, always trusts, always hopes, always perseveres.

These four qualities summarize the way that love responds to other people. The repetition of *always* emphasizes that we are to act this way despite anything that anyone may do to us.

The Greek word translated *protects* comes from the word for "roof." Thus love protects others (from threatening situations or negative talk), as a roof protects what is inside a building.

Love *always trusts.* This certainly does not mean that we are to be naive, believing everything that we are told or chasing after every strange idea that appears on the horizon. The point here is that love gives us a positive attitude toward others that makes us eager to believe the best, not the worst, about people. Love continues to believe that God has ways of reaching out and saving wayward souls. It gives us an optimistic, patient perspective toward life.

Love also *always hopes* and *always perseveres.* Love looks toward the future positively. It refuses to fold in the face of difficult people or circumstances. It is thoroughly loyal—to God and to others.

III. Permanence of Love (1 Corinthians 13:8-13)
A. It Never Fails (v. 8)

8 Love never fails. But where there are prophecies, they will cease; where there are tongues, they will be stilled; where there is knowledge, it will pass away.

In verses 1-3 Paul declared that even the most coveted spiritual gifts and the most commendable actions, if exercised without love, are empty and meaningless. In verses 4-7 he listed the qualities and actions of love that make it the "most excellent way." Now in the closing verses of this chapter he shows that love is superior to the spiritual gifts because *love* is permanent, while the gifts are temporary.

B. It Reflects Maturity (vv. 9-12)

9 For we know in part and we prophesy in part,

Knowledge and prophecy refer back to two of the spiritual gifts that were mentioned in 1 Corinthians 12:8 and 10. Although Paul, as an apostle, had received by revelation a special knowledge of God's purposes in Christ (Galatians 1:11, 12), he readily recognized that his understanding was only partial. There were at least two reasons for this. First of all, God in his infinite wisdom had not chosen to reveal all of his mysteries at that time. Second, if he had, man in his human weakness would not have been able to comprehend it. In the same way, the ability to *prophesy* resulted in only partial understanding. Peter confirms the partial understanding of the prophets in Peter 1:10-12.

10 . . . but when perfection comes, the imperfect disappears.

This verse has been the source of considerable discussion. Some understand *perfection* to refer to the revelation of the New Covenant embodied in the New Testament Scriptures. The special spiritual gifts were necessary in the first century and shortly thereafter to authenticate this new and final revelation of God's will to man. (See the reference to how the Lord "confirmed his word" in Mark 16:20.) According to this view, the gifts ceased once the New Testament was completed.

Another view is that *perfection* looks to the second coming of Christ. When he who is the perfect revelation of God returns, then special gifts will no longer be needed.

Still others believe that *perfection* means "maturity," as it does in various passages (Colossians 1:28; James 3:2). As such, it may refer to a mature individual or a mature church. When a person or congregation has attained "unity in the faith and in the knowledge of the Son of God" and "the whole measure of the fullness of Christ" (Ephesians 4:13), there will no longer be a need for the gifts of knowledge and prophecy. Or when the church as a whole becomes "mature," it no longer needs the foundational gifts of the apostles and prophets (Ephesians 2:20).

¹¹ When I was a child, I talked like a child, I thought like a child, I reasoned like a child. When I became a man, I put childish ways behind me.

Paul elaborates on the point he made in the previous verse. The *child* represents the time in which Paul was writing (first century) while the *man* points to maturity at some time future to Paul. As noted under verse 10, the time represented by this analogy varies according to one's view of what the "perfection" is. Under the first view—and probably the third—we are in that time now. But if one takes the perfection to be the return of Christ, then that time is, obviously, still future to us today.

¹² Now we see but a poor reflection as in a mirror; then we shall see face to face. Now I know in part; then I shall know fully, even as I am fully known.

A *mirror* in Paul's day was not made of glass but of polished metal. With such a mirror one's *reflection* would be dim and distorted. But at some future time *we shall see face to face.* To use a contemporary illustration, we might compare a person's photograph to the person himself. A photograph may show certain aspects of a person accurately, but it in no way adequately shows the real person. When "perfection comes" (v. 10), we will have more complete knowledge about those matters that we now *know in part.*

Again, one's understanding of when this happens depends on his interpretation of what "perfection" means. Those who believe it refers to the return of Jesus would say that at that time we will see him face to face. Those who say that "perfection" designates the completion of the New Testament or the attainment of maturity may take a more symbolic understanding of *face to face.* Some will combine both views, seeing the arrival of "perfection" as beginning a process that makes the foundational gifts unnecessary before Christ returns, but not necessarily granting full knowledge, *even as I am fully known,* until the Lord's return.

C. It Lasts Forever (v. 13)

¹³ And now these three remain: faith, hope and love. But the greatest of these is love.

The closing verse of this chapter brings Paul's discussion to a fitting conclusion. The spiritual gifts that had created so much controversy in the Corinthian church were not permanent. What really matters are the qualities of *faith, hope,* and *love.* This triad sums up quite succinctly the crucial elements that lie at the heart of Christian living.

In one sense, faith will not be needed in the next world, for then we shall "walk by sight." But in another sense it will exist there as fulfilled faith. The same is true of hope. Hope is a wonderful source of encouragement in this life, but in Heaven we will no longer need that kind of hope. However, it will exist as hope that has been realized and rewarded.

The greatest of these is love. Love is greater than faith and hope, because in Heaven it will be most necessary. Faith and hope are not divine attributes, but human ones. God does not need faith and hope; we do. But "God is love" (1 John 4:8), and if we are to relate to him throughout eternity, then we must possess love above all else.

VICTORY THROUGH CHRIST'S RESURRECTION (1 CORINTHIANS 15:51-58)

Establishing the Groundwork

After his lengthy discussion of spiritual gifts in 1 Corinthians 12–14, Paul raises another topic that was causing some tension within the Corinthian church: the resurrection of the dead. He begins chapter 15 by reminding the Corinthians of the gospel that he had first preached to them and that they had received. The basic facts of that message included Christ's death, burial, and resurrection (vv. 1-4). Paul then lists some of the appearances of Jesus after his resurrection (vv. 5-8), including his appearance to Paul, "as to one abnormally born" (v. 8).

Having highlighted the importance of Jesus' resurrection, Paul proceeds to describe the devastating consequences that result if Christ has not been raised from the dead (vv. 12-19). He then examines the resurrection from the standpoint of its place in God's redemptive plan, including the statement, "For as in Adam all die, so in Christ all will be made alive" (v. 22). Furthermore, Paul addresses the claim of some skeptics that one cannot know the precise nature of the resurrected body; therefore, belief in a resurrection is futile. He points out that nature provides an example of resurrection in the seed that is sown and the plant that later springs forth from the ground (vv. 35-38). The human "natural body" that is "sown" in the ground (buried) "is raised a spiritual body" (vv. 42-44).

In concluding his defense of the resurrection of Jesus and of his followers, Paul sounds a note of triumph and praise for the victory provided through

Jesus' resurrection. That victory, however, does not mean that Christians can rest on their laurels and "coast" to Heaven. Christ's victory over death means that his followers have a job to do!

Examining the Text

I. A Great Mystery (1 Corinthians 15:51-53)
A. Sudden Transformation (vv. 51, 52)

51 Listen, I tell you a mystery: We will not all sleep, but we will all be changed—

In the vocabulary of the New Testament, *a mystery* is not a puzzle that we can solve by clever detective work. A mystery is something we cannot know unless someone tells us. Paul proposes to *tell* us this one.

Here the word *sleep* is a figure of speech (note Jesus' use of the term with Jairus's daughter in Mark 5:39 and with Lazarus in John 11:11-14). It is an appropriate figure, for Paul is about to emphasize the fact that literal death is not permanent. That comes in the next verse; here in verse 51 we read that not everyone will die. Some will still be living in their natural bodies when the last trumpet sounds. Those natural bodies that have not died will *be changed* into spiritual bodies along with those who will be raised from the dead. (See also 1 Thessalonians 4:13-17.)

52 . . . in a flash, in the twinkling of an eye, at the last trumpet. For the trumpet will sound, the dead will be raised imperishable, and we will be changed.

The forthcoming change will not be a long, drawn-out process. The phrases *in a flash* and *in the twinkling of an eye* imply a sudden occurrence. It will be completed before the sound of the *trumpet* dies away. People long *dead* and people who have never died will stand together. (See also Matthew 24:31 and Revelation 11:15.)

B. Significant Truth (v. 53)

53 For the perishable must clothe itself with the imperishable, and the mortal with immortality.

Using language similar to that found in verse 42, Paul summarizes that which is best about the spiritual bodies: they are immortal, never to die. And they are *imperishable*—they will not even be sick or subject to weakness. Paul says nothing about how handsome, intelligent, strong, or skillful these spiritual bodies are. But we cannot imagine that any one of them is deficient in any way. They are perfectly suited for eternity in Heaven.

II. A Glorious Moment (1 Corinthians 15:54-58)

"The last enemy to be destroyed is death" (1 Corinthians 15:26). When God's people rise triumphant over death, that will indeed be the final victory. The conflict between good and evil, wide as the world and long as human history, will be over. So our text ends with a brief song of victory.

A. Conquest of Death (vv. 54-57)

54 When the perishable has been clothed with the imperishable, and the mortal with immortality, then the saying that is written will come true: "Death has been swallowed up in victory."

Here Paul uses the words of Isaiah 25:8. A glance at that passage shows us that the victory over death is God's doing, not our own: "He will swallow up death forever. The Sovereign Lord will wipe away the tears from all faces."

55 "Where, O death, is your victory? Where, O death, is your sting?"

Now Paul quotes from Hosea 13:14. *Death* has been frightening humanity ever since Adam and Eve, but it should hold no terror for Christians. Why should we be afraid to turn loose of these frail bodies when we know we shall receive imperishable bodies in exchange? Death is an enemy, to be sure, but it is a defeated enemy.

56 The sting of death is sin, and the power of sin is the law.

What makes us afraid of *death?* Our sins do. We know we have earned eternal condemnation instead of everlasting life. And *the law* gives our sins the power to terrify us, because the law makes our sins so undeniable. Yet we are not terrified. We are Christians. We are forgiven. Our sins are taken away. We are not in line for the wages of sin, but for the gift of God. Eternal life is ours (Romans 6:23).

57 But thanks be to God! He gives us the victory through our Lord Jesus Christ.

We have seen that *the victory* is God's, not ours. Now we see that it is ours, too—not in the sense that we won it, but because God gives it to us *through our Lord Jesus Christ.* So *thanks be to God!*

B. Challenge to Disciples (v. 58)

⁵⁸ Therefore, my dear brothers, stand firm. Let nothing move you. Always give yourselves fully to the work of the Lord, because you know that your labor in the Lord is not in vain.

Our resurrection hope is not just a dream for the future; it is also a source of inspiration for the present. It motivates us to serve the Lord *fully* and faithfully now as we await his final triumph over death. Our *labor in the Lord is not in vain*, for the impact we make on lives will last for eternity!

How to Say It

ACHAIA. Uh-*kay*-uh.

ADRIATIC. Ay-dree-*at*-ic.

AEGEAN. A-*jee*-un.

AGAPE *(Greek).* Uh-*gah*-pay.

APHRODITE. Af-ruh-*dite*-ee.

APOLLO. Uh-*pah*-low.

APOLLOS. Uh-*pahl*-us.

AQUILA. *Ack*-wih-luh.

ARAMAIC. *Air*-uh-*may*-ik (strong accent on *may*).

ATHENS. *Ath*-unz.

CEPHAS. *See*-fus.

CHLOE. *Klo*-ee.

CORINTH. *Kor*-inth.

CRISPUS. *Kris*-pus.

EPHESUS. *Ef*-uh-sus.

GAIUS. *Gay*-us.

GALLIO. *Gal*-ee-o.

HEROD. *Hair*-ud.

HYPERBOLE. high-*per*-buh-lee.

JAIRUS. *Jye*-rus or *Jay*-ih-rus.

LAZARUS. *Laz*-uh-rus.

PELOPONNESUS. *Pell*-uh-puh-*ness*-us (strong accent on *ness*).

PILATE. *Pie*-lut.

PRISCILLA. Prih-*sil*-uh.

STEPHANAS. *Stef*-uh-nass.

Chronological Chart of the New Testament Epistles

Epistle	Writer	Occasion	Date
1 & 2 Thessalonians	Paul	See p. 136	AD 52
1 Corinthians	Paul	See p. 136	AD 56
2 Corinthians	Paul	See p. 136	AD 57
Galatians	Paul	See p. 136	AD 57/58
Romans	Paul	See p. 136	AD 58
James	James, half-brother of Jesus	Written, probably from Jerusalem, to encourage Jewish Christians scattered throughout the world (cf. Acts 8:1).	c. AD 62
Ephesians	Paul	See p. 136	AD 63
Philippians	Paul	See p. 136	AD 63
Colossians	Paul	See p. 136	AD 63
Philemon	Paul	See p. 136	AD 63
Hebrews	Various suggestions; traditionally ascribed to Paul.	Written to encourage Jewish believers not to forsake Christianity and return to Judaism. Almost certainly written before AD 70, as no mention is made of the destruction of the temple. If Paul is the author, it was likely written near the end of his first imprisonment in anticipation of a visit to Jerusalem.	c. AD 63
1 Peter	Peter	Written to Jewish believers as an exhortation to endure Roman persecution.	AD 64
1 Timothy	Paul	See p. 136	AD 65
Titus	Paul	See p. 136	AD 65
2 Timothy	Paul	See p. 136	AD 67
2 Peter	Peter	Similar in purpose to 1 Peter, though possibly written in anticipation of the apostle's death. Tradition holds that Peter and Paul were executed on the same day.	AD 67/68
Jude	Jude (Judas), half-brother of Jesus	Written to encourage Jewish believers, the book has many parallels with 2 Peter.	c. AD 75
1, 2, & 3 John	John	Written from Ephesus, before John's exile to Patmos, to warn the church of a growing heresy that threatened the church.	c. AD 90ff.

Chapter 9

Living and Giving as Reconciled People: Studies in 2 Corinthians, Galatians, and Ephesians

2 Corinthians 5:11-21; 9:1-13; Galatians 5:22–6:10; Ephesians 2:8-22

THE MINISTRY OF RECONCILIATION (2 CORINTHIANS 5:11-21)

Establishing the Groundwork

Second Corinthians was likely written in the year AD 56 or 57, some months after 1 Corinthians. First Corinthians 16:5-8 indicates that that letter was written from Ephesus before Pentecost (in the spring). Second Corinthians would likely have been written later that same year or possibly near the beginning of the next. Second Corinthians 2:13 and 7:5 indicate that this letter was written from Macedonia. Apparently the Ephesian "uproar" led to Paul's departure from Ephesus (Acts 20:1) earlier than he had intended when he wrote 1 Corinthians. At the same time, he was very concerned about how the Corinthians had received the earlier letter and sent Titus to Corinth ahead of him (2 Corinthians 2:1-4, 12, 13; 7:5-9). This letter was then written after Paul had received Titus's report and was sent, probably with Titus, in part to prompt the Corinthians to prepare the offering they would be sending to the saints in Jerusalem (2 Corinthians 8:16-24).

As noted in the previous chapter, Paul's first epistle to the church at Corinth dealt with certain issues that were troubling the Christians there. Some of Paul's words were rather stern (1 Corinthians 5:1-13; 11:17), but they were written from the heart of a father to his spiritual children (4:14-16). While most of the Corinthians accepted Paul's rebuke and repented (2 Corinthians 7:8, 9), some of them apparently took offense at Paul's tone and words. Some were asking, in effect, "Who does Paul think he is, talking to us like that?" Considering how strongly Paul defends his apostleship in 2 Corinthians, some of the scoffers must have been challenging his credentials, perhaps noting that he was not one of the original Twelve, or that he had once been a persecutor of the church. In some cases, Paul goes on the defensive in behalf of himself and his ministry. See, for example, 2 Corinthians 3:1, 2; 4:1, 2; 6:3; 7:2; 10:7–11:33; 12:17-19.

However, in chapter 5 (from which the following text comes), Paul takes the offensive. He challenges friend and foe at Corinth to put aside their bruised feelings and petty fussing in order that they might concentrate on the higher calling that God has put before all Christians. Paul challenges the Corinthians, not to fight him, but to join him as partners in the ministry of reconciliation.

Examining the Text

I. A Mission to Accomplish (2 Corinthians 5:11-15)
A. Not for Personal Gain (vv. 11-13)

[11] Since, then, we know what it is to fear the Lord, we try to persuade men. What we are is plain to God, and I hope it is also plain to your conscience.

In response to his critics at Corinth who challenged his authority and his motives, Paul begins this section of 2 Corinthians by explaining his devotion to preaching. He has taken on an evangelistic ministry of trying to *persuade men* to accept Christ. He does this, not for his own sake, but for the sake of those whom he persuades.

In the preceding verse, Paul has mentioned that all must "appear before the judgment seat of Christ." For those outside of Christ, that will be a time to view with *fear,* but for those in Christ it will be an occasion of joy. Paul did not want the judgment to be a fearful experience for anyone, so he urged everyone to come to Christ.

The charges being made against Paul were patently false. He had no ulterior motives or insatiable ego behind his ministry. Paul declared that his life and ministry were *plain* to both *God* and man. He was not operating under any "hidden agenda."

[12] We are not trying to commend ourselves to you again, but are giving you an opportunity to take pride in us, so that you can answer those who take pride in what is seen rather than in what is in the heart.

We are not trying to commend ourselves to you again. Several times in 2 Corinthians, Paul provides details regarding his ministry, his background, and his apostolic authority. But Paul insisted that he was not providing any new information to the Corinthians; instead, he was simply reminding them of what they already knew. He hoped that his reminder would provide them with *an opportunity to take pride in us,* that is, it would encourage them to speak up for him when his critics became especially spiteful.

Paul's critics are described as those who *take pride in what is seen rather than in what is in the heart.* Apparently some of their criticism of Paul was grounded in certain external matters that they found objectionable. Perhaps there was something about Paul's appearance that they did not like. Some believe that

Paul's "thorn in the flesh" (2 Corinthians 12:7-10) was a physical abnormality, though this is only speculation. Perhaps there was something about Paul's speaking style that his critics found wanting, since he himself acknowledged that he did not speak with the "eloquence or superior wisdom" that some valued so highly (1 Corinthians 2:1-5).

13 If we are out of our mind, it is for the sake of God; if we are in our right mind, it is for you.

Apparently Paul's mental stability was also being challenged. Paul's response was to turn the charge around and make it look ridiculous. Are we *out of our mind?* Then it would be because we are "crazy" about God. Of course, Paul was not admitting any incompetence; he was simply responding tongue in cheek to the critics' charge. The second part of the verse expresses what was closer to reality. Paul saw himself as someone of *right mind,* which was evident in the way he had devoted his life to serving God and others rather than himself.

B. Compelled by Love (vv. 14, 15)

14 For Christ's love compels us, because we are convinced that one died for all, and therefore all died.

Paul develops a logical argument in this verse and the next. It actually begins with the premise *that one died for all,* a reference to Christ dying on the cross for all sinners. If this is true (and we know it is), then it implies that *all died.* How so? Paul is picturing Christ's death as a substitutionary atonement. We sinners had a penalty we owed to God because of our sin. Christ was willing to pay that penalty for us as our substitute. We would expect the penalty that he paid to be the same as the penalty we owed. Therefore, Paul is reasoning, if what Christ did for us was to die, then this reveals the condition that Christ came to remedy as our substitute: *all died.*

Why such clever reasoning here? Paul was simply explaining his motive for ministry. Since he along with everyone else was once "dead in sin" until Jesus paid his penalty for him, he felt a great burden in his heart to find some way to "repay" Jesus for loving him enough to do what he did at Calvary. As Paul says, *Christ's love compels us.*

15 And he died for all, that those who live should no longer live for themselves but for him who died for them and was raised again.

Now Paul completes his logical progression by arguing that every person for whom Christ died should feel in his heart the same constraint that Paul feels toward his preaching. All who have been saved by the death of Christ should feel compelled to serve with full devotion the One who saved them.

II. A Motive to Inspire (2 Corinthians 5:16, 17)
A. Not Limited by What We See (v. 16)

16 So from now on we regard no one from a worldly point of view. Though we once regarded Christ in this way, we do so no longer.

Paul had come to realize that the *worldly point of view* was an inadequate standard by which to measure any individual. At one time he had *regarded Christ in this way.* But all of this had changed. Paul *no longer* judged people by the world's perspective; instead, he saw them the way God sees them. He learned to view every person the same way, as someone created in God's image with dignity and value. Christ considered that individual so valuable that he was willing to give up everything he had in Heaven in order to save him. Paul's thought was, "How can I do any less?"

B. Seeing What We Can Become (v. 17)

17 Therefore, if anyone is in Christ, he is a new creation; the old has gone, the new has come!

Once we begin to see others from God's perspective, we will not only see their inherent dignity but also their potential *in Christ.* Those we can persuade to yield to Christ in faith will have their inner character completely reworked. The Corinthians could easily have testified to the dramatic change that being a *new creation* could produce. Some of them had been sordid characters of the worst kind (1 Corinthians 6:9-11). But they had been "washed" in the blood of the Lamb, "sanctified," and "justified in the name of the Lord Jesus Christ and by the Spirit of our God" (v. 11).

III. A Message to Proclaim (2 Corinthians 5:18-21)
A. God's Actions (vv. 18, 19)

18 All this is from God, who reconciled us to himself through Christ and gave us the ministry of reconciliation:

To understand the *ministry of reconciliation,* we must first understand the concept of reconciliation. The basic idea is to take two persons who are in disagreement and help them resolve their differences so that they can resume their normal relationship. For example, when management and labor are in a contract dispute, their normal working relationship is interrupted. When negotiations reach an impasse, a mediator is brought in to help them resolve their differences. The mediator's job is essentially to listen as each side states his case, determine where each has legitimate claims against the other, and then help the two sides work out a reasonable solution to which both can agree.

At Calvary Jesus acted as the mediator between God and sinful man. We had no legitimate charge against a holy God, for he has never done us wrong. But because of our sin against God, he did have just cause for punishing us with death. The mediator's judgment against us would have been devastating, but he graciously offered to pay the penalty for us in order to bring a resolution to this dispute. This offer was above and beyond the duty of a mediator; but then, Christ is no ordinary mediator. So it is that all sinners who agree to these terms and allow Christ to pay their death penalty for them can be *reconciled* to God, restored to a peaceful relationship with the one our sins have alienated.

We who have been reconciled to God by Christ are not to rest comfortably in our new standing. We have been given *the ministry of reconciliation.* We have a duty to announce to others what they need to do if they want to be reconciled to God as we have been.

> [19] *. . . that God was reconciling the world to himself in Christ, not counting men's sins against them. And he has committed to us the message of reconciliation.*

No one should ever imagine that God was a bystander at Calvary, observing what went on, then deciding how to respond. The cross was part of God's "set purpose and foreknowledge" (Acts 2:23). God was *reconciling the world to himself.* Reconciliation was neither our idea nor our doing; it was entirely of God.

Because of the work of Christ on behalf of his people, God is no longer *counting men's sins against them.* We need to understand that our biggest obstacle to a relationship with God is the guilt of our sin. The idea of being guilty means to deserve punishment because one has done wrong. Sin makes us guilty in the eyes of God and deserving of his punishment. (It should be noted that we do not always feel guilty, but we are in fact guilty just the same.) For those of us who through faith claim the death of Christ for our sins, God will not "count" the guilt of our sins; instead, he will mark our debt "paid."

B. Our Appeal (vv. 20, 21)

> [20] *We are therefore Christ's ambassadors, as though God were making his appeal through us. We implore you on Christ's behalf: Be reconciled to God.*

Here is one way to summarize our gospel message to the world: *Be reconciled to God.* Paul's phrasing is intended to add one more thought to the picture of two disputing parties in mediation. After a mediator works out a plan for reconciliation, each party in negotiation must then decide whether or not to agree to the terms. Usually as one party agrees to the terms, he reaches his hand out across the table for a handshake that will "seal the deal." He has decided that he is ready to be reconciled to his adversary. He now asks his adversary to do the same, to "be reconciled" to him.

In a spiritual sense, God stands even now with his hand reaching out across the table. He has agreed to the terms of Christ the mediator. He has accepted his substitutionary death at Calvary. He is ready to shake hands and "seal the deal." Through our preaching, he is pleading with sinful man: *be reconciled to God.* There is nothing more that God needs to do for our salvation. It now remains for each individual to decide whether or not to accept the terms of reconciliation.

This wonderful news will not be communicated unless those who have already been reconciled do so. Thus we Christians are *Christ's ambassadors* or royal representatives. We speak in his behalf a message he has given. We are not permitted to modify or compromise it, for it is not our message. We speak what Christ has told us to say. It is the same message that was once delivered to us: "Be reconciled to God."

[21] *God made him who had no sin to be sin for us, so that in him we might become the righteousness of God.*

The sinless character of Jesus is clearly affirmed in Scripture (Hebrews 4:15; 7:26) and supported by the Gospel accounts of his life. Yet at Calvary Jesus was *made . . . to be sin for us.* This is another reference to the substitutionary atonement, by which Jesus assumed the guilt of our sins and paid their penalty. This should not be read so as to imply that Jesus actually became a real sinner. Jesus took the place of sinners, and he was punished as a sinner should be punished, though he himself remained the one *who had no sin.* As the footnote in the *New International Version*® tells us, the word *sin* here can also be understood as "sin offering." Jesus became "the atoning sacrifice for our sin" (1 John 2:2).

And never forget the other side of the substitution. Christ took on the guilt of our sins so that *in him we might become the righteousness of God.* We could never pass the judgment bar of God on the basis of our own record of good deeds; for no matter how much good we could show, it would never be enough to make up for our sins against God. That is why God's grace allows us to assume Christ's perfect record even as he assumes our guilt. We stand before God fully reconciled to him, not on the basis of our good deeds, but because he allows us to wear the righteousness of Christ.

PRINCIPLES OF CHRISTIAN GIVING (2 CORINTHIANS 9:1-13)

Establishing the Groundwork

Some of the studies from the book of Acts in this volume called attention to the high degree of commitment and compassion that characterized the early followers of Jesus. In particular, see the comments on Acts 2:44, 45; 4:32-37; and 11:27-30. The latter passage notes how the Christians in Antioch (many of whom were Gentiles) sent financial help to the impoverished Jewish believers in Jerusalem, "each according to his ability" (Acts 11:29).

A more substantial collection for Jewish Christians became a major project of Paul's third missionary journey. He promoted it among the churches of Galatia, and while in Ephesus he sent instructions for the collection of funds in Corinth and the surrounding territory of Achaia (1 Corinthians 16:1-3). Titus became Paul's emissary to encourage the project in Macedonia, where it was very successful, as well as in Achaia (2 Corinthians 8:1-7, 16-24). In fact, Paul used the example of the Macedonians to spur the Corinthians on to fulfill their good intentions to help the Christians in Jerusalem (2 Corinthians 8:1-7); and he used the Corinthians' example to challenge the Macedonians (9:1-5)!

In the ninth chapter of 2 Corinthians, Paul provided further and more detailed instructions about giving. The contents of this chapter (in fact, the contents of both chapters 8 and 9) offer a helpful study in Christian giving.

Examining the Text

I. Challenges to Give (2 Corinthians 9:1-5)
A. Paul's Commendation (vv. 1, 2)

[1, 2] There is no need for me to write to you about this service to the saints. For I know your eagerness to help, and I have been boasting about it to the Macedonians, telling them that since last year you in Achaia were ready to give; and your enthusiasm has stirred most of them to action.

In the previous chapter Paul mentioned that he was sending Titus and two other brothers to Corinth to oversee the collection for the *service to the saints—* that is, to help the Jerusalem Christians (vv. 18-22). Since Paul had come under attack by some in the Corinthian church, he wisely limited his involvement in this activity, lest his enemies would have an occasion to bring further charges against him. By sending these well-known and respected men, Paul removed the likelihood that any could challenge his integrity. We today would be wise to follow his example to "do what is right, not only in the eyes of the Lord but also in the eyes of men" (2 Corinthians 8:21).

There is no need for me to write to you. In this way Paul complimented the Corinthians on their *eagerness* to fulfill their ministry to the Jerusalem Christians. In fact, he had been *boasting* about the generosity of the churches in *Achaia* (the province in which Corinth was located) to the churches in Macedonia (the province in northern Greece where cities such as Philippi and Thessalonica were located). Paul noted that his words had had an impact on these other churches: *your enthusiasm has stirred most of them to action.*

B. The Church's Preparation (vv. 3, 4)

³ But I am sending the brothers in order that our boasting about you in this matter should not prove hollow, but that you may be ready, as I said you would be.

Titus and the two other *brothers* had been sent on ahead to make the necessary preparations for receiving the collection. After Paul had commended the generosity of the Corinthians, he did not want his words to *prove hollow*.

⁴ For if any Macedonians come with me and find you unprepared, we—not to say anything about you—would be ashamed of having been so confident.

Paul said that some of the *Macedonians* might accompany him when he returned to Corinth. (We cannot say for sure whether they did or not, but we do know from Acts 20:4 that three Macedonians were accompanying him just after this visit.) Should that happen, Paul said, then not only those in Corinth but also he and his companions would have been embarrassed because of how *confident* Paul had been concerning the Corinthians.

C. Paul's Concern (v. 5)

⁵ So I thought it necessary to urge the brothers to visit you in advance and finish the arrangements for the generous gift you had promised. Then it will be ready as a generous gift, not as one grudgingly given.

Paul wanted the Corinthians' collection to be *ready* before he arrived so that he would not have to press upon them the issue of giving. If he should have to coerce them or plead with them to give, it would appear as though he were trying to obtain the money for himself. (In that day it was not uncommon for itinerant teachers to extort money from their students.) Paul wanted to avoid any controversy about his motives, for this would only further antagonize those in Corinth who were already critical of him.

II. Principles of Giving (2 Corinthians 9:6-13)
A. Sowing Bountifully (v. 6)

⁶ Remember this: Whoever sows sparingly will also reap sparingly, and whoever sows generously will also reap generously.

Paul's words sound like a proverb; however, nothing resembling this saying can be found in the book of Proverbs. His observation is quite apparent: a farmer who plants a small plot probably will not enjoy as large a harvest as the farmer who plants a large plot. Likewise, if one skimps on seeds in order to save money, he is not likely to enjoy the abundant harvest of one who plants the necessary amount of seeds.

We should not understand Paul to mean that one should give much in order to get much in return. More important than the amount one gives is his motive in giving (a point that Paul will touch on shortly). Jesus commended the poor widow who gave only two small coins ("all she had to live on") rather than the rich men who "gave their gifts out of their wealth" (Luke 21:1-4).

B. Giving Cheerfully (v. 7)

⁷ Each man should give what he has decided in his heart to give, not reluctantly or under compulsion, for God loves a cheerful giver.

When one is cajoled or pressured into giving, his gift is likely to be given *reluctantly*. One who gives *what he has decided in his heart to give* is more likely to give generously and certainly more cheerfully than one who has been pressured or manipulated into giving.

Giving from the heart, however, does not mean that giving should be based entirely on emotions. Good Christian stewardship requires that we give intelligently as well as emotionally. In fact, long-lasting joy is more likely to result from intelligent giving than from giving that is the product of spur-of-the-moment emotions.

C. Trusting God's Promises (vv. 8-11)

⁸ And God is able to make all grace abound to you, so that in all things at all times, having all that you need, you will abound in every good work.

Some argue that if we give generously, God will reward us generously. This may seem to be true in some cases. When we are seriously committed to Christ and give generously to his church, we are likely to be better off financially, in part because we no longer need or want many of the expensive "toys" that have become status symbols in our culture. But that is not Paul's point here. God provides *all things at all times* in order that we may *abound in every good work.* In other words, he blesses us that we may use those blessings to help others, not to better ourselves.

> *⁹ As it is written:*
> *"He has scattered abroad his gifts to the poor;*
> *his righteousness endures forever."*

Paul reinforced his point with a quotation from Psalm 112:9. *He has scattered abroad.* In the context of the Psalm, this statement is describing a righteous man. One mark of such a man is his generosity. Because of his deep concern for others, as reflected in the fact that he has given unselfishly *to the poor, his righteousness endures forever.* This *righteousness* refers to good deeds that often have positive consequences long after the initial gift has been given. For example, a child may give money to support a missionary who carries the gospel to some who had never heard it. These converts pass their faith on to their children, who do the same with their children, and so forth, resulting in many generations' becoming Christians. Only eternity will measure the worth and the impact of the child's gift.

> *¹⁰ Now he who supplies seed to the sower and bread for food will also*
> *supply and increase your store of seed and will enlarge the harvest of your*
> *righteousness.*

This verse seems to reflect in part Isaiah 55:10. Here the word *he* refers to God, rather than to a righteous man. Such a man who is also generous does not really create the wealth that he shares with others. Both the *seed* and the *bread* come from God. Paul is reminding us that as we have freely received from God, so we should freely share with others our blessings. God will *enlarge* the impact of our giving beyond anything we can imagine.

> *¹¹ You will be made rich in every way so that you can be generous on every*
> *occasion, and through us your generosity will result in thanksgiving to God.*

The contributions that the Corinthians and others were sending to the saints in Jerusalem would provide relief for some of their physical needs. But it would also benefit the givers, providing them the joy that comes from helping others. Furthermore, this gift would lead the recipients to render *thanksgiving to God.* No doubt the Jerusalem Christians had prayed for help in their time of need. The fact that their prayers had been answered through the *generosity* of the Gentile churches would strengthen their faith in God and help dispel any reservations they may have had toward Gentile Christians.

D. Meeting Needs (v. 12)

12 This service that you perform is not only supplying the needs of God's people but is also overflowing in many expressions of thanks to God.

In this verse Paul reiterated two important blessings that resulted from the Gentile churches' generosity (and should accompany ours as well). First, they were *supplying the needs of God's people;* that is, they supplied what the Jerusalem Christians needed. Second, their giving was the source of *many expressions of thanks to God*—a point that Paul elaborates on in verse 13.

E. Glorifying God (v. 13)

13 Because of the service by which you have proved yourselves, men will praise God for the obedience that accompanies your confession of the gospel of Christ, and for your generosity in sharing with them and with everyone else.

The Jerusalem Christians would *praise God*, being convinced of the Corinthians' *obedience* as demonstrated by their *generosity in sharing* their resources. The phrase *with everyone else* reminds us that while Christians have a special responsibility to those of the "family of believers," their benevolence must not be limited to fellow Christians (Galatians 6:10).

IN STEP WITH THE SPIRIT (GALATIANS 5:22–6:10)

Establishing the Groundwork

While Romans is considered Paul's greatest work, many would rank Galatians a close second. Some have called this book Paul's "Magna Carta." Others have labeled it the "Christian Declaration of Independence."

Unlike the majority of Paul's letters, Galatians was not written to a specific church in a city. It was written to a group of churches in a province called Galatia. This province received its name from the Gauls who settled in what is now northern Turkey in 279 BC. Later, in 25 BC, the Romans captured that area, joined it with another area to the south, and named the entire province Galatia.

Bible students debate whether Paul was writing Galatians to the earlier and more northern area where the Gauls first lived or had the southern and newer part of the Roman province in mind. Most scholars have settled on the southern area as the more likely option. This fits very well with events recorded in Acts, as the area of southern Galatia included the cities of Iconium, Lystra, Derbe, and Antioch of Pisidia, where Paul established churches during his first missionary journey with Barnabas, recorded in Acts 13 and 14. The letter was clearly written after the Jerusalem Conference discussed in Acts 15 and alluded to in Galatians 2. That conference is usually dated as AD 50 or 51. It must, then, have been written while Paul was on his second or third missionary journey, AD 52-58. Because of the book's similarity with Romans, many scholars date the two letters as written at about the same time, around AD 58, probably from Macedonia.

Two primary issues underlie the book of Galatians. The first is that Paul himself is under attack. Some of his opponents were claiming that he was not a real apostle and therefore had no real authority. Paul spends a great deal of time, particularly in the opening chapter of this letter, defending his apostleship; for if his authority is undermined, so is his message.

This leads to the second problem the book addresses. The Galatians had accepted the gospel Paul preached, but they were being seduced into thinking that they had to embrace all the law of Moses to be saved. The uniqueness of the gospel of grace was being compromised.

The passage to be examined from Galatians includes Paul's discussion of the fruit of the Spirit and of the others-oriented lifestyle that those who are guided by the Spirit should manifest. In such a lifestyle one finds true freedom, in contrast to the "acts of the sinful nature" (5:19-21) that can lead only to the cruelest kind of slavery.

Examining the Text

I. The Spirit and the Christian (Galatians 5:22-26)
A. Fruit of the Spirit (vv. 22, 23)

22 But the fruit of the Spirit is love, joy, peace, patience, kindness, goodness, faithfulness,

The *fruit of the Spirit* is the harvest of virtues that is produced in the Spirit-filled life. While these characteristics are natural products of the Spirit, we must also actively cultivate them. It is not enough to put aside the destructive works of the flesh (listed in verses 19-21); these must be replaced by something better.

Love is the primary Christian virtue. It does not count the cost or calculate the profit. Like God's own love, it is not restricted to recipients who are lovable. *Joy* is our spontaneous, happy response to life in Christ. It is not a pleasant feeling brought on by favorable circumstances; true joy defies circumstances. *Peace* is more than the absence of war; it is the sense of well-being that comes from knowing we have all we need in Christ. Jesus spoke of such peace to his disciples as his crucifixion drew closer (John 14:27; 16:33). Paul could speak of peace, even when writing from a prison (Philippians 4:6-9).

Patience is the ability to keep from losing our tempers with other people. The Bible presents God himself as patient (2 Peter 3:9). The variety of circumstances and people that we encounter in our lives helps us to develop this virtue. Someone has remarked that the incidents in our lives that we refer to as "interruptions" (and usually do not welcome) are really God's appointments that he brings our way for a purpose. Often our spiritual growth is part of that purpose.

Kindness is the sweet disposition that wants to serve the needs of people. *Goodness* involves both correct morals and a generous heart—it is more active than gentleness. *Faithfulness* includes integrity in our dealings with one another and in being reliable.

²³ *. . . gentleness and self-control. Against such things there is no law.*

The world sometimes mistakes *gentleness* for weakness. The Christian, following the example of Jesus, is ready to yield his or her own rights for the good of others. Gentleness involves holding oneself under control. *Self-control* is the ability of one's spirit to control one's flesh. It is far more than moderation in practicing one's vices; it is the kind of spiritual discipline that is possible only when one is led by the Spirit. Law is designed to restrain evil, but *there is no law* or limitation on these virtues! When these are our pursuit, we are completely free.

B. Life in the Spirit (vv. 24–26)

²⁴ *Those who belong to Christ Jesus have crucified the sinful nature with its passions and desires.*

This statement is similar in meaning to Paul's declaration in Galatians 2:20: "I have been crucified with Christ." To say that we *belong to Christ Jesus* means that we have repented utterly and completely of our old way of life, which is patterned after the *sinful nature*, or the flesh. We are to repudiate totally the *passions and desires* associated with that lifestyle. The word *crucified* emphasizes how drastic and decisive we must be about breaking ties with sin and determining to serve Christ.

²⁵ *Since we live by the Spirit, let us keep in step with the Spirit.*

In this verse, Paul uses a very specific word for *keep in step*. It describes keeping in step as a military unit would do when marching. To place this verse together with the previous one gives us a very useful definition of Christian maturity. We must say no to what is evil by crucifying the flesh, and we must say yes to what is good by walking in step with the Spirit.

26 *Let us not become conceited, provoking and envying each other.*

While this verse appears at the end of Galatians 5, it also serves to introduce the teaching found in the next chapter about relationships within the body of Christ. Paul warns Christians not to *become conceited*; that is, we should not become so self-centered and self-righteous that we take pleasure in *provoking* one another (to unnecessary and fruitless arguments) and *envying each other.*

Notice that both extremes of our potential responses to people are included in this verse. On the one hand, we may look at our neighbor with pride, thinking that we are better than he or she. On the other hand, we may view our neighbor with envy, thinking that he or she is better (or more talented, more popular, etc.) than we are. Neither attitude is appropriate for someone led by the Spirit.

II. The Spirit and Others (Galatians 6:1-10)
A. Restoring the Fallen (v. 1)

1 *Brothers, if someone is caught in a sin, you who are spiritual should restore him gently. But watch yourself, or you also may be tempted.*

Here Paul describes a circumstance that provides an excellent test of whether or not we are walking in step with the Spirit. How do we react *if someone is caught in a sin?* When a believer is overtaken in a fault and found to be guilty of some specific transgression, that person is not to be cast aside as a reject. Those who are recognized as *spiritual* leaders should go and try to restore that person. The spiritual rescue squad must do their work *gently* and lovingly, in the spirit of meekness. They must not be heavy-handed or domineering, but should *watch* out for their own lives, realizing that they also *may be tempted.*

B. Bearing Others' Burdens (vv. 2-5)

2 *Carry each other's burdens, and in this way you will fulfill the law of Christ.*

Like soldiers in an army, "we are all in this together." We do not gloat or rejoice when we see a fellow soldier fall in battle; we realize that we are diminished by his fall. Therefore, we help each other when the going gets rough. We step in to *carry each other's burdens* whenever we see that the load has become heavier than a brother or sister can bear (Romans 15:1). In this way we *fulfill the law of Christ* (John 15:12).

³ *If anyone thinks he is something when he is nothing, he deceives himself.*

Here Paul addresses an attitude that could hinder some from bearing the burdens of others (v. 2). Some may think themselves too important or too busy to help another in need. That attitude adds up to *nothing* in God's eyes. We are deceiving ourselves with such thinking; we are certainly not fooling God and probably not many people.

⁴ *Each one should test his own actions. Then he can take pride in himself, without comparing himself to somebody else,*

Rather than trying to judge and critique others, let *each* person simply *test* himself or herself. We may think ourselves better than someone else until we compare ourselves with God. Taking *pride* in ourselves comes as we grow according to his standard, not our own flawed, self-made standards.

⁵ *. . . for each one should carry his own load.*

Does this verse contradict what Paul said in verse 2: "Carry each other's burdens"? Not at all. It completes the thought of that verse. I ought to help you with your burden. That's part of my responsibility, my *load*. But you are responsible for your load whether I help you or not. Likewise you ought to help me with my burden, but I am responsible for it whether you help me or not. That is the reason I should examine my own work and you should examine yours. For eternity we will be judged by what we do (2 Corinthians 5:10), and here and now we can improve what we do.

C. Showing Generosity (vv. 6-10)

⁶ *Anyone who receives instruction in the word must share all good things with his instructor.*

People who are given *instruction in the word* have a responsibility they ought to carry. Their teachers have the burden of supporting their families while they spend their lives teaching. Therefore, those who are taught should *share all good things with* their *instructor.* Jesus himself taught that "the worker is worth his keep" (Matthew 10:10). Paul said that those who preach the gospel "should receive their living from the gospel" (1 Corinthians 9:13, 14).

⁷ *Do not be deceived: God cannot be mocked. A man reaps what he sows.*

This principle can apply to a variety of areas, including Christian stewardship (2 Corinthians 9:6-8). In this context, Paul's words should be understood in light of what he has stated about living in the flesh and living in the Spirit in chapter 5 (and in the next verse as well).

⁸ The one who sows to please his sinful nature, from that nature will reap destruction; the one who sows to please the Spirit, from the Spirit will reap eternal life.

We should not sow to *please* the *sinful nature*, because if we do that we will surely *reap destruction*. That destruction includes both the physical and spiritual consequences of choosing to live in sin. The positive application of the principle is this: *the one who sows to please the Spirit . . . will reap eternal life.*

⁹ Let us not become weary in doing good, for at the proper time we will reap a harvest if we do not give up.

All of us at times grow weary in what we are *doing* for the Lord. Perhaps Paul switches to the first person (*us* and *we*) because he is fighting his own weariness. We try to do what pleases God, but it goes unappreciated. We try to live moral lives, and the world laughs. While we struggle to make enough money to be able to contribute to the work of the kingdom, the wicked prosper. Like the psalmist, we are envious of the foolish when we see "the prosperity of the wicked" (Psalm 73:3).

But there will be a day of reckoning. *At the proper time*, a time known only to God, we will *reap* our *harvest*. Our eternity will stretch out before us in Heaven. We cannot *give up*, lose heart, or tire out. The prize for the winners is too great to lose.

¹⁰ Therefore, as we have opportunity, let us do good to all people, especially to those who belong to the family of believers.

Paul challenges us to use every *opportunity* we have to *do good*. We should seek to help *all people*, but we have as Christians a special responsibility to help those within *the family of believers*. It is a sign of spiritual maturity if Christians are willing to do good to all people and surely a sign of immaturity if they will not do good to those with whom they share the common bond of faith and fellowship in Jesus.

ONENESS IN CHRIST (EPHESIANS 2:8-22)

Establishing the Groundwork

The book of Ephesians is thought by many Bible students to have been a circular letter—that is, that it was addressed to a group of churches rather than to one specific congregation. Three reasons are often cited for this conclusion.

The first is a command by Paul in Colossians 4:16. He tells the Colossians to send their letter on to the Laodiceans when they have read it and to read his letter that was to come from Laodicea. Apparently Paul did expect at least some of his letters to circulate. (We do not know what has happened to this letter to the Laodiceans.)

The second piece of evidence for believing that Ephesians was a circular letter is the lack of personal information and references included in the letter. Paul was closely associated with the Ephesian church—he spent three years in Ephesus (Acts 20:31)—yet this letter does not contain the kind of warm, personal language that one would expect to see.

The third piece of evidence is that the earliest copies of the book do not have the words "in Ephesus" in the opening verse. Why, then, did the letter come to be called the book of Ephesians? The church in Ephesus may have been the largest one or most prominent among the group of churches to which the letter was sent. Perhaps it was the church that took custody of the letter.

Ephesians, Philippians, Colossians, and Philemon are usually called Paul's prison epistles. Most likely they were written in AD 63. What is perhaps most striking about these four letters is Paul's positive attitude in all of them. It is surely an insight into the apostle's relationship with Christ that he could maintain such a vibrant faith while in prison. Paul himself may have been in bonds, but his spirit was always free—with the freedom that only Jesus can give.

In the following text, Paul emphasizes that Christ died for both Jew and Gentile—to bring an end to the separation between the two. He encourages us to remember that we are all sinners who have been reconciled to God by Jesus' death on the cross. If we have been thus accepted by God, then we must accept each other.

Examining the Text

I. Saved! (Ephesians 2:8-10)
A. By Grace Through Faith (vv. 8, 9)

8 For it is by grace you have been saved, through faith—and this not from yourselves, it is the gift of God—

In spite of the questions that this verse has often raised, we marvel at how concisely Paul explains the substance of the gospel, drawing attention to salvation, grace, and faith in one verse. Certainly the verse offers much comfort in the assurance that *by grace you have been saved.* This frees us from trying to earn or deserve Heaven, which we can never do.

A certain amount of controversy has arisen over the words *this not from yourselves, it is the gift of God.* What is it that is not from ourselves? What exactly is the gift of God? Some believe that *faith* itself is the gift of God. They maintain that those who respond to God were first given the gift of faith by the Holy Spirit so that they would believe; thus it is impossible for them not to believe. (It would then be equally impossible for anyone to believe without this gift.) This position, however, diminishes the factor of man's free will, which is emphasized in "whoever" passages such as John 3:16 and Revelation 22:17.

There is also a linguistic problem with this position. In the Greek text the pronoun *this* (in *this not from yourselves*) is a neuter pronoun. It cannot, then, refer to *faith* because *faith* is feminine in gender. *This* refers not to any actual word in the text but to the concept expressed, that is, to the entire process of salvation. Our salvation is a gift from God. That this understanding is the better way to view this verse becomes clearer when the next verse is considered—"not by works." Good works are important, but not as the source of our salvation. Paul addresses the role of works in verse 10.

> *⁹ . . . not by works, so that no one can boast.*

One of the consequences of understanding that we are saved by grace should be a sense of genuine humility. The plan of salvation is the work of God, *so that no one can boast.* No one can ever say that he is going to Heaven on the basis of his own *works.*

B. For Good Works (v. 10)

> *¹⁰ For we are God's workmanship, created in Christ Jesus to do good works, which God prepared in advance for us to do.*

While salvation is "not by works," we must never think that works are meaningless. However, they must be understood in proper relationship to our faith. In order to emphasize the significance of *good works,* Paul points out that *God prepared in advance* that we should *do* them. It is God's will for us as Christians that in this life we should display good works and thus let our light shine (Matthew 5:16). Thus works do not justify us, but they do identify us.

This verse also describes Christians as *God's workmanship.* The Greek word used here carries the connotation of a "work of art." (It is the source of our word "poem.") Perhaps we could translate it as "God's masterpiece."

II. Reconciled! (Ephesians 2:11-18)

In this section of the passage, Paul deals with what we might call our "double alienation": we are separated from God and from each other.

A. A Great Chasm (vv. 11, 12)

¹¹ Therefore, remember that formerly you who are Gentiles by birth and called "uncircumcised" by those who call themselves "the circumcision" (that done in the body by the hands of men)—

Paul reminded his Gentile readers what their condition was like before they knew Christ. They were *called "uncircumcised"* as a derisive way of noting that they lacked the covenant sign of Israelite males.

Circumcision was first commanded of Abraham (Genesis 17:10-14). Eventually the practice became to the Jews a symbol of their presumed superiority to the *Gentiles.* Peter, for example, was accused of going to uncircumcised men and eating with them following his visit to the house of Cornelius (Acts 11:1-3). Paul, however, explained that Christ has provided a new kind of circumcision. In Colossians 2:11 Paul wrote that Christians are "circumcised . . . not with a circumcision done by the hands of men." To the Philippians, he wrote, "For it is we who are the circumcision, we who worship by the Spirit of God, who glory in Christ Jesus, and who put no confidence in the flesh" (Philippians 3:3).

¹² . . . remember that at that time you were separate from Christ, excluded from citizenship in Israel and foreigners to the covenants of the promise, without hope and without God in the world.

At that time (before they became Christians), the Gentiles were *separate from Christ.* They were *excluded from citizenship in Israel.* They were not part of God's chosen people and did not share in *the covenants of the promise* made with individuals such as Abraham, Moses, and David, and given to the nation of Israel. Gentiles were both hopeless and godless. It is hard to imagine a more desperate situation.

B. A Greater Bridge (vv. 13-18)

¹³ But now in Christ Jesus you who once were far away have been brought near through the blood of Christ.

Verse 13 introduces a much brighter picture, thanks to the phrase *but now.* (Other significant uses of this phrase are found in Romans 6:22; 7:6; and Colossians 3:8.) The Gentiles, who for so long had been *far away* have now been *brought near* to God *in Christ Jesus.* Those who have been "on the outside looking in" have seen the barriers come down. No separation exists between God and the Gentiles; therefore no separation exists between Jew and Gentile. How did this happen? It happened through the cross, where Jesus shed his *blood.*

Today there is considerable concern about the divisions—racial, social, economic, and others—that exist in our society. We need to keep in mind the degree of hostility that was present between Jew and Gentile in Paul's day. Read the book of Acts to see how challenging it was for the church, which began among the Jews, to understand that God wanted to save Gentiles as well. A gathering of the leadership (recorded in Acts 15) was required to settle the issue, and even that did not put the issue to rest. No less a figure than the apostle Peter had trouble living out the new understanding of God's love for Gentiles as well as Jews. (See Galatians 2:11-14.) Yet it is one of the impressive accomplishments of the gospel of Christ that it could and did transcend such formidable barriers. Can anything but the gospel heal the divisions present in our fragmented world?

> *14 For he himself is our peace, who has made the two one and has destroyed the barrier, the dividing wall of hostility,*

Paul does not say merely that Jesus brought peace, but that *he himself is our peace.* There are two ways Paul describes the difference Jesus has made. First, he *has made the two one.* Any differences between Jew and Gentile mean nothing now. Second, Paul says that Christ *destroyed the barrier, the dividing wall of hostility.* The Greek word rendered *barrier* is a general term that can refer to any kind of wall or fence, including a wall that was used to protect a vineyard (Mark 12:1). Perhaps Paul was thinking of the "wall" that existed in the Jerusalem temple, where gates leading into the inner courts displayed warning signs barring Gentiles from going any farther. Violation of this warning was punishable by death. Recall the uproar that resulted when Paul was accused of bringing Gentiles into a forbidden area of the temple (Acts 21:27-36).

> *15 . . . by abolishing in his flesh the law with its commandments and regulations. His purpose was to create in himself one new man out of the two, thus making peace,*

Jesus is described as *abolishing in his flesh the law with its commandments and regulations.* Some see this statement as contradictory to Jesus' declaration that he did not "come to abolish the Law or the Prophets . . . but to fulfill them" (Matthew 5:17). These two verses simply offer two different perspectives on what Jesus did concerning the law. Jesus fulfilled the law by living according to its standards of righteousness and by emphasizing its underlying principles (as seen throughout the Sermon on the Mount). Through his coming the law's purpose was fulfilled in that it is meant to "lead us to Christ" (Galatians 3:24).

In this passage from Ephesians, Paul seems to place special emphasis on the ceremonial aspects of the law—*commandments and regulations*. These are the portions of the law (including such matters as feast days, food regulations, and rituals) that drove a wedge between Jew and Gentile. Colossians 2:14 says that Jesus "canceled the written code, with its regulations, that was against us and that stood opposed to us; he took it away, nailing it to the cross."

Under the New Covenant, the portions of the law concerning moral issues (for example, the Ten Commandments) can still provide guidance as a standard of conduct, but not a means of salvation. Only Jesus' death supplies that. His sacrifice has allowed those who have broken the law to be forgiven.

The impact of Jesus' death is described as making *one new man out of the two*. Some believe that this is to be taken in a corporate sense, picturing the church as God's new humanity that includes both Jews and Gentiles. Others see the phrase as descriptive of the new individual or "new creation" in Christ (2 Corinthians 5:17). This person is neither Jew nor Gentile; he is a Christian!

16 . . . and in this one body to reconcile both of them to God through the cross, by which he put to death their hostility.

Since the cross has done away with what once separated Jews and Gentiles, and has reconciled them *to God,* they can now be reconciled to each other.

17 He came and preached peace to you who were far away and peace to those who were near.

This verse tells us that Jesus *came and preached peace* to those *far away* (Gentiles) and *to those who were near* (Jews). But Jesus' earthly ministry was primarily for the sake of "the lost sheep of Israel" (Matthew 15:24). When did he preach peace to Gentiles? Probably Paul is describing the impact of Jesus' ministry, particularly his death and resurrection, on all peoples, to whom his followers are told to go and preach (Mark 16:15). Thus Peter could speak to the Gentiles in the house of Cornelius of "the message God sent to the people of Israel, telling the good news of peace through Jesus Christ" (Acts 10:36). He then concluded, "Everyone who believes in him receives forgiveness of sins through his name" (Acts 10:43).

18 For through him we both have access to the Father by one Spirit.

Through Jesus all peoples, Jews and Gentiles alike, have *access* to God as their *Father.* The Greek word rendered *access* is related to a word that describes the official who would usher someone into a king's presence. Now *both* Jews and Gentiles can walk in daily fellowship with the King of Heaven. Both Jews and Gentiles have the gift of the same indwelling *Spirit* (Acts 2:38, 39).

III. Included! (Ephesians 2:19-22)

In this portion of the text, Paul uses what might be called a mixed metaphor. He combines the figures of a nation, a family, and a building to illustrate that Christians (both Jews and Gentiles) belong together because they belong to God.

A. In God's Family (v. 19)

19 Consequently, you are no longer foreigners and aliens, but fellow citizens with God's people and members of God's household,

Paul offers a before-and-after picture of what we were before Christ's coming and what we are now, thanks to him. We were *foreigners and aliens*; we had no place among *God's people.* But that is *no longer* true; now we have been designated *fellow citizens.* We enjoy the full privileges of being citizens of the kingdom of Heaven and *members of God's household* (family).

B. In God's Temple (vv. 20-22)

20 . . . built on the foundation of the apostles and prophets, with Christ Jesus himself as the chief cornerstone.

Paul now pictures Christians as building blocks in a great temple that God is constructing. He describes the *apostles and prophets* as the *foundation* of this building. This makes sense, since the apostles and prophets were instrumental in delivering the first inspired messages to the early church.

Then Paul designates *Christ Jesus himself as the chief cornerstone.* Today cornerstones are largely symbolic. In the first century, however, the cornerstone was a vital part of the construction of a building. Great care was taken to be sure the cornerstone was perfectly square and level. It then stood as a standard of reference for all the measurements relating to the construction of the rest of the building.

21 In him the whole building is joined together and rises to become a holy temple in the Lord.

Each Christian might be called a "brick" in God's *building.* Paul pictures this building as in the process of constant growth. Anyone who becomes a Christian is added to the structure. Every part belongs; every part has purpose.

Together the parts constitute *a holy temple in the Lord*—his dwelling place (1 Corinthians 3:16).

> **²² And in him you too are being built together to become a dwelling in which God lives by his Spirit.**

Now Paul goes a step farther. Not only is this great building—this holy temple—being *built* by God, but he himself dwells in it *by* the presence of *his Spirit*. Of course, Paul is not talking about a literal building. Just as God has created "one new man" including both Jews and Gentiles (v. 15), so he has constructed one new building—his church, composed of the people (both Jews and Gentiles) in whom he *lives* through his Spirit.

How to Say It

ABRAHAM. *Ay*-bruh-ham.

ACHAIA. Uh-*kay*-uh.

ANTIOCH. *An*-tee-ock.

CALVARY. *Kal*-vuh-ree.

COLOSSIANS. Kuh-*losh*-unz.

CORNELIUS. Cor-*neel*-yus.

DERBE. *Der*-be.

EPHESIAN. Ee-*fee*-zhun.

EPHESUS. *Ef*-uh-sus.

GALATIA. Guh-*lay*-shuh.

GAULS. Gawlz.

GENTILES. *Jen*-tiles.

ICONIUM. Eye-*ko*-nee-um.

ISRAELITE. *Iz*-ray-el-ite.

LAODICEA. Lay-*odd*-uh-*see*-uh (strong accent on *see*).

LAODICEANS. Lay-*odd*-uh-*see*-unz (strong accent on *see*).

LYSTRA. *Liss*-truh.

MACEDONIA. Mass-eh-*doe*-nee-uh.

MACEDONIANS. Mass-eh-*doe*-nee-unz.

MOSES. *Mo*-zes or *Mo*-zez.

PENTECOST. *Pent*-ih-kost.

PHILIPPI. Fih-*lip*-pie or *Fil*-ih-pie.

PISIDIA. Pih-*sid*-ee-uh.

THESSALONICA. *Thess*-uh-lo-*nye*-kuh (strong accent on *nye*; *th* as in *thin*).

TITUS. *Ty*-tus.

Chapter 10

Living Faithfully in Preparation for Christ's Return: Studies in Ephesians, Philippians, Colossians, and 1 Thessalonians

Ephesians 4:1-16; 5:22–6:4; Philippians 3:7-16;
Colossians 1:15-20; 1 Thessalonians 4:13-18

BUILDING UP THE BODY OF CHRIST (EPHESIANS 4:1-16)

Establishing the Groundwork

The study from Ephesians that concluded the previous chapter was taken from the doctrinal portion of the letter (chapters 1-3). Chapter 4 begins with a more practical portion of the letter, in which Paul addresses concerns relevant to Christian living. (Most of Paul's letters could be outlined as doctrinal first and then practical.)

At the same time, what Paul considers at the beginning of the chapter is closely tied to the preceding material. (Note the word *then* in verse 1.) The doxology at the close of chapter 3 (vv. 20, 21) includes the phrase "to [God] be glory in the church and in Christ Jesus." In chapter 4 Paul proceeds to address how the church can bring glory to God. His initial topic of concern is unity in Christ—a matter that the church must make a top priority.

Examining the Text

I. Recognizing Unity (Ephesians 4:1-6)
A. Essential Attitudes (vv. 1-3)

¹ As a prisoner for the Lord, then, I urge you to live a life worthy of the calling you have received.

Paul's use of the word *urge* indicates the critical nature of his discussion of unity. He begins his plea by expressing his desire that his readers *live a life worthy*—"practice what they preach," or "walk the talk." In fact, Paul uses the metaphor of "walking" (not reflected in the translation) in this passage. He wants the believers' walk to reflect *the calling* they *have received.* All Christians are called to cultivate the attitudes that follow.

² Be completely humble and gentle; be patient, bearing with one another in love.

Here Paul begins to describe what it means to live a life worthy of our calling. He wants followers of Jesus to *be patient, bearing with one another in love.* Working together with others requires patience; and if we are going to have that kind of patience, then we must possess the related qualities of being *humble and gentle.* People will inevitably disappoint us and will tax our patience at times. What we must never forget is how much we need people to be patient with us.

³ Make every effort to keep the unity of the Spirit through the bond of peace.

Notice that *unity* and *peace* are linked in this verse. In a sense, peace is the by-product of unity; peace, in turn, serves to keep unity alive and well. This unity is said to be *of the Spirit.* Elsewhere Paul tells us, "We were all baptized by one Spirit into one body . . . and we were all given the one Spirit to drink" (1 Corinthians 12:13). The Spirit is also the source of the gifts (1 Corinthians 12:4, 7, 11) that are to be used to achieve "unity in the faith" (Ephesians 4:13).

B. Essential Principles (vv. 4-6)

What follows is a seven-part statement of Christian unity. It seems more than coincidental that Paul lists seven items, since seven is a frequent symbol in the Scriptures for completeness.

⁴ There is one body and one Spirit—just as you were called to one hope when you were called—

The *one body,* of course, is the church. Today the various denominations that exist make it difficult for many to see the church as one body. This was not the case in Paul's day, and this is not the case in God's eyes. In spite of the divisions created by man, to him there is still only one body.

The *one Spirit* is the Holy Spirit. Every Christian has the gift of the Holy Spirit (Acts 2:38; 5:32). It is one of the tragedies of our time that the purpose for which the Spirit was given (to glorify Jesus, according to John 16:14) has been lost amid numerous questions and controversies concerning the Spirit's work.

The *one hope* to which we are *called* is no doubt the hope of eternal life. This hope is firmly grounded in the resurrection of Jesus, who declared, "Because I live, you also will live" (John 14:19).

⁵ . . . one Lord, one faith, one baptism;

It is obvious that the *one Lord* is Jesus himself. What does Paul mean by *one faith?* It may refer to the fact that Christians "have been saved, through faith" (Ephesians 2:8). However, it could also describe the substance of what we believe. A similar usage is found in the phrase "the faith that was once for all entrusted to the saints" (Jude 3).

Paul also mentions *one baptism.* Many might respond to Paul's claim by saying, "But there are many baptisms mentioned in the Bible: John the Baptist's baptism, baptism in the Holy Spirit, and water baptism." However, since Jesus included water baptism as part of what should be preached to all the world (Matthew 28:19, 20; Mark 16:16) and since Paul describes it as the act by which one is brought "into Christ" (Romans 6:3, 4; Galatians 3:27), it seems clear that the one baptism is water baptism.

This, however, does not end the discussion. A question might be raised concerning the mode of baptism—that is, how it is done. Some use sprinkling, others believe in pouring, and still others advocate immersion. Which is the *one baptism?* When we consider the meaning of the word *baptism* (the verb form means "to dip or plunge") and the evidence provided in the book of Acts (Acts 8:38, 39, for example, where Philip and the eunuch "went down into the water" and "came up out of the water"), it is clear that originally baptism was done by immersion.

⁶ . . . one God and Father of all, who is over all and through all and in all.

Last in Paul's description of the basics of Christian unity (though first in prominence and authority) is *God* himself. He is described as the *Father of all,* and his authority is affirmed in the phrase *who is over all and through all and in all.*

Notice in these verses the mention of the three persons of the Trinity: one Spirit (v. 4), one Lord, Jesus (v. 5), and one God (v. 6).

II. Respecting Diversity (Ephesians 4:7-12)
A. Source of Our Gifts (vv. 7-10)

⁷ But to each one of us grace has been given as Christ apportioned it.

Paul now moves from stating the principles of unity to considering the expression of unity in church life. He reminds his readers that *each one of us . . . has been given* some kind of spiritual gift that can be exercised in some ministry of the church. Here Paul describes these gifts as given by *Christ,* but these are also gifts of the Holy Spirit, as noted in 1 Corinthians 12:7-11.

⁸ This is why it says:
"When he ascended on high,
he led captives in his train
and gave gifts to men."

Here Paul cites a passage from the Old Testament (Psalm 68:18). The text pictures a conquering hero rising up a mountain and then giving of the spoils of his victory as *gifts* to his people. Paul's main point is to affirm that the church has been given gifts by our Conqueror, Christ Jesus, who has *ascended* into Heaven. Each person has been given a gift, and all gifts are to be exercised for the good of the church.

What is meant by the phrase *he led captives in his train*? Some believe that the captives are those who march in triumph behind the victorious Christ and are the recipients of his gifts. (A similar idea is expressed in 2 Corinthians 2:14.) More likely, however, the phrase here describes Jesus' victory over his spiritual enemies. Colossians 2:15 supports this view by noting that Jesus, "having disarmed the powers and authorities, . . . made a public spectacle of them, triumphing over them by the cross."

Of special note in considering Paul's quotation from Psalm 68:18 is that it varies from the text found there, which reads, "You *received* [not *gave*] gifts from [the Hebrew more accurately reads "on behalf of"] men." Perhaps Paul recognized that the gifts Christ gives to his church have been given to him by God; however, in this verse he chooses to emphasize what Christ has given, since he has alluded to what Christ has "apportioned" in verse 7. However we understand what Paul is saying, we can trust that, under the inspiration of the Holy Spirit, he is providing the correct understanding and application of the verse from Psalms.

⁹ (What does "he ascended" mean except that he also descended to the lower, earthly regions?

Since the passage Paul cited spoke of Christ's having *ascended*, then he must *also* have *descended*. To where did Christ descend? Paul says he *descended to the lower, earthly regions*, but that phrase is also confusing. What does Paul mean?

Some believe that this refers to the earth itself and is speaking of what happened in the incarnation: Jesus left the glories of Heaven, "became flesh and made his dwelling among us" (John 1:14), and then later ascended back to Heaven. Others claim that *the lower, earthly regions* refers to the grave or to Hades, the abode of the dead. Those who hold this view often cite 1 Peter 3:18-20 for support.

¹⁰ He who descended is the very one who ascended higher than all the heavens, in order to fill the whole universe.)

When he had accomplished his Father's task ("after he had provided purification for sins," Hebrews 1:3), Jesus *ascended higher than all the heavens* to "the right hand of the throne of God" (Hebrews 12:2). He is in this position of authority and prominence *in order to fill the whole universe*—perhaps a reference to his giving of the Holy Spirit (Acts 2:33) and the gifts that accompany the Spirit's presence. Paul now proceeds to describe some of these gifts and their purpose.

B. Variety of Our Gifts (v. 11)

¹¹ It was he who gave some to be apostles, some to be prophets, some to be evangelists, and some to be pastors and teachers.

This verse describes some of the people whom God has gifted in order to help the church fulfill its mission. It is not surprising that this list begins with the office of the *apostles.* They were the men commissioned by Jesus to lead in the proclamation of the gospel and the establishment of the church.

Next, Paul mentions the *prophets.* Prophets were inspired by God to utter special proclamations of divine truth. A good example is Agabus, mentioned in Acts 11:28 and 21:10, 11. Both apostles and prophets make up what Paul calls the "foundation" of the church (Ephesians 2:20).

Following the prophets is the office of *evangelists.* This word comes from a Greek verb meaning "to bring good news." An evangelist proclaims the good news found in the gospel. It would seem that the main focus of the evangelist's work is to reach lost people with the gospel. (Perhaps evangelists could be considered the equivalent of today's church planters.) Only one person in the Bible is given the title of *evangelist,* and that is Philip (Acts 21:8). Timothy is told to "do the work of an evangelist" (2 Timothy 4:5), so many conclude that the title properly belongs to him as well.

Paul also mentions *pastors and teachers.* Frequently in modern usage, the word *pastor* is used to refer to the preaching minister of a congregation. While the preaching minister may perform a variety of pastoral duties, such duties are usually associated in the New Testament with the office of elder (also called "overseer"). The Greek word for *pastor* literally means "shepherd," and it is the elders who are exhorted to "be shepherds" of the church (Acts 20:17, 28; 1 Peter 5:1, 2).

In the Greek text, each of these offices has a definite article except *teachers.* Most students believe this indicates that the last two terms describe one office ("pastor-teachers" or "teaching elders"), not two. This office may well describe the "elders . . . whose work is preaching and teaching" (1 Timothy 5:17).

All of the leadership gifts mentioned in this verse are given for a special purpose, which Paul goes on to explain.

C. Purpose of Our Gifts (v. 12)

12 . . . to prepare God's people for works of service, so that the body of Christ may be built up

What are these gifted leaders supposed to accomplish? They are *to prepare God's people for works of service*. The Greek word translated *prepare* was used in New Testament times to describe the setting of a broken bone. It is used in the New Testament itself to describe the mending of nets (Matthew 4:21). But the idea of "repair" is not the primary meaning. More important is the idea of making something or someone ready for a purpose. Even the repair is not a cosmetic repair, but a functional one. The expression here conveys the idea of "equipping" the saints for performing some valuable service.

One of the most important tasks of the leaders in any church is to encourage those in the congregation to exercise their gifts, carry out their ministries effectively, and thus bless the church. This, of course, does not mean that the church will ever outgrow the need for a vocational ministry. There is far too much work to do in the church for anyone in that position to work himself out of a job. It is true, however, that all Christians are ministers in the sense of being "servants." And as all exercise their gifts and fulfill their ministries, they will fulfill the purpose for which Christ has given these gifts: *so that the body of Christ may be built up*.

III. Reaching Maturity (Ephesians 4:13-16)
A. The Process (vv. 13, 14)

13 . . . until we all reach unity in the faith and in the knowledge of the Son of God and become mature, attaining to the whole measure of the fullness of Christ.

The church achieves *unity* in Christ and becomes *mature* when each Christian is willing to use his or her gift or gifts to help others grow toward *the whole measure of the fullness of Christ*. To be like Jesus—this is the true measure of our progress.

14 Then we will no longer be infants, tossed back and forth by the waves, and blown here and there by every wind of teaching and by the cunning and craftiness of men in their deceitful scheming.

To be childlike in humility is commended by Jesus (Matthew 18:1-4), but here the immaturity of *infants* is something to be avoided. Paul wants Christians to be knowledgeable enough not to be unstable. Proverbs 18:17 says, "The first to present his case seems right, till another comes forward and questions him." The mature

Christian knows enough to ask questions rather than just accept everything anyone says without careful consideration. Like the noble Bereans, he or she examines what a teacher says against the Scriptures (Acts 17:11).

Christians should beware of both questionable doctrines and the men who use *cunning and craftiness* to deceive others. The mature must not be taken in by spiritual con artists and their clever words. They should know the Word well enough to be able to recognize the "counterfeit" message of the dishonest teacher or preacher.

B. The Product (vv. 15, 16)

15 Instead, speaking the truth in love, we will in all things grow up into him who is the Head, that is, Christ.

Truth without *love* can come across as harsh and vindictive. Love without truth can come across as sloppy and undisciplined sentimentality. The combination of both is necessary in order to enhance the process of growth toward the likeness of *Christ*.

16 From him the whole body, joined and held together by every supporting ligament, grows and builds itself up in love, as each part does its work.

Paul uses various medical terms in this verse to describe a *body* that is healthy and fully functioning. *Each part* is important to the whole. *Love* enables the parts to work together so that the body *grows and builds itself up*. Of course, it is *from* Christ the Head (v. 15) that the health of the body comes. When all parts of the body respect his headship, the body will demonstrate the unity that will lead others to believe in Jesus (John 17:21).

CHRISTIAN LIVING IN THE HOME (EPHESIANS 5:22–6:4)

Establishing the Groundwork

After teaching about building up the body of Christ (Ephesians 4:11-16), Paul calls followers of Jesus to "put off" the way of living associated with their pre-Christian lifestyles (v. 22) and to "put on the new self, created to be like God in true righteousness and holiness" (v. 24). Paul then gives a series of exhortations concerning a Christian's conduct (vv. 25-32).

The text to be examined in this study, taken from portions of chapters 5 and 6, continues these exhortations, with a special emphasis on responsible conduct in the home. In each of these areas of life, we have a duty to live by the highest standards of behavior—the standards of Christ himself.

Examining the Text

I. The Wife's Place (Ephesians 5:22-24)
A. What She Is to Do (v. 22)

²² Wives, submit to your husbands as to the Lord.

Here Paul applies the principle of submission, introduced in verse 21, to *wives.* When Paul admonishes wives to *submit to your husbands, as to the Lord,* he does not mean that a wife should treat her husband as if he were Jesus. Paul is saying that a wife's submission to her husband is a service that she does unto the Lord, or for the Lord's glory. A similar phrase is used in encouraging servants to obey their masters "just as you would obey Christ" (Ephesians 6:5-7).

B. Why She Is to Do It (v. 23)

²³ For the husband is the head of the wife as Christ is the head of the church, his body, of which he is the Savior.

The authority given to the *husband* is not absolute. That he is *the head of the wife* does not give him license to coerce his wife into submission. The standard against which his headship is measured is clear: *as Christ is the head of the church.* This indicates that marriage is truly "holy matrimony," meant to give both husband and wife a deeper appreciation of their relationship to Christ.

Notice the close ties between home and church: the order in the home is to reflect how Christ and the church are related. Whether or not a man really knows Christ and follows his example will be evident from the state of his household. Thus one quality to be found in an elder is that he "manage his own family well" (1 Timothy 3:4). The next verse then asks, "If anyone does not know how to manage his own family, how can he take care of God's church?" This defines "management," both for the elder and for the husband, as "taking care of."

C. How She Is to Do It (v. 24)

²⁴ Now as the church submits to Christ, so also wives should submit to their husbands in everything.

Paul's teaching that *wives should submit to their husbands in everything* is not meant to demean women. (It is important to remember that Christianity brought to women a sense of dignity that the pagan world of the first century had not provided.) His teaching establishes a sense of order in the home. It does not mean that men are smarter or more valuable than women. In a football team the quarterback may not be the smartest player; however, order in the huddle requires someone to take the role of leader. In an army the general may not be more intelligent than the private, yet the necessity of discipline and order in a military unit requires that someone be in charge. Paul is establishing a similar arrangement of authority in the Christian home, modeled on the arrangement that every Christian understands: the submission of the church to Jesus.

II. The Husband's Place (Ephesians 5:25-33)
A. The Model (vv. 25-27)

25 Husbands, love your wives, just as Christ loved the church and gave himself up for her

While *submit* is the primary command to *wives,* the priority for *husbands* is *love.* Paul's command is followed with an extraordinary standard for husbands to follow. Husbands are to love their wives *just as Christ loved the church.* How did he love the church? He *gave himself up for her.* That is the kind of sacrificial love with which husbands are to treat their wives.

26 . . . to make her holy, cleansing her by the washing with water through the word,

Paul then comments briefly on the degree with which Jesus loves the church and desires what is best for her. He says that Jesus gave himself in order *to make her holy* and provided for her *cleansing . . . by the washing with water through the word.* Most likely this cleansing with water is a reference to Christian baptism (cf. Acts 22:16). *The word* is the word of God (the gospel), which Peter describes as the "imperishable" seed that produces the new birth (1 Peter 1:23-25).

27 . . . and to present her to himself as a radiant church, without stain or wrinkle or any other blemish, but holy and blameless.

Jesus also wants his *church* (his bride) to be *a radiant church, without stain or wrinkle or any other blemish.* As the loving husband, Jesus took it upon himself to do what was necessary to make his bride beautiful. He took care of all the spots, wrinkles, and blemishes caused by sin through his sacrifice on the cross.

B. The Love (vv. 28-30)

28, 29 In this same way, husbands ought to love their wives as their own bodies. He who loves his wife loves himself. After all, no one ever hated his own body, but he feeds and cares for it, just as Christ does the church—

Paul applies Christ's love for the *church* to the *love* of *husbands* for their *wives.* He says that husbands *ought to love their wives as* they do *their own bodies.* Many men have bought into the self-centered spirit of our time and have abandoned their responsibilities at home. Believing that these duties stood in the way of their personal happiness, they have selfishly pursued interests outside the home and family. Here Paul declares that a man's love of self and of his wife are interconnected: *he who loves his wife loves himself.* For the husband to love his wife *just as Christ does the church* is in his own best interests and brings him the greatest sense of fulfillment as a man.

Some may ask whether (or to what degree) Paul's teaching is applicable in situations in which the husband or the wife is not a Christian. Guidance for proper conduct in these situations is provided in such Scriptures as 1 Corinthians 7:12-16 and 1 Peter 3:1-6. Certainly Paul's teaching should encourage us to take seriously his words about not being "yoked together with unbelievers" (2 Corinthians 6:14-18). Our youth need to receive special instruction in these matters to avoid substantial heartache in the future.

30 . . . for we are members of his body.

Love has a "boomerang effect" in the church and in a marriage. We must never forget that how a husband treats his wife is how he is treating a member of the church, and how he treats a member of the church is how he is treating Jesus; for the church is *his body.* Jesus takes it personally when the husband does or does not love his wife. A person in the body of Christ cannot mistreat another part of the body without doing harm to himself.

C. The Union (vv. 31-33)

31 "For this reason a man will leave his father and mother and be united to his wife, and the two will become one flesh."

The verse Paul cites at this point comes from Genesis 2:24. The passage describes three factors that are seen in the kind of caring, loving, upbuilding relationship that makes *one flesh* of two.

First, there is "leaving." A married man does not stop respecting *his father and mother.* He does not necessarily move to another town. But he must not let attachment to his parents mar in any way his close, intimate relationship with his wife. Second, there is "cleaving," which is captured in the idea of being *united to his wife.* Husband and wife not only live with each other but for each other. Third, there is "weaving": *the two will become one flesh.* This refers to both physical intimacy and relational interdependence. The first can happen during the honeymoon; the second takes time to develop. Husband and wife come to depend on each other emotionally, mentally, socially, and financially. Neither is complete without the other.

32 This is a profound mystery—but I am talking about Christ and the church.

Again, Paul reminds us that the husband/wife relationship is built on the model of *Christ and the church.*

33 However, each one of you also must love his wife as he loves himself, and the wife must respect her husband.

Since Christ's love for the church family is our example, a husband's *love* should mirror that love. The wife's reaction should mirror the church's expected reaction to Christ. The husband's love is the starting point; the *respect* of the *wife* is the corresponding response. That is the formula for harmony in marriage.

III. Children and Parents (Ephesians 6:1-4)
A. What a Child Is to Do (vv. 1-3)

1-3 Children, obey your parents in the Lord, for this is right. "Honor your father and mother"—which is the first commandment with a promise—"that it may go well with you and that you may enjoy long life on the earth."

Children are admonished to *obey* their *parents.* They are to do so *in the Lord,* or as part of their duty to the Lord. Similar language occurs in connection with the wife's submission to her husband (Ephesians 5:22) and with slaves' obedience of their masters (6:5-7).

Paul strengthens his words with a *promise* from the Ten Commandments (Deuteronomy 5:16): *that it may go well with you and that you may enjoy long life on the earth.* This is not a guarantee of long life to all obedient children, but it does call attention to the fact that obedient, God-fearing children are far less likely to engage in the kind of behavior that shortens so many lives.

B. What a Father Is to Do (v. 4)

4 Fathers, do not exasperate your children; instead, bring them up in the training and instruction of the Lord.

Fathers held a position of great authority in the ancient world. In some cases they possessed an almost dictatorial power over their *children.* Paul tells Christian fathers that in the exercise of their leadership they must not *exasperate* their children. All children will get angry at times, and no parent can avoid that. Paul is encouraging fathers not to be the source of such anger by their hasty words or thoughtless actions. Remember, fathers, that our children's perception of the heavenly Father will depend in large part on the kind of fathers we are!

PRESSING ON TOWARD THE GOAL (PHILIPPIANS 3:7-16)

Establishing the Groundwork

The church in the city of Philippi, located in the province of Macedonia, was the first established by Paul in what we now know as Europe. Acts 16 tells of what transpired there. Thus began what became a strong and generous congregation. The church at Philippi sent gifts to help Paul when he moved on to Thessalonica (Philippians 4:16) and later when his journeys took him to Corinth (2 Corinthians 11:9).

That spirit of generosity was still present approximately ten years later, when, while Paul was a prisoner at Rome, the Philippian church sent Epaphroditus, one of their leaders, with a substantial gift. Epaphroditus stayed for a time as a helper to Paul, but he became seriously ill while he was there. When Epaphroditus was able to travel, Paul sent him home with the letter of thanks and encouragement that we have come to call the epistle to the Philippians (Philippians 2:25-30).

Among Paul's writings, this one is especially notable for its warm and affectionate tone and for its persistent expression of rejoicing in Christ. Chapter 1 presents Jesus as the focus and goal of Paul's life: "For to me, to live is Christ" (1:21). Chapter 2 presents Christ as the perfect example of the self-sacrificing spirit that will build the church in peace and unity. Chapter 3 opens with an exhortation to "rejoice in the Lord" (a command that Paul repeats in 4:4). Paul then warns the Philippians of certain "dogs" (3:2), or false teachers, who are encouraging people to put their "confidence in the flesh" (outward conformity to Jewish law) rather than in Christ. He proceeds to list some of the items in his own background that gave him more than enough reason to have such confidence (v. 4). He does so to emphasize that such dependence on the flesh can never make a person right with God. Only by following the course that is urged in the succeeding verses can we be made right with God.

Examining the Text

I. The Goal Is Christ (Philippians 3:7-11)

In Philippians 3:4-6, the apostle has noted that his "bragging rights" in relation to the Jewish law were far better than those of others who depended on the law for their acceptance with God. All of that, however, constituted a *program* to be carried out. For Paul that program had been replaced with a *Person* to be loved, honored, and served for time and eternity.

A. Counting Everything Loss (vv. 7, 8)

⁷ But whatever was to my profit I now consider loss for the sake of Christ.

Paul recognized that any part of his background or reputation that encouraged reliance on anything but *Christ* for his salvation was a handicap to him. The more desirable these items had been, the greater would be their potential to become a hindrance. They must now be moved from the *profit* side of his personal and spiritual ledger to the *loss* side *for the sake of* his relationship with Christ. A Christian must ask himself occasionally which of his "assets" have become liabilities because they compete with Christ for top priority in his time and attention.

⁸ What is more, I consider everything a loss compared to the surpassing greatness of knowing Christ Jesus my Lord, for whose sake I have lost all things. I consider them rubbish, that I may gain Christ

To know and serve and be with Christ is a blessing so great as to be sought at any and all costs. It begins with considering the information about Jesus found in the Gospels; it moves to an acceptance of Jesus as Savior and Lord; it then grows into the kind of intimacy described by Paul as *the surpassing greatness of knowing Christ Jesus my Lord.* Thus does one become prepared for the further intimacy of an eternity with Jesus.

Note that Paul was not promising some price that he would pay; he was giving a sober account of what he had already paid. His position in the Jewish community; his family and friends; his home with all its comforts and security—these and other assets had been tossed aside that he might *gain Christ.* Did the apostle miss these items and mourn their loss? To the contrary, he rejoiced in his glorious exchange, regarding the losses as *rubbish,* or material for the garbage can.

B. Having His Righteousness (v. 9)

⁹ . . . and be found in him, not having a righteousness of my own that comes from the law, but that which is through faith in Christ—the righteousness that comes from God and is by faith.

Paul says it again: a person's *righteousness,* or becoming right with God, comes not through outward conformity to *the law* of Moses but through belief in and commitment to God through his Son Jesus. The phrase *in him* describes a vital and intimate relationship with *Christ* that begins in time and continues throughout eternity.

If one could become acceptable with God through obedience to the law, then his salvation would be by means of his good behavior and thus an earned reward. But that is impossible, because no one—except Jesus—has yet fully kept the law. Paul recognized the hopelessness of his position under the law (in spite of his own "faultless" standing before the law; see v. 6), and recognized that his salvation must come not from himself but *from God* through Christ. It must be received *by faith*—the belief that expresses itself through complete trust and obedience.

C. Knowing Him (vv. 10, 11)

10 I want to know Christ and the power of his resurrection and the fellowship of sharing in his sufferings, becoming like him in his death,

To *know Christ* was Paul's constant passion and purpose. In order to attain such an intimate acquaintance, the apostle was willing to share to the greatest possible degree the experiences of his Lord and Savior. If he was to experience the *power* that raised Christ from the dead, he would need to follow Jesus through the giving of his life daily in service to God (note his statement, "I die every day," in 1 Corinthians 15:31), and also through a willingness even to die in the service of Jesus (Revelation 2:10). This was no halfhearted effort!

11 . . . and so, somehow, to attain to the resurrection from the dead.

The Scriptures teach that a *resurrection from the dead* will be shared by both saint and sinner—the one to life eternal and the other to condemnation (John 5:28, 29; Acts 24:15). Resurrection to life with Christ is a goal worth more than whatever can be invested in striving toward it.

Attain here signifies the arrival at a chosen destination. Paul had his eye on the goal and was on his way to reaching it. This does not mean, however, that eternal life is achieved on the basis of one's personal effort. It is a gift from God to be accepted and received. One's appreciation of its value increases, however, as the recipient grows in his familiarity with the provider.

II. The Approach Is Commitment (Philippians 3:12-16)
A. Pressing On (v. 12)

12 Not that I have already obtained all this, or have already been made perfect, but I press on to take hold of that for which Christ Jesus took hold of me.

Paul described himself as *not . . . made perfect.* He was not yet a finished product of God's workmanship. That, however, did not keep him from pursuing his goal patiently to the end. Instead he would *press on* as a patient hunter tracks his game. Paul resolved to stay the course with dogged persistence.

Here was Paul's fervent desire: *to take hold of that for which Christ Jesus took hold of me.* The action is comparable to a drowning person's being seized by his rescuer and enabled to grasp the rope he hadn't known was there. The lifesaving is accomplished by the rescuer, but it requires the cooperation of the rescued one. The Lord has laid hold on all of us through the gospel; through the same gospel we lay hold on him and are saved.

B. Forgetting and Expecting (vv. 13, 14)

13, 14 Brothers, I do not consider myself yet to have taken hold of it. But one thing I do: Forgetting what is behind and straining toward what is ahead, I press on toward the goal to win the prize for which God has called me heavenward in Christ Jesus.

What a thought to grasp all at once! Let us consider its most important ingredients one by one. The term *brothers* shows that Paul regarded his readers as equals with him in the family of God. He and they had shared in the opportunities and responsibilities of the gospel. We share in them, too!

Paul had not yet reached his *goal:* he did not claim *to have taken hold of* his reward. He had not yet crossed the finish line in the Christian race, but he was committed to going all out to reach it.

One thing I do! The Greek text does not include the words *I do,* and is really more powerful without it. "This is it!" Paul seems to say. "Nothing else matters!"

Forgetting what is behind—this could include much of the "rubbish" from Paul's past: his Jewish heritage and cultural advantages; his sins and failures; his impressive array of accomplishments. None of these must be allowed to divert his attention from the opportunities before him.

Straining toward. As a runner leans forward and extends himself to the limit, Paul was exerting the utmost effort to reach his objective.

I press on toward the goal. Paul was not following a general compass direction of "living a good life." His eyes were fixed on a specific goal.

Verse 14 concludes with Paul's description of his goal: *the prize for which God has called me heavenward in Christ Jesus.* On reaching that goal Paul would receive the everlasting, never-fading "crown of righteousness" (1 Corinthians 9:25; 2 Timothy 4:8) given to those who are "faithful, even to the point of death" (Revelation 2:10). If there is anything more wonderful than being *in Christ*, it will be the joy of being *with Christ!*

C. Preserving the Gains (vv. 15, 16)

15 All of us who are mature should take such a view of things. And if on some point you think differently, that too God will make clear to you.

Having presented clearly his own position and perspective, the apostle recommended the same course to the *mature* Christians among his readers. Any who considered themselves to be grown up in their spiritual development were exhorted to *take such a view of things.* However, if some differences of viewpoint still remained, Paul would leave the matter to *God,* trusting that he would *make clear* what the less mature needed to know. Such individuals required further teaching, perhaps by experience, perhaps by a more complete understanding of Christ and his Word, or perhaps by the example of mature Christians. Agreement would not be compelled, even by an apostle.

16 Only let us live up to what we have already attained.

Even those who have not yet *attained* the level of maturity that others have should not stand around doing nothing while God is bringing them "up to speed." Let them *live* by the truth they have already learned. Thus they will not lose the ground they have gained, but will be in a position to advance—learning more, doing more, and growing more toward the likeness of Christ.

THE SUPREMACY OF CHRIST (COLOSSIANS 1:15-20)

Establishing the Groundwork

This study includes a portion of the first chapter of Paul's letter to the Colossians. This letter, like Ephesians, Philippians, and Philemon, is one of Paul's "prison epistles" and, like the rest, was probably written from Rome around AD 63. Like Ephesians, it was sent by the hand of Tychicus (Colossians 4:7-9).

The city of Colosse was located some 100 miles east of Ephesus, in what is modern-day Turkey. We do not know when the church there was formed, for Colosse is never mentioned in the book of Acts. Probably it was established during Paul's ministry at Ephesus. Luke tells us that Paul used the school of Tyrannus as his headquarters in Ephesus for two years, and that as a result "all the Jews and Greeks who lived in the province of Asia heard the word of the Lord" (Acts 19:9, 10). Otherwise, all we know of the Colossian church is what we can learn from this letter and from Paul's letter to Philemon, which was carried by Onesimus, who most likely lived in Colosse (Colossians 4:9).

It is important to note the similarities between Colossians and Ephesians. They cover the same basic topics and exhibit a similar structure. In some instances the wording is very similar (compare, for example, Colossians 4:7-9 and Ephesians 6:21, 22). Probably they were written at the same time, with Tychicus delivering Ephesians first and then going to Colosse to deliver Colossians.

Despite the similarities between Ephesians and Colossians, there are important differences, many of which can be attributed to the reason Paul wrote this letter. Apparently Paul had received some disturbing news from Epaphras (mentioned in Colossians 1:7 and 4:12) that certain false doctrines were being propagated in the Colossian church, including an early form of what would later be known as Gnosticism.

The name *Gnosticism* comes from a Greek word meaning "knowledge." Gnostics believed that they possessed a secret knowledge of spiritual truth that the average or "unenlightened" person could not possess. That is the reason Paul, in writing to the Colossians, emphasizes that in Christ alone are "all the treasures of wisdom and knowledge" (Colossians 2:3; cf. 1:9, 10). Only in Christ (not in the Gnostics' doctrine) is God's true "mystery" revealed (1:26, 27; 2:2).

Gnostics also believed that material things, including the physical world itself, were evil, created by an evil god. There was also a good god, they believed, who was spirit only, for only the spirit was good. They believed in a spiritual world full of divine beings (one of whom was Jesus) who came forth from this good god. Apparently some of these emanations became confused with angels, resulting in the actual worship of angels among some in the Colossian church. Paul warns against this practice in Colossians 2:18.

As he does with his letter to the Ephesians, Paul begins his epistle to the Colossians with a tribute of praise to the Lord Jesus Christ. In the passage to be studied, the apostle presents Jesus as creator and reconciler.

Examining the Text

I. Christ, Our Creator (Colossians 1:15-18)
A. His Identity (v. 15)

15 He is the image of the invisible God, the firstborn over all creation.

Jesus is described as *the image of the invisible God.* The Greek word translated *image* is a word that gives us our English word *icon.* It could describe an image on a coin or a person's reflection in a mirror. Thus does Paul counter the false teaching that Jesus was simply one of many beings who came from God. Jesus was Immanuel—"God with us." Later Paul will affirm that in Christ "all the fullness of the Deity lives in bodily form" (Colossians 2:9). The nature of God is perfectly represented in Jesus.

Jesus is also *the firstborn over all creation.* Although this phrase may seem to portray Jesus as a created being, we should understand the term *firstborn* to highlight the role of Christ, not his origin. It was common in the first century to bestow on the firstborn special rights and obligations. Paul thus sets the stage for his declaration in the next two verses that Jesus Christ is Lord over all of the created world.

B. His Activity (v. 16)

16 For by him all things were created: things in heaven and on earth, visible and invisible, whether thrones or powers or rulers or authorities; all things were created by him and for him.

As one with the Father, Jesus was involved in the creation of this world. (See John 1:1-3.) This verse counters the Gnostic notion of the world's creation by an evil god. Notice also that Paul places Christ above all *thrones or powers or rulers or authorities*. These include the authorities *in heaven and on earth*. The reference to heavenly powers may reflect Paul's concern about the worship of angels within the Colossian church.

C. His Supremacy (vv. 17, 18)

17 He is before all things, and in him all things hold together.

Christ is not only superior in that he existed *before* the created world, but it is through him that the entire created world is sustained. Jesus is the "glue" of this universe. If not for Jesus, there would be chaos.

18 And he is the head of the body, the church; he is the beginning and the firstborn from among the dead, so that in everything he might have the supremacy.

Not only is Christ the head of the created world, but he is specifically *the head of the body, the church*. The idea of the church as a body with Jesus as the head is one of Paul's favorite images of the church. It has been wisely said that the church is not just an organization; it is an organism.

Whereas Jesus was described as "the firstborn over all creation" in verse 15 (indicating his supremacy as creator of all things), here he is called *the firstborn from among the dead*. This is obviously referring to his resurrection. Jesus raised certain individuals from the dead; however, they were brought back in their physical bodies and eventually died again. Jesus was the first to rise from the dead, never to die again. Because he is "the firstfruits of those who have fallen asleep" (1 Corinthians 15:20), it is the "blessed hope" (Titus 2:13) of all followers of Jesus to be resurrected and to be "clothed with . . . immortality" when he returns (1 Corinthians 15:51-54; Romans 8:11).

The resurrection is the primary reason that Jesus has been given *supremacy.* Paul says that Jesus was "declared with power to be the Son of God by his resurrection from the dead" (Romans 1:4).

II. Christ, Our Reconciler (Colossians 1:19, 20)
A. Possessing God's Fullness (v. 19)

19 For God was pleased to have all his fullness dwell in him,

The phrase *to have all his [God's] fullness dwell in him [Jesus]* refers to the incarnation of Christ. The Word through whom all things were created (John 1:1-3) "became flesh and made his dwelling among us. We have seen his glory, the glory of the One and Only, who came from the Father" (v. 14). This is another point at which Paul refutes the Gnostics' belief that Jesus was one of many spirit beings who came from God (cf. Colossians 1:15). *All* the fullness of God is found in Jesus—and in no one else!

B. Reconciling All Things (v. 20)

20 . . . and through him to reconcile to himself all things, whether things on earth or things in heaven, by making peace through his blood, shed on the cross.

This verse also calls attention to the purpose for which Jesus "became flesh": *to reconcile to himself all things.* The means of this reconciliation was *his blood, shed on the cross* (note the similarity to Ephesians 2:16). It is through Jesus' death and our acceptance that what happened there happened for us that we are able to be at *peace* with God.

Why does Paul mention both *things on earth* and *things in heaven* being reconciled? Probably he is indicating how far-reaching is the impact of Jesus' death. Just as "by him all things were created: things in heaven and on earth" (v. 16), now all things are reconciled to God by him. That "the whole creation" is affected by the work of Christ is clear from Romans 8:19-22. Again, Paul's words are similar to his teaching in Ephesians: that God will one day "bring all things in heaven and on earth together under one head, even Christ" (1:10).

THE SECOND COMING OF CHRIST (1 THESSALONIANS 4:13-18)

Establishing the Groundwork

Thessalonica was a city of some 200,000 residents, located about 100 miles west of Philippi in the Roman province of Macedonia. Paul, Silas, and Timothy arrived there on Paul's second missionary journey after their tumultuous experience in Philippi (Acts 16:11-40). What transpired in Thessalonica is recorded in Acts 17:1-9.

It is hard to know how long Paul and his companions were in Thessalonica, but they were there long enough for the following to occur: (1) they established a viable church and built some lasting friendships (1 Thessalonians 1:2-4); (2) Paul established himself in a self-sustaining occupation (1 Thessalonians 2:9); and (3) Paul received financial gifts at least twice from the Philippian Christians (Philippians 4:16).

Paul became deeply concerned for the welfare of the Thessalonian church and desired to visit there (1 Thessalonians 2:17, 18). When those plans did not materialize, he sent Timothy so that he could encourage the believers and then report to Paul on their condition (1 Thessalonians 3:1-8). Paul was in Athens when he dispatched Timothy on this mission (3:1, 2). His good news regarding the Thessalonians' continued faithfulness in the face of persecution (1 Thessalonians 3:6-8) was most encouraging to Paul. The report also seems to have included bad news of the Jews' ongoing campaign to discredit the church by slandering those who had first brought the gospel to Thessalonica.

One area in which instruction was especially needed concerned the Thessalonians' understanding of the second coming of Christ. Every one of the five chapters in 1 Thessalonians closes with a reference to Christ's return. A critical misunderstanding that Paul had to address was the fear that anyone who died before Jesus' return would have no part in that glorious occasion. The passage included in this study was written to correct that error.

First Thessalonians is one of the earliest writings that are part of the New Testament. The year was approximately AD 52; the place of writing was most likely Corinth.

Examining the Text

I. Emphasis on Christ's Return (1 Thessalonians 4:13-17)
A. Source of Hope (vv. 13, 14)

13 Brothers, we do not want you to be ignorant about those who fall asleep, or to grieve like the rest of men, who have no hope.

Paul was not willing to leave the Thessalonians *ignorant* on such an important topic as the return of Jesus. The phrase *those who fall asleep* refers to those who have died. It suggests rest from one's labors and the expectation of resurrection.

Paul's words are not meant to speak against grieving for those who have died. Even Jesus wept at the tomb of Lazarus (John 11:35). There is a great difference, however, between the bitter emptiness of those who can see nothing beyond a final heartbeat, and those whose faith in Jesus provides an infinitely joyous expectation of a new beginning. The sorrow of the latter group is vastly different in every way from those *who have no hope*. Such a difference, when exhibited in circumstances of death or suffering, can provide a persuasive testimony to the power of Christian faith.

14 We believe that Jesus died and rose again and so we believe that God will bring with Jesus those who have fallen asleep in him.

Here Paul begins to address the primary question troubling the Thessalonians. What had become, and what would become, of those who had already died in Christ? The answer is this: *God will bring with Jesus those who have fallen asleep in him*.

This statement can be understood one of two ways. The first possibility is that *those who have fallen asleep in* Jesus will be included among those "holy ones" who will return with Jesus when he comes (1 Thessalonians 3:13). The second possibility involves taking the word *bring* to refer to what will happen to the dead after Jesus has returned; that is, God will *bring* them back to Heaven with Jesus. With either understanding comes the assurance that the future of those who die in Christ is secure. Believing that God will bring Christians from the grave is surely not difficult after knowing that he has brought Jesus from the tomb.

B. Series of Events (vv. 15-17)

15 According to the Lord's own word, we tell you that we who are still alive, who are left till the coming of the Lord, will certainly not precede those who have fallen asleep.

The highest possible authority is cited for Paul's declaration in this verse: *the Lord's own word*. This likely came, either by some otherwise unrecorded teaching of Jesus during his earthly ministry (compare the statement of Jesus mentioned in Acts 20:35) or by direct revelation to Paul himself (Galatians 1:11, 12; 2:2; Ephesians 3:3).

The word is this: at *the coming of the Lord*, those *who are still alive* will *certainly not precede those who have already fallen asleep* in Christ. Thus, those Christians who have died will share fully in the glory of Christ's return; they will not miss out on any of the benefit.

Some have claimed that this statement shows that Paul believed that the return of Jesus would take place in his lifetime. However, it is more accurate to say that he believed that it *could* take place in his lifetime; on the other hand, were Paul to die before that day, he was perfectly content to "depart and be with Christ" (Philippians 1:23).

> [16] *For the Lord himself will come down from heaven, with a loud command, with the voice of the archangel and with the trumpet call of God, and the dead in Christ will rise first.*

The Lord himself will come down from heaven, fulfilling what the angels had spoken at the time of his ascension (Acts 1:10, 11). The *loud command* is like the bold command of an officer addressing his troops. Thus did Jesus command Lazarus to come forth from the grave (John 11:43). It is also possible that the shout will come from the *archangel*, heralding the coming of Jesus. (The only named archangel in the Bible is Michael, mentioned in Jude 9.) The trumpet call of God will call forth those who have died (1 Corinthians 15:52). The *dead in Christ* will be *in Christ* as surely in death as they were in life. Death cannot separate anyone from the love of God (Romans 8:38, 39).

> [17] *After that, we who are still alive and are left will be caught up together with them in the clouds to meet the Lord in the air. And so we will be with the Lord forever.*

The spirits of those who have died in Christ will have been alive all the time, although absent from their bodies (see 2 Corinthians 5:8; Philippians 1:23, 24). At Christ's return, their bodies will arise and be clothed with immortality (1 Corinthians 15:53). These saints will thus be prepared to "inherit the kingdom of God" (v. 50). They will then be joined by the saints *who are still alive and who are left*, but who will be instantly changed into their glorified spiritual bodies (vv. 51, 52). Together, both the dead and the living will *meet the Lord in the air* and *will be with the Lord forever!*

II. Encouragement to Believers (1 Thessalonians 4:18)

> [18] *Therefore encourage each other with these words.*

It is not enough for the *words* of Scripture to instruct, establish, and encourage the people who read them. Those same Scriptures are to be shared, reviewed, and discussed in gatherings of the church (Hebrews 10:25) and in personal contacts, so that all may be encouraged by their message. Let us use these words to quiet anxieties over the situation of departed saints, to strengthen faith in the promises of God, and to *encourage* the kind of living that prepares us to receive those promises.

How to Say It

AGABUS. *Ag*-uh-bus.

BEREANS. Buh-*ree*-unz.

COLOSSE. Ko-*lahss*-ee.

COLOSSIANS. Kuh-*losh*-unz.

DEUTERONOMY. Due-ter-*ahn*-uh-me.

DOXOLOGY. dox-*ahl*-uh-jee.

EPAPHRAS. *Ep*-uh-frass.

EPAPHRODITUS. Ee-*paf*-ro-*dye*-tus (strong accent on *dye)*.

EPHESIANS. Ee-*fee*-zhunz.

GNOSTIC. *Nahss*-tick.

GNOSTICISM. *Nahss*-tih-*sizz*-um (strong accent on *Nahss*).

HADES. *Hay*-deez.

IMMANUEL. Ih-*man*-you-el.

INCARNATION. *in*-car-*nay*-shun (strong accent on *nay*).

MACEDONIA. Mass-eh-*doe*-nee-uh.

ONESIMUS. O-*ness*-ih-muss.

PHILEMON. Fih-*lee*-mun or Fye-*lee*-mun.

PHILIPPI. Fih-*lip*-pie or *Fil*-ih-pie.

SILAS. *Sigh*-luss.

THESSALONICA. *Thess*-uh-lo-*nye*-kuh (strong accent on *nye*; *th* as in *thin*).

TIMOTHY. *Tim*-o-thee (*th* as in *thin*).

TYCHICUS. *Tick*-ih-cuss.

TYRANNUS. Ty-*ran*-nus.

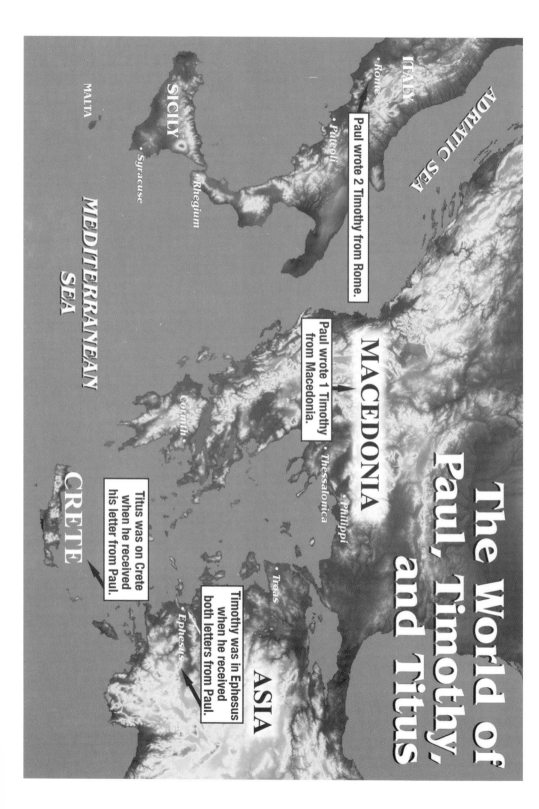

The World of Paul, Timothy, and Titus

Paul wrote 2 Timothy from Rome.

Paul wrote 1 Timothy from Macedonia.

Titus was on Crete when he received his letter from Paul.

Timothy was in Ephesus when he received both letters from Paul.

ADRIATIC SEA

ITALY
• Rome
• Puteoli

SICILY
• Syracuse
• Rhegium

MALTA

MEDITERRANEAN SEA

MACEDONIA
• Thessalonica
• Philippi

• Corinth

• Troas

CRETE

• Ephesus

ASIA

Chapter 11

Staying the Course in Trying Times: Studies in 1 and 2 Timothy and Hebrews

1 Timothy 3:1-13; 2 Timothy 3:10-17; 4:1-8;
Hebrews 1:1-4; 2:5-18; 11:1-6

QUALIFICATIONS OF LEADERS IN THE CHURCH (1 TIMOTHY 3:1-13)

Establishing the Groundwork

Apparently 1 Timothy was written after Paul's period of "house arrest" in Rome (Acts 28:16, 30, 31) had ended, which would have been in the year AD 63. (That Paul expected to be released from this imprisonment may be seen from his statements in Philippians 1:19, 25.) Paul then resumed his travels, visiting such places as Macedonia, from which he seems to have written 1 Timothy (1 Timothy 1:3). He may even have made his way to Spain, fulfilling a desire he had expressed in Romans 15:24, 28.

During this period of time, Paul would have written the letter to Titus as well as 1 Timothy. First Timothy may be dated in the year AD 65, with Titus being written the same year or possibly the next. Both of these letters, along with 2 Timothy, are commonly referred to as Pastoral Epistles. The pastoral tone is especially apparent in 1 Timothy and Titus (the surroundings from which Paul wrote 2 Timothy were quite different as we will note in the introduction to that letter). Both letters include instructions, warnings, and counsel appropriate for someone in a pastoral setting. For example, both 1 Timothy and Titus contain the qualifications for leaders in the Lord's church (1 Timothy 3:1-13; Titus 1:5-9). Paul's counsel to Timothy on this issue comprises the first passage drawn from the Pastoral Epistles for this study.

Examining the Text

I. Qualifications of Elders (1 Timothy 3:1-7)

Perhaps the most crucial position of leadership described in the New Testament is that of elder. This office is also known as an "overseer." The Greek words *presbyteros* (translated "elder") and *episkopos* (translated "overseer") are both used in describing this office in Acts 20:17, 28 and Titus 1:5, 7.

In 1 Timothy 3:1-7, Paul gives a list of qualifications that provide a profile of an exemplary Christian leader. Some are very similar to one another and therefore related. There is also a great deal of overlap, as previously noted, with Titus 1:5-9.

A. Having the Desire (v. 1)

¹ Here is a trustworthy saying: If anyone sets his heart on being an overseer, he desires a noble task.

When Paul cites this *trustworthy saying*, is he quoting an old adage, quoting a previous teaching of his own with which Timothy is familiar, or creating a new saying as he writes? We cannot be sure. What is most important is the truthfulness of the saying itself: it is indeed *a noble task* to function as a Christian leader. It is possible for someone acting out of purely selfish ambition (Luke 22:24-27) to set *his heart on being an overseer,* but that is not the humble desire and willingness to shepherd the Lord's flock that Paul is commending.

B. Blameless and Faithful (vv. 2a, 2b)

²ᵃ Now the overseer must be above reproach,

The general idea of being *above reproach* cannot, of course, be taken as an absolute—otherwise we would expect leaders to be perfect! It is more the idea that no one should look at a prospective elder and think, "Oh, no! Not him!" Perhaps what Paul specifically means by *above reproach* can be found in the list that follows.

²ᵇ . . . the husband of but one wife,

This phrase has sparked much debate. Most students agree that it means that an elder must be, or must have been, married. Is Paul making that an absolute requirement? If so, neither he nor Jesus could have been an elder. (And, of course, neither of them was an elder!) There is no doubt that some qualities of pastoral care are learned best in the context of family life.

What about those who were once married but are no longer? Very few believe that Paul meant to exclude widowers. Literally, *husband of but one wife* is a "one-wife man" or even a "one-woman [kind of] man." (The word for *wife* in the Greek is simply the word for "woman.") We can be certain that a bigamist or a man with a mistress could not be considered. The issue the church struggles with today is whether or not a divorced man may be an elder. If we take this phrase to mean "a one-woman [kind of] man," then the issue is the man's own personal faithfulness. Even if a man's wife has been unfaithful, *he* may still very well be a one-woman man.

Many churches look at this issue on a case-by-case basis. What is indisputable is that the quality of a person's marriage affects his ability to lead.

C. Disciplined and Hospitable (vv. 2c, 2d)

2c . . . temperate, self-controlled, respectable,

This verse continues with virtues that almost speak for themselves. Being *temperate* and *self-controlled* both point to the ability to control one's desires. (See also Titus 1:8.) *Respectable* includes the idea of living an honorable life.

2d . . . hospitable,

To be *hospitable* literally means to be a "lover of strangers." It refers to the willingness to give food or shelter to travelers or visitors. In New Testament times, traveling prophets and evangelists were in particular need of such hospitality.

D. Able to Communicate the Scriptures (v. 2e)

2e . . . able to teach,

Being *able to teach* does not require an elder to be a distinguished orator or dynamic speaker. But he should be capable of communicating the Scriptures. The phrase does not explain the precise way in which this is to be done. It may be in a public or private setting. Some teachers may feel more comfortable in one setting than the other, and it is certainly helpful if a church has elders who are able to teach in either environment.

E. Self-controlled (v. 3)

3 . . . not given to drunkenness, not violent but gentle, not quarrelsome, not a lover of money.

Wine was common in the ancient world, and its dangers were well known then as now. Passages such as Proverbs 21:17; 23:20, 21, 29-32 are very clear on the dangers of alcohol. There are practical and spiritual reasons for modern Christians to practice total abstinence, but that subject is not addressed here. Paul's restriction logically may be extended to all unhealthy addictions to the various legal and illegal drugs that we hear about in news reports every day.

There is a certain overlap between the ideas of being *violent* and *quarrelsome,* and the latter can lead to the former. We perhaps should not see these ideas as unconnected from the discussion of drunkenness earlier in this verse when we consider that those who abuse alcohol are frequently the ones who get into fights.

Someone who is *a lover of money* undoubtedly is in violation of the Tenth Commandment (Exodus 20:17). We should be careful to remember that the acquisition of wealth is not a sin in and of itself. But both those who need money and those who already have plenty are in danger of developing a sinful attitude. (See 1 Timothy 6:10.)

F. Orderly Family (vv. 4, 5)

4, 5 He must manage his own family well and see that his children obey him with proper respect. (If anyone does not know how to manage his own family, how can he take care of God's church?)

Once again there is a point of controversy here. Does this verse mean that the elder must have *children,* or is Paul simply discussing the typical or normal situation? There are men today who will not allow themselves to be considered for the office of elder because they take what Paul says quite literally.

It is certainly true that lessons learned from managing one's *own family* can affect how well a man serves as an elder. If a church leader has not displayed leadership in his home, he will find it difficult to exercise leadership in the *church.* Many leadership and interpersonal skills learned in the home will apply to work in the church.

G. Spiritual Maturity (v. 6)

6 He must not be a recent convert, or he may become conceited and fall under the same judgment as the devil.

The danger of selecting a *recent convert* to be an elder is quite clear, and the Bible talks about the issue of pride (being *conceited*) in numerous places (see Proverbs 11:2; 13:10; 16:18; Romans 12:16). Spiritually mature believers truly know what it means to bear the responsibility of being an elder. This knowledge will create the humility that a leader needs.

H. Good Reputation (v. 7)

7 He must also have a good reputation with outsiders, so that he will not fall into disgrace and into the devil's trap.

Leaders should be respected. This should be true not just among Christians, but also by the community as a whole. Can the church really have a good witness if its leaders are known scoundrels?

The devil's trap is probably the sin of pride (note verse 6). It is assumed that the besetting sin of the devil, the sin that caused him to be cast from Heaven, was pride.

II. Qualifications of Deacons (1 Timothy 3:8-13)

Another important office in the New Testament church was that of deacon. This comes from a Greek word that can mean "servant" in a general sense, but in certain contexts it refers to a specific office of the church. At some point in the expansion of first-century Christianity, local churches came to have both elders (or overseers) and deacons (see Philippians 1:1).

Many students think that the very first deacons are listed in Acts 6:1-6, although the specific word *deacon* does not occur there. Many of the qualifications of a deacon overlap with the qualifications of an elder, so it will not be necessary to discuss those that are repeated.

A. Respectable and Sincere (v. 8a)

⁸ᵃ Deacons, likewise, are to be men worthy of respect, sincere,

An important way for a deacon to become *worthy of respect* is by conducting himself with dignity. A godly deacon is also *sincere*; he is not someone who says one thing to one person and something completely different to another.

B. Self-controlled (v. 8b)

⁸ᵇ . . . not indulging in much wine, and not pursuing dishonest gain.

See the previous discussion of verse 3. Although elders have the greater authority, deacons must meet the same high standards.

C. Having a Pure Conscience (v. 9)

⁹ They must keep hold of the deep truths of the faith with a clear conscience.

The deep truths that were a great mystery to those who lived in Old Testament times have now been more fully revealed as the gospel of Christ (Romans 16:25, 26). What was once hidden is now made known (Colossians 1:26). Paul desperately wants all believers to know these truths (Ephesians 3:1-6). Deacons need to understand these great *truths of the faith* and believe them *with a clear conscience.*

D. Tested (v. 10)

¹⁰ They must first be tested; and then if there is nothing against them, let them serve as deacons.

Some students think that the idea of *being tested* suggests that an apprenticeship for deacons is appropriate. Whatever means of testing is used, the end result must be that *nothing* is able to be said *against* potential deacons—the same requirement for potential elders (see the comments on verse 2).

E. Family Conduct (vv. 11-13)

11 In the same way, their wives are to be women worthy of respect, not malicious talkers but temperate and trustworthy in everything.

The conduct of a potential deacon's wife will reveal the quality of his home life. As with an elder, a deacon is very unlikely to be able to take care of the church if his home life is chaotic (see the comments on verse 4 and the comments on the following two verses).

12, 13 A deacon must be the husband of but one wife and must manage his children and his household well. Those who have served well gain an excellent standing and great assurance in their faith in Christ Jesus.

Again, the ideas here mirror what Paul has already said about elders in verse 4. After reminding Timothy that deacons are also to be good husbands and fathers, Paul commends deacons for their significant work. Does the mention of an *excellent standing and great assurance* speak to the deacon's being respected in the eyes of God, the eyes of the church, or the eyes of the community? It could be all three.

We should pause to note that there is nothing in these verses to indicate that the office of *deacon* is to be considered some kind of stepping-stone to the office of elder. Some might remain deacons for the rest of their lives. Each office has a purpose in the church. The two have different functions, but both are important.

ENCOURAGEMENT TO REMAIN FAITHFUL (2 TIMOTHY 3:10-17)

Establishing the Groundwork

In the "Establishing the Groundwork" section of the previous passage, it was noted that 1 Timothy and Titus were written fairly close to each other, likely within a year of each other. The third of the Pastoral Epistles, 2 Timothy, was written some time later, perhaps in the year AD 67. By this time, the Roman emperor Nero had intensified his persecution of Christians. Paul probably was arrested as a consequence of these efforts.

Chronologically, 2 Timothy is the last of Paul's epistles in the New Testament. He speaks forthrightly about his impending death in 2 Timothy 4:6-8 and urges Timothy to come to him quickly (v. 9), pleading "Do your best to get here before winter" (v. 21). Conditions were far different in this imprisonment in Rome from what they were during Paul's earlier "house arrest," when Paul was allowed to have frequent visitors (Acts 28:30, 31). During this second imprisonment, one of Paul's friends had difficulty even locating him (2 Timothy 1:17). Paul asked for his cloak (4:13), perhaps because of the damp conditions in which he was being kept. Yet, in spite of the dismal surroundings, Paul's faith and hope in Jesus Christ were as vibrant as ever. He did not view himself as facing death, but rather a "departure" (v. 6) as he prepared to leave this world and receive "the crown of righteousness" (v. 8).

Of course, Paul also wrote to encourage Timothy not to allow his own faith to waver, regardless of what was happening to Paul. Timothy must speak boldly and without shame (1:8). He must keep "the pattern of sound teaching" (1:13). He must be strong and endure hardship (2:1-3). He must remember that Jesus was raised from the dead and that his persecuted people will be as well (2:8, 11). He must do his best to correctly handle the word of truth (2:15).

The power of that word of truth as found in the Scriptures is the subject of the first passage to be examined from this letter.

Examining the Text

I. Learning from Paul (2 Timothy 3:10-13)
A. Sufferings of Paul (vv. 10, 11)

10 You, however, know all about my teaching, my way of life, my purpose, faith, patience, love, endurance,

Paul did not expect to be on earth to guide Timothy much longer (2 Timothy 4:6-8). He wanted this young man to remember and follow the example that Paul had given in past years. First, Paul mentions his *teaching*. Timothy must remember the "sound teaching" he had heard from Paul (1:13) and pass it on to "reliable men who will be qualified to teach others" (2:2).

In his *way of life*, Paul had always tried to please the Lord (2 Corinthians 5:9). Timothy must make that his passion as well. Paul's *purpose* included a number of goals: to do God's will, to preach the gospel where it had not been heard before (Romans 15:20), and to win the prize for which God had called him in Christ (Philippians 3:12-14).

Faith can describe personal belief, faithfulness, or a system of doctrines (as in Jude 3). Paul's *patience* in the midst of his many sufferings for Christ (which he will describe further in verse 11) and in confronting the frequent criticism that he received would have been well known to Timothy. There is little difference between patience and *endurance*; perhaps patience describes Paul's attitude toward difficult people, while endurance refers to his ability to handle circumstances in a Christ-honoring way. Timothy should determine that he will be no less faithful during whatever trials he may experience. *Love* is the trademark that should characterize any follower of Jesus (John 13:35), but especially those who lead his church.

> *11 . . . persecutions, sufferings—what kinds of things happened to me in Antioch, Iconium and Lystra, the persecutions I endured. Yet the Lord rescued me from all of them.*

Paul had become acquainted with Timothy in *Lystra* (which was probably Timothy's hometown), where Paul was stoned by hostile opponents and left for dead (Acts 14:19). *Antioch* (of Pisidia) and *Iconium* were nearby cities, visited by Paul during his first missionary journey (Acts 13:14, 51). Angry protesters had driven Paul out of those towns as well (Acts 13:50; 14:5, 6). Timothy was aware of these *persecutions*. He would need courage to endure similar *sufferings*. He could take heart from Paul's reassuring words: *The Lord rescued me from all of them.*

B. Sufferings of All Christians (vv. 12, 13)

> *12 In fact, everyone who wants to live a godly life in Christ Jesus will be persecuted,*

Jesus had warned his disciples, "If they persecuted me, they will persecute you also" (John 15:20). The persecution of Christians did not begin with the Roman emperor Nero. All the sufferings mentioned by Paul in 2 Corinthians 11:24-27 occurred at earlier times. Still earlier, Paul himself had been one of the persecutors of Christians, when he was known as Saul (Acts 8:3). It appears that Christians were *persecuted* to some extent in most places (1 Thessalonians 2:14, 15; Hebrews 10:32-34; James 1:2). Timothy could expect his share of persecution as well, but that must not deter him from the goal of living *a godly life in Christ Jesus.*

> *13 . . . while evil men and impostors will go from bad to worse, deceiving and being deceived.*

The presence of Christianity will not make *evil* people better if they do not want to be made better. The presence of the Christian witness may simply make such people more determined to go *from bad to worse*. Not only will these people be *deceived*, they will deceive others. The ability to lie to others and to themselves seems to characterize evil people.

II. Learning from Scripture (2 Timothy 3:14-17)
A. Trustworthy Teachers (v. 14)

14 But as for you, continue in what you have learned and have become convinced of, because you know those from whom you learned it,

Paul's charge to Timothy was to *continue in what* he had *learned* and was *convinced of*. Timothy would be encouraged to do this as he remembered who had taught him. His grandmother Lois and his mother Eunice had been godly examples, and he had learned much from them (2 Timothy 1:5). Timothy may have been led to faith in Christ by Paul; if not, he certainly was mentored by the apostle and encouraged to grow in his faith. Timothy could depend on the teaching he had received from these sources.

B. Trustworthy Teachings (vv. 15-17)

15 . . . and how from infancy you have known the holy Scriptures, which are able to make you wise for salvation through faith in Christ Jesus.

Timothy's grandmother and mother had likely instilled within him a knowledge of the *Scriptures*, which helped prepare him to understand later their fulfillment in *Jesus* (see John 5:39). Today our Scriptures include both Old and New Testaments, and they are still able to *make* the earnest reader *wise for salvation through faith in Christ Jesus.*

16 All Scripture is God-breathed and is useful for teaching, rebuking, correcting and training in righteousness,

All Scripture ultimately comes from *God*. Working through human writers, God was the author and source. Second Peter 1:21 tells us, "Men spoke from God as they were carried along by the Holy Spirit." We can take comfort in the fact that "the Scripture cannot be broken" (John 10:35).

Scripture is valuable in so many ways! Nothing can match the Bible as a source of *teaching* about God and man, sin and salvation, righteousness and truth. It also provides *rebuking* and *correcting* to guard us against wrong, misguided teachings. Ultimately Scripture provides *training in righteousness* so that we can both live and think as God desires.

17 . . . so that the man of God may be thoroughly equipped for every good work.

While Paul's concerns in this letter were primarily for Timothy, what he says about the purpose of Scripture applies to every follower of Jesus. When he states that the purpose of Scripture is to make us *thoroughly equipped for every good work*, he means that the Scripture provides all we need to become mature Christians and to become what God created us to be.

PREACH THE WORD (2 TIMOTHY 4:1-8)

Establishing the Groundwork

We may refer to the closing chapter of 2 Timothy as Paul's "farewell address." There we learn that no one was with Paul except for Luke (2 Timothy 4:11). Some of his companions apparently had been sent away to carry out other tasks in the Lord's service. He encourages Timothy to bring John Mark, the former "deserter" (Acts 13:13; 15:37, 38) whom Paul now saw as "helpful" in his ministry (2 Timothy 4:11). A tragic note surrounds the absence of Demas, who had deserted Paul "because he loved this world" (v. 10). While urging Timothy to join him in Rome and to "get here before winter" (v. 21), Paul also encouraged his "dear son" (1:2) to remain faithful in his ministry.

Examining the Text

I. Paul's Charge to Timothy (2 Timothy 4:1-5)
A. Crucial Task (vv. 1, 2)

¹ In the presence of God and of Christ Jesus, who will judge the living and the dead, and in view of his appearing and his kingdom, I give you this charge:

Paul gives to Timothy the solemn *charge* of faithfully carrying out his ministry. This sacred responsibility is not based on any personal whim. It is made *in the presence of God and of Christ Jesus*; it is based on the highest authority.

Numerous passages in the New Testament declare that Jesus will judge the world (both *the living and the dead*) when he returns (Matthew 25:31-33; John 5:22, 25-27; Acts 10:40-42; Romans 2:16; 2 Corinthians 5:10). *His appearing* refers to that return. That event will signal the consummation of Christ's *kingdom*. All Christians are in that kingdom now (Colossians 1:13); they look forward to its magnificent, heavenly fulfillment (2 Timothy 4:18; 2 Peter 1:10, 11).

² Preach the Word; be prepared in season and out of season; correct, rebuke and encourage—with great patience and careful instruction.

The charge to *preach the word* must be carried out not only when it is convenient to do so, but always. To *be prepared in season and out of season* means that Timothy should be prepared to preach the Word at all times, whether it is convenient or not.

Notice that preaching the Word includes the responsibilities to *correct, rebuke and encourage*. There are preachers who specialize in correcting and rebuking, but rarely do any encouraging. Others encourage but never rebuke. Biblical preaching requires that we do both. And just as God has shown *great patience* to us (2 Peter 3:9), so our preaching is to be done with patience.

B. Coming Times (vv. 3, 4)

³ For the time will come when men will not put up with sound doctrine. Instead, to suit their own desires, they will gather around them a great number of teachers to say what their itching ears want to hear.

The phrase *the time will come* seems reminiscent of Paul's words about the "last days," beginning in 2 Timothy 3:1. It should be recognized, however, that a lack of sound doctrine has always been a problem against which the church has had to struggle. Acts 20:29, 30 records Paul's words to the elders of the church at Ephesus, warning them that "from your own number men will arise and distort the truth in order to draw away disciples after them."

⁴ They will turn their ears away from the truth and turn aside to myths.

Paul had previously issued warnings about *myths* to both Timothy (1 Timothy 4:7) and Titus (Titus 1:14). During the period of time between the Old and New Testaments, Jewish writers had created many fanciful tales. Greek myths went back even farther than that. But the New Testament writers always insisted that their teachings rested on historical foundations, unlike myths and legends. If Jesus did not actually live, die, and rise from the dead, what hope do we have? (See 1 Corinthians 15:12-19.)

C. Consistent Temperament (v. 5)

⁵ But you, keep your head in all situations, endure hardship, do the work of an evangelist, discharge all the duties of your ministry.

Once again, Paul cautions Timothy (as he had done previously in 1:8; 2:3; and 3:12) to be prepared to *endure hardship* as he carries out his *ministry*. The *work of an evangelist* is to share the good news of salvation with sinners, in order to bring them into a saving relationship with Jesus Christ. While some may indeed be specially gifted to carry on this responsibility, evangelism should be the concern of every Christian.

II. Paul's Acceptance of Death (2 Timothy 4:6-8)
A. His Awareness (v. 6)

⁶ For I am already being poured out like a drink offering, and the time has come for my departure.

The expression *being poured out like a drink offering* calls to mind certain practices under the Old Testament law. When an animal was offered on the altar, a vessel of wine was poured out as the final act of the sacrificial ceremony (Numbers 15:1-10). By using this figure, Paul was indicating that the final act of his personal living sacrifice (Romans 12:1) to Jesus had begun. As Paul had offered his life to Jesus, he now offered his death in one final expression of devotion.

The word *departure* was an especially meaningful way for Paul to view his death. The Greek word was used of loosing the harness of an animal that had been yoked for working in the fields. It was used of loosing the moorings of a vessel that had been in port. It was also used of a soldier tearing down his tent so that he could embark on a march. Paul was prepared to rest from his labors for Christ and ready to set out on the journey that would lead him into Christ's presence.

B. His Achievement (v. 7)

⁷ I have fought the good fight, I have finished the race, I have kept the faith.

Here, as in his other writings, Paul uses language drawn from the athletic arena and from the battlefield (see 1 Corinthians 9:24-27; Ephesians 6:10-18). The phrase *fought the good fight* probably would have called the attention of Paul's readers to a wrestling or boxing match, or perhaps a contest between gladiators. Paul had *finished the race*; he was now in a position to receive the "prize" to which he had alluded during his earlier imprisonment in Rome (Philippians 3:14).

Keeping *the faith* may refer to Paul's faithful proclamation of the gospel and the "sound teaching" that he had encouraged Timothy to "keep" (2 Timothy 1:13). He may also be alluding to his personal commitment to the task that Jesus had given him to be his messenger to the Gentiles (Acts 9:15; 22:21). In spite of the warning that accepting this call would mean much suffering (Acts 9:16), Paul had accepted the call and had never looked back.

C. His Assurance (v. 8)

⁸ Now there is in store for me the crown of righteousness, which the Lord, the righteous Judge, will award to me on that day—and not only to me, but also to all who have longed for his appearing.

The word rendered *crown* does not refer to the gem-encrusted symbol of royalty, but to the simple laurel wreath that was awarded to a victorious athlete. The *crown of righteousness* was much more than a simple wreath of leaves. It symbolized eternal life (Revelation 2:10) and would never wither or fade, as the athlete's crown eventually would. Whereas in most races there is only one winner, in the Christian race there are many winners. Paul knew that he had no exclusive claim on the crown of righteousness; it is reserved for *all who have longed for* Christ's *appearing*.

THE SUPERIORITY OF THE SON (HEBREWS 1:1-4)

Establishing the Groundwork

Commentators have suggested that the epistle to the Hebrews "begins like a treatise, proceeds like a sermon, and closes like a letter." While some controversy has surrounded this book, it occupies a crucial place in the New Testament.

The main controversy concerning Hebrews deals with its authorship. Many have ascribed this book to Paul. However, unlike the epistles that bear Paul's name, Hebrews is unsigned. Nor can we give an exact date for its writing. It seems obvious, however, that it was written before AD 70. The Romans destroyed Jerusalem and the temple in that year, ending the worship services that had been conducted there. Had Hebrews been written after that date, the writer almost certainly would have mentioned the temple's destruction because of the book's various references to temple activities.

We are not told of the specific destination of this epistle. But clearly it seems to be aimed at Jewish Christians, specifically those then living in Palestine. The purpose of the letter was to encourage them to remain faithful in spite of the persecutions they had endured. The writer seems concerned that they might be tempted to abandon Christianity and return to Judaism. For that reason *better* is a key word throughout the letter. Christ is better than any of the forefathers who had spoken in the past (such as Moses) or the angels. Furthermore, Christians have a better hope (7:19), a better covenant based on better promises (8:6), a better sacrifice (9:23), and in Heaven a better inheritance (10:34).

Examining the Text

I. How God Has Spoken (Hebrews 1:1, 2)
A. In Past Days (v. 1)

¹ In the past God spoke to our forefathers through the prophets at many times and in various ways,

A fundamental proposition of both Judaism and Christianity is that *God has spoken* to the human race. Our God is not some remote, obscure deity who observes our activities from afar with little or no involvement.

The fact that God has spoken *at many times* means that he has never locked himself into a predictable timetable for his numerous revelations. But one thing is certain: he always has revealed himself when humanity has needed for him to do so. There have also been *various ways* through which God has spoken. He has, of course, used people *(the prophets)*—sometimes speaking to them in an audible voice, at other times through dreams or visions. But he has also used other means of communicating to the *forefathers*. He revealed his will through a burning bush (Exodus 3:2), through a pillar of fire and a pillar of cloud (Exodus 40:38), and even through a donkey (Numbers 22:22-35).

B. In These Last Days (v. 2)

² . . . but in these last days he has spoken to us by his Son, whom he appointed heir of all things, and through whom he made the universe.

Frequently the Bible divides the history of God's redemptive work into two segments of time. The Old Testament era is considered the "former days," or as in Hebrews 1:1, "in the past." The New Testament era, beginning with Christ's first coming and ending with his return, is viewed as the *last days*. For other uses of this phrase and similar terminology in the New Testament, see Acts 2:16, 17; 1 Corinthians 10:11; Hebrews 9:26; 1 Peter 1:20; and 1 John 2:18.

Jesus has been *appointed heir of all things*. We should not think of this inheritance as one in which the father must die before the son can receive it. This expression indicates the close relationship of the divine Son to the heavenly Father. One aspect of this kinship is the Son's participation in the creation of all things. This doctrine is stated, not only in this verse, but in other New Testament passages as well (see John 1:1-3; 1 Corinthians 8:6; Colossians 1:15-17).

II. How God's Son Is Superior (Hebrews 1:3, 4)
A. Who He Is (v. 3a)

³ᵃ The Son is the radiance of God's glory and the exact representation of his being, sustaining all things by his powerful word.

This statement summarizes some of the more important aspects of the relationship between the Father and *the Son* through a series of striking phrases. First, the Son is *the radiance of God's glory*. John 1:14 affirms this same idea: "We have seen his glory, the glory of the One and Only, who came from the Father."

Second, the Son is *the exact representation of* God's *being*, much as the image on a coin is an exact match of the image on the die. Hear Jesus' own words: "Anyone who has seen me has seen the Father" (John 14:9).

Furthermore, the Son is described as *sustaining all things by his powerful word.* Paul wrote to the Colossians that in Jesus, "all things hold together" (Colossians 1:17). He is not only the Creator; he is also the Sustainer.

B. What He Has Done (vv. 3b, 4)

³ᵇ After he had provided purification for sins, he sat down at the right hand of the Majesty in heaven.

The writer of Hebrews then notes that as majestic as the Son was, he humbled himself and came to earth for the purpose of providing *purification for sins.* Through his death on the cross he has paid the price required by God's holiness and justice (Romans 3:21-26). Once this mission was accomplished, *he sat down at the right hand of the Majesty in heaven*, indicating his eternal reign with the Father. That Jesus sat down, indicating his work was completed, will be contrasted later with the ministry of the Old Testament priest, who "day after day . . . stands and performs his religious duties" (Hebrews 10:11, 12).

⁴ So he became as much superior to the angels as the name he has inherited is superior to theirs.

During the centuries between the Old and New Testaments, Jewish writers created much speculation about the work of *angels.* Although angels are heavenly beings and are messengers for God, they are inferior to the Son. One clear point of evidence that this is so is that they have not received his more excellent *name*, that is, Son of God. The remainder of chapter 1 provides additional evidence of the Son's superiority.

CHRIST, THE AUTHOR OF OUR SALVATION (HEBREWS 2:5-18)

Establishing the Groundwork

With the portion of Hebrews covered in the following text, the writer takes a somewhat surprising turn. To this point, he has been providing evidence of Jesus' superiority. Now he begins to describe Jesus' humiliation. When Jesus became a human being, he was "made a little lower than the angels" (Hebrews 2:9). He became subject to the weaknesses of the flesh, including suffering and death. Therein lies part of the "mystery of godliness" (1 Timothy 3:16). It does not seem rational to the human mind that Jesus could be exalted by being humiliated through suffering and death, and yet that is the point of the following passage from Hebrews 2. The highest and mightiest laid aside his highness and mightiness to dwell among us, that he might triumph as the author of our salvation.

Examining the Text

I. Christ's Superiority (Hebrews 2:5-9)
A. The World's Subjection (v. 5)

⁵ It is not to angels that he has subjected the world to come, about which we are speaking.

The Son was involved in the creation of the physical world (John 1:3; Colossians 1:16; Hebrews 1:2). He also has power over *the world to come.* The writer of Hebrews is firmly convinced that when Christ came in the flesh, he inaugurated a new era. The new era will reach its fulfillment when Jesus returns in triumph to bring about the new heavens and new earth—the world to come. (See also Ephesians 1:20, 21; Revelation 21:1.) *Angels* are, and forever will be, involved and active in this new era, but there is no doubt that the Son is in charge.

B. The Psalmist's Testimony (vv. 6-8)

⁶⁻⁸ᵃ But there is a place where someone has testified:
"What is man that you are mindful of him,
the son of man that you care for him?
You made him a little lower than the angels;
you crowned him with glory and honor
and put everything under his feet."

To say *there is a place where someone has testified* may strike us as a strange way to quote Scripture. But we need to remember that in those days the Scriptures were not conveniently divided into chapters and verses as our Bibles are today. Furthermore, the readers would be familiar enough with this passage (which is taken from Psalm 8:4-6) that they did not need book, chapter, and verse references to recognize that it came from the Scriptures.

Many Bible students believe that this part of Psalm 8 has two "layers" of interpretation. First, the psalmist (David) speaks of man in the strictly human sense. In this sense the word *man* is generic, referring to males and females. At the same time, as verse 9 indicates, David was speaking prophetically of a specific man: the Messiah, who was to come. Jesus often used the title *son of man* to describe himself in the Gospels. The writer of Hebrews quotes from this section of Psalm 8 in a context that many believe maintains these same two "layers" of interpretation. First, it applies to Jesus, as can be seen from verse 9. At the same time the phrase "son of man" as used in Psalm 8:4 (and as reapplied here in Hebrews 2:6) can refer to mortals.

The question *What is man?* is just as relevant today as it was when it was originally written. Many today consider humans to be no more than the product of a long evolutionary process. But neither the psalmist nor the writer of Hebrews sees humanity that way. Humans have unique worth in God's sight. We are *a little lower than the angels* in that we are subject to some restrictions (such as death) that angels do not face while we are on the earth. Jesus took on these same limitations when he came as a man, making him also a little lower than the angels for a while.

However, there is more to the story. Being *lower than the angels* was a temporary condition for Jesus, and it is meant to be for us. After Christ's resurrection and ascension into Heaven, his earthly limitations disappeared when he was *crowned* with *glory and honor* and set over all the works of God's hands. We who are followers of Jesus await our transformation from "lowly bodies" to bodies "like his glorious body" (Philippians 3:20, 21).

> ⁸ᵇ *In putting everything under him, God left nothing that is not subject to him. Yet at present we do not see everything subject to him.*

On God's great, final day, the world will be in subjection to the redeemed of humanity (1 Corinthians 6:2, 3). Even so, all things ultimately will be subjected to Christ; *everything* will be put *under him.* Those final victories are not immediately obvious to us. Limited as we are by human frailties, it may appear to us that Satan is triumphant. The harmony God intended for human beings to enjoy has not yet been fully restored: *at present we do not see everything subject to* Christ.

C. Christ's Sacrifice (v. 9)

> ⁹ *But we see Jesus, who was made a little lower than the angels, now crowned with glory and honor because he suffered death, so that by the grace of God he might taste death for everyone.*

Much of the language here repeats that of verse 7. By coming in the flesh, Jesus was *made a little lower than the angels.* His humiliation became even greater when he *suffered death.* As a result of all this, he was *crowned with glory and honor.* Paul expresses this same idea of humiliation then exaltation in Philippians 2:8, 9.

Jesus' death had a specific purpose; it was a sacrificial *death for everyone*—for "the sins of the whole world" (1 John 2:2). As a result, we have a responsibility to share this good news of the *grace of God* with everyone.

II. Christ's Work and Position (Hebrews 2:10-18)
A. Work of Salvation (v. 10)

¹⁰ In bringing many sons to glory, it was fitting that God, for whom and through whom everything exists, should make the author of their salvation perfect through suffering.

God desired to create a family of *sons* who would one day dwell with him in glory. To accomplish this, *it was fitting* that he *make the author of their salvation perfect through suffering.* Of course, the idea of a suffering Messiah was repugnant to the Jews; Paul calls the crucifixion of Christ a "stumbling block" to them (1 Corinthians 1:23).

That Jesus was made *perfect through suffering* does not refer to moral perfection, because Jesus was without sin. The word translated here as perfect means "to bring to completion." It does not speak of Christ's character as much as it speaks of his calling. Until Jesus suffered and died, he was incomplete in the sense that his mission to save humanity had not been fulfilled.

B. Position of Brother (vv. 11-13)

¹¹ Both the one who makes men holy and those who are made holy are of the same family. So Jesus is not ashamed to call them brothers.

What a glorious truth to know that Jesus Christ considers us to be his *brothers!* Through his sacrifice for us, he gave us the opportunity to be *made holy,* or set apart for service to God. Being holy does not mean that one is perfect or never sins. It does mean that an individual has made a commitment to become more Christlike. This thought is captured in the phrase: "Not perfect, but progressing." No one is alone in seeking to attain this goal; all Christians are part of *the same family,* desiring to do all things to God's glory (1 Corinthians 10:31). We need to encourage one another continually in these efforts—a point the writer of Hebrews later makes (Hebrews 10:25).

¹², ¹³ He says,
"I will declare your name to my brothers;
in the presence of the congregation I will sing your praises."
And again,
"I will put my trust in him."

And again he says,
"Here am I, and the children God has given me."

The writer now uses three quotations from the Old Testament to show that God has always had a "family plan" in mind. The first comes from Psalm 22:22. Notice that the family relationship (*brothers*) that the writer introduces takes place in the context of the church (the *congregation*). It is significant to note that much of the first portion of this Psalm (vv. 1-21) provides details concerning the crucifixion of Christ (see especially verses 1, 7, 8, 15-18). With verse 22, quoted here, the Psalmist (David) begins to describe what the writer of Hebrews sees as the consequences of Christ's suffering. That suffering has been one of his primary themes in this passage (see verses 9 and 10).

C. Work of Destruction (vv. 14-16)

14 Since the children have flesh and blood, he too shared in their humanity so that by his death he might destroy him who holds the power of death— that is, the devil—

Our struggle with Satan is a spiritual struggle (Ephesians 6:12). But because we are made of *flesh and blood,* Satan directs many of his attacks upon us through the flesh. Thus if Christ was to be "tempted in every way, just as we are" (Hebrews 4:15), it was necessary that he join us in the flesh and share in our *humanity.*

Through his death and resurrection, Christ destroyed *the power of death* wielded by *the devil.* For this reason Paul can hail Christ's resurrection with these triumphant words: "Where, O death, is your victory? Where, O death, is your sting?" (1 Corinthians 15:55).

15 . . . and free those who all their lives were held in slavery by their fear of death.

People dread the idea of being *in slavery* or bondage. For many, death is the most feared slave master—feared because its bondage seems so final. But because of our Lord's victory over the devil, we can view death as a defeated enemy. Christ is now the one who holds the "keys of death and Hades" (Revelation 1:18).

16 For surely it is not angels he helps, but Abraham's descendants.

Christ's birth was heralded by *angels,* but he did not come as an angel. When Jesus was born, he came as a human being—specifically as a Jew and one of *Abraham's descendants.* Through Jesus, Christians are counted as "Abraham's seed" when they come to Jesus by faith (Galatians 3:29). The link with Abraham would have been important to the Jewish Christians addressed by the writer of Hebrews.

D. Position of High Priest (vv. 17, 18)

17 For this reason he had to be made like his brothers in every way, in order that he might become a merciful and faithful high priest in service to God, and that he might make atonement for the sins of the people.

The writer's thoughts now move to Jesus' ministry as our *high priest*, a topic he will develop in more detail shortly (see Hebrews 4:14–5:10; 8:1-6). In the Old Testament the high priest was selected from among the people; he was one of them (Hebrews 5:1). Since Jesus shared in our humanity (v. 14), he could be a *merciful* high priest, sympathetic to our weaknesses (Hebrews 4:15). He was *faithful* in two ways: *to God*, because he faithfully carried out the mission God sent him to accomplish, and to all *people*, for he faced death on the cross on their behalf and made *atonement* for their *sins*.

18 Because he himself suffered when he was tempted, he is able to help those who are being tempted.

Because Jesus *was tempted* "in every way, just as we are" (Hebrews 4:15), he can not only sympathize with us; *he is able to help* us when we are *tempted*. We are told of certain temptations that he faced (Matthew 4:1-11), but certainly there were many others. Indeed, because he was the Son of God, Jesus faced the full fury of Satan in a way that no human being can ever face. Because he passed successfully through the fires of temptation, he can now offer support to his people who face similar fires. What an encouragement to know that there is always "grace to help us in our time of need" (Hebrews 4:16)!

LIVING BY FAITH (HEBREWS 11:1-6)

Establishing the Groundwork

As noted previously, the author of Hebrews was writing to Jewish Christians who were in danger of abandoning their Christian faith and embracing Judaism once again. The author marshals several arguments to convince the readers to remain true to their Christian commitment. Frequent warnings are issued (2:1-4; 3:7-19; 6:4-6; and 10:26-31, for examples). He also demonstrates that the new covenant is better than the old in having a better high priest, a better sacrifice, and a better hope.

While we do not know all the reasons that the readers may have had for wanting to abandon Christianity, the fear of persecution or hardship is very likely. In Hebrews 10:32-39, the writer notes how initially these followers of Jesus had gladly endured hardship and deprivation for Jesus' sake. He encourages them to persevere and not to "throw away your confidence" (vv. 35, 36). In Hebrews 11 (the "faith chapter" of the Bible), the inspired writer turns to Jewish history to demonstrate that great heroes of the past had faced all kinds of challenges to their faith. But they had prevailed in spite of the danger.

Examining the Text

I. Elements of Faith (Hebrews 11:1-3)
A. Faith and Certainty (vv. 1, 2)

¹ Now faith is being sure of what we hope for and certain of what we do not see.

This is certainly one of the most important verses in the entire Bible. If we do not understand what *faith* is, we will forfeit our *hope* for the life to come. Faith as described here conveys the idea of confidence in what one believes. Faith is not just vague wishful thinking; it is the complete certainty that God's promises will be fulfilled.

² This is what the ancients were commended for.

The ancients were those who had lived in the past. They are probably the same as the "forefathers" mentioned in Hebrews 1:1. Not all of these *were commended*, however. Adam and Eve were expelled from the Garden of Eden for rebellion. Cain was the first murderer. But some were obedient and received God's blessings as a result. It was by faith that these were able to serve in such a way that they received God's approval.

B. Faith and Creation (v. 3)

³ By faith we understand that the universe was formed at God's command, so that what is seen was not made out of what was visible.

Some modern scientists scoff at the idea that *the universe was formed at God's command*. They insist that they alone can give us a scientific or "reasonable" explanation of its existence. For example, some propose the "Big Bang" theory for the beginnings of the universe. Even if this theory were true, it does not tell us where the original matter and energy came from to produce such a great explosion. At this point the scientist has to fall back on some kind of *faith* to tell us about the origins of matter and energy.

Since both Christians and non-Christians must rely on faith to answer these ultimate questions, we have a right to ask whose faith is more likely to be valid. Which is more reasonable: to have faith that the material used to form the universe somehow just "always existed," or to have faith in a God who is able to create from nothing? (See Romans 4:17.)

II. Examples of Faith (Hebrews 11:4-6)
A. Abel (v. 4)

⁴ By faith Abel offered God a better sacrifice than Cain did. By faith he was commended as a righteous man, when God spoke well of his offerings. And by faith he still speaks, even though he is dead.

The account of *Abel* and *Cain* is found in Genesis 4:1-15. Both brothers brought sacrifices to God. Cain brought "some of the fruits of the soil," while Abel brought "fat portions from some of the firstborn of his flocks" (vv. 3, 4). God accepted Abel's sacrifice, but rejected Cain's. This so angered Cain that he murdered his brother.

This verse gives us a clue regarding God's perspective on this incident. We are told that Abel offered *a better sacrifice* because he was *righteous.* It appears that the problem was not with the sacrifice itself, whether animal or grain. The important issue was that of attitude. Abel offered his sacrifice *by faith* with a humble heart, while Cain offered his grudgingly or arrogantly. As a result of his godly example, Abel *still speaks* to us *even though he* has been *dead* for thousands of years.

B. Enoch (vv. 5, 6)

⁵ By faith Enoch was taken from this life, so that he did not experience death; he could not be found, because God had taken him away. For before he was taken, he was commended as one who pleased God.

There are two men named *Enoch* in Genesis. Genesis 5:21-24 allows us to conclude that the Enoch being discussed was the son of Jared and the father of Methuselah. The most important information we learn about him in that passage is that he "walked with God" (v. 24). This is significant because in Enoch's day most people were walking away from God, not with him.

Enoch's *faith* is the reason the writer of Hebrews mentions him as an example. As a result of his faith, Enoch *did not experience death* in the usual sense, for "God took him away" (Genesis 5:24; compare the case of Elijah in 2 Kings 2:11).

⁶ And without faith it is impossible to please God, because anyone who comes to him must believe that he exists and that he rewards those who earnestly seek him.

Without faith in *God*, the heroes and heroines mentioned in Hebrews 11 would not have been pleasing to him, nor would they have been able to perform their heroic deeds. The twofold aspects of faith are reaffirmed here. Faith believes that God *exists*. Faith also provides a foundation for the confidence that God *rewards those who earnestly seek him.* What was true for these faithful men and women of old was true for the Jewish Christians in the first century, and it is also true for us today.

How to Say It

ABEL. *Ay*-buhl.

ANTIOCH. *An*-tee-ock.

CAIN. Cane.

DEMAS. *Dee*-mus.

ELIJAH. Ee-*lye*-juh.

ENOCH. *Ee*-nock.

EPISKOPOS *(Greek).* eh-*pis*-koh-poss.

EUNICE. U-*nye*-see or *U*-nis.

ICONIUM. Eye-*ko*-nee-um.

JARED. *Jair*-ud.

JUDAISM. *Joo*-duh-izz-um or *Joo*-day-izz-um.

LOIS. *Lo*-is.

LYSTRA. *Liss*-truh.

MACEDONIA. Mass-eh-*doe*-nee-uh.

METHUSELAH. Muh-*thoo*-zuh-luh (*th* as in *thin*).

PISIDIA. Pih-*sid*-ee-uh.

PRESBYTEROS *(Greek).* prez-*bew*-ter-oss.

Chapter 12

Putting Action to Our Faith:
Studies in James, 1 Peter, 2 Peter, and 1 John

James 1:19-27; 2:14-26; 1 Peter 2:1-10; 3:13-17;
2 Peter 3:1-10; 1 John 4:7-16

HEARING AND DOING (JAMES 1:19-27)

Establishing the Groundwork

Who was the James who wrote the letter that bears his name? Modestly he calls himself "a servant of God and of the Lord Jesus Christ" (James 1:1). Most likely he is "James, the Lord's brother" (Galatians 1:19). James is named first among Jesus' brothers in both Matthew (13:55) and Mark (6:3), perhaps indicating that he was the oldest of those siblings.

The Gospels indicate that after more than two years of miracles and teaching, Jesus' brothers still did not believe that he was the Christ (John 7:5). In fact, they did not become convinced until he rose from the dead. First Corinthians 15:7 mentions Jesus' appearance to James after his resurrection; and since James is mentioned in addition to the apostles, it is likely that this James is Jesus' brother. According to the book of Acts, Jesus' brothers were among those who were gathering to pray in Jerusalem after Jesus had ascended into Heaven (Acts 1:13, 14). Later, Paul named James along with two of the apostles as "pillars" of the church (Galatians 2:9). During an important doctrinal debate, it was James who stated the conclusion reached by the apostles, the elders, and the church at Jerusalem (Acts 15:13-29).

When we look at the book of James, then, we are seeing a letter from one of the strongest, wisest, and most trusted leaders of the first-century church in Jerusalem. He writes "to the twelve tribes scattered among the nations" (James 1:1), which is most likely a reference to Jewish Christians.

Examining the Text

I. The Need for Hearers (James 1:19-21)
A. General Principles (vv. 19, 20)

19 My dear brothers, take note of this: Everyone should be quick to listen, slow to speak and slow to become angry,

In James 1:18, James stated that God has given us spiritual birth through the word of truth. Since that is the case, verse 19 then stresses the importance of every person's being *quick to listen* to that word. This could also apply to our relationships with people. Many times we are all too slow to listen and quick to speak so that we can get our point across before others have the opportunity to do the same. However, we usually learn more when we are listening than when we are talking. James will have much more to say about the proper use of the tongue in James 3:1-12.

James also advises that we should be *slow to become angry*. One who speaks quickly is often quick to lose his temper. Frequently the wisdom of Proverbs supports James' counsel, as it does here in Proverbs 16:32: "Better a patient man than a warrior, a man who controls his temper than one who takes a city."

20 . . . for man's anger does not bring about the righteous life that God desires.

Man's anger does not lead him to become more *righteous*. Quite the contrary, it hinders one's spiritual growth. There is a time and a place for one to exhibit righteous indignation, but even those occasions need to be carefully examined to make sure that one's attitude and behavior honor God.

B. Specific Command (v. 21)

21 Therefore, get rid of all moral filth and the evil that is so prevalent and humbly accept the word planted in you, which can save you.

James urges his readers to *get rid of all moral filth* and *evil*. The verb *get rid of* literally means "to put off," as one would remove a dirty garment. Unless we are willing to do this, we cannot receive the *word* of God that he desires to become *planted* in our hearts. This word includes the message of salvation and provides all we need both to do and to become all that God wants us to do and be (see 2 Timothy 3:15).

II. The Need for Doers (James 1:22-25)
A. Command (v. 22)

22 Do not merely listen to the word, and so deceive yourselves. Do what it says.

Christian teaching is designed to plant God's Word into our minds and hearts (v. 21), to make it a vital part of our thinking and our emotions. But one is only deceiving himself if he thinks he is a good Christian when he has *the word* in his mind and heart but not in his hands and feet.

B. Comparison (vv. 23, 24)

23, 24 Anyone who listens to the word but does not do what it says is like a man who looks at his face in a mirror and, after looking at himself, goes away and immediately forgets what he looks like.

Usually you don't look in a *mirror* just for the privilege of admiring yourself for a few seconds. You look to see if you need to comb your hair, adjust your tie, or renew your makeup. If any of these is needed, you provide it without delay. That is what makes the use of the mirror worthwhile.

But some people, even some Christians, hear the *word* from Scripture as it points out some error or sin in their behavior; then they go on their way and forget what they just heard! In that case the hearing is worthless. A change to better conduct is what gives value to the hearing.

C. Challenge (v. 25)

25 But the man who looks intently into the perfect law that gives freedom, and continues to do this, not forgetting what he has heard, but doing it—he will be blessed in what he does.

God's Word is called *the perfect law that gives freedom* (note also James 2:12), because those who hear it and obey it are made free (John 8:31, 32). They are made free from the bondage of sin (John 8:34) and free from the punishment of sin (Romans 6:23). If anyone looks into God's Word and changes his conduct to match God's teaching and continues to live by that teaching, *he will be blessed in what he does.* Our godly actions and deeds do not "earn" this blessing, of course, but they do demonstrate the sincerity of our faith (a point that James will later make in James 2:14-26).

III. The Nature of True Religion (James 1:26, 27)
A. Control of the Tongue (v. 26)

26 If anyone considers himself religious and yet does not keep a tight rein on his tongue, he deceives himself and his religion is worthless.

Picture a man who goes to church every Sunday, who perhaps leads in prayer when he is asked, and who may even be an elder or a deacon. But he fails to control *his tongue.* Perhaps he frequently repeats unfounded gossip. Perhaps he is cruel and loud in judging others. Perhaps he often loses his temper and occasionally curses. Such a person may fool himself, thinking himself to be a good Christian. But when he lets his tongue run wild, he shows that in truth his *religion is worthless.*

B. Compassion and Purity (v. 27)

²⁷ Religion that God our Father accepts as pure and faultless is this: to look after orphans and widows in their distress and to keep oneself from being polluted by the world.

James has just called attention to one mark of a phony Christian: an unruly tongue. Now he highlights two marks of a genuine Christian. The first is generosity in taking care of *orphans and widows*—people who are often taken advantage of because of their circumstances. The Old Testament frequently connects these two groups of people as being some of the most helpless and vulnerable in the ancient world (examples can be found in Exodus 22:22-24; Deuteronomy 10:18; and Deuteronomy 14:28, 29).

The second mark is keeping *oneself* morally pure, avoiding *being polluted by the world.* The Christian is not to be characterized by any of the world's selfishness or lust. Moral purity is an important theme in the New Testament (see 1 Timothy 5:22; 6:14; Titus 2:12; James 1:21; 2 Peter 1:4; 2:20; 3:14); without it, our effectiveness as witnesses for Christ is badly damaged.

FAITH AND WORKS (JAMES 2:14-26)

Establishing the Groundwork

In a previous study from Hebrews 11:1-6, the importance of faith was noted. "Without faith it is impossible to please God," Hebrews 11:6 tells us. But a faith that is completely intellectual and devoid of any commitment to service is useless. It is, as James bluntly states it, "dead." In the first few months and years of its existence, the church certainly understood this. The record in Acts provides examples of how closely related faith and works were in the lives of the early Christians (Acts 2:44, 45; 4:32-37; 11:27-30).

Apparently something changed during the years that followed. If the Christians James was addressing had continued to demonstrate their faith by their works, James would not have had to write the admonition that we find in the text to be examined below. We do not know why this change came about, but some suggestions can be offered. Very often the zeal and enthusiasm of new converts begins to wane after time. Perhaps the change occurred because many of the most zealous members of the Jerusalem church had been imprisoned or had fled from the city to escape persecution.

Whatever the reason, James thought it necessary to remind his readers that genuine faith cannot be separated from works. It is a reminder that every follower of Jesus needs to hear and heed.

I. Faith and Works Separated (James 2:14-19)
A. The Issue Raised (v. 14)

14 What good is it, my brothers, if a man claims to have faith but has no deeds? Can such faith save him?

In this verse, James returns to the subject that he had dealt with in James 1:22-27. Again he emphasizes the importance of practical Christian living. Some people in James's day may have interpreted the doctrine of justification by *faith* to mean that good *deeds* were not necessary; or perhaps some had simply become apathetic in doing what they knew to be right. In either case, it was important that such an error be exposed. James asks, *Can such faith* [without deeds] *save* a person? This is a rhetorical question, the answer to which is obviously no. A faith that does not lead to good works is clearly not a saving faith.

B. The Issue Illustrated (vv. 15-18)

15, 16 Suppose a brother or sister is without clothes and daily food. If one of you says to him, "Go, I wish you well; keep warm and well fed," but does nothing about his physical needs, what good is it?

To make sure no one misunderstands the point that he is making, James gives his readers an example. He asks them to imagine *a brother or sister* in Christ who is *without clothes and daily food*. Of course, helping a stranger is no less proper than helping a brother or a sister; but, as Paul indicates in Galatians 6:10, our primary duty as Christians is to "the family of believers." Instead of supplying what the individual really needs, suppose that the person who notices the need supplies only words: "Go in peace; may your needs be met. Praise the Lord!" One can almost hear the sarcasm dripping from James's words as he writes.

It is true that there may be occasions when all we can offer or all that are needed are kind words. But James does not have this kind of a situation in mind. He is describing a situation in which a person has the means to help and offers only words. In that case, *what good* are words?

17 In the same way, faith by itself, if it is not accompanied by action, is dead.

Previously James had asked if a *faith . . . not accompanied by action* can save a person (v. 14). Here he makes it clear that not only can such faith not save a person; in reality it does not even exist!

¹⁸ But someone will say, "You have faith; I have deeds."
Show me your faith without deeds, and I will show you my faith by what I do.

Here James's example challenges an empty profession of orthodoxy, a claim to have *faith* with nothing to substantiate or validate it. We must act upon what we claim to believe, so that our faith may be alive and productive, not dead. This is how we become the salt and light that Jesus desires us to be (Matthew 5:13-16).

C. The Issue Reinforced (v. 19)

¹⁹ You believe that there is one God. Good! Even the demons believe that— and shudder.

Again, James wants to emphasize that the issue at hand is not the content of one's faith; it is whether one is translating that content into action. To further illustrate this point, he uses the touchstone of the Jewish faith—the belief in *one God* (Deuteronomy 6:4). The *demons* are allies of Satan, opposed to everything that the one God stands for. They certainly *believe* in him, for they consider him their archenemy; but it is just as certain that they are not going to obey him. Thus their belief in God leads them to *shudder*—and nothing more. James challenges his readers to move beyond this level of faith to a faith that produces useful fruit.

II. Faith and Works United (James 2:20-26)
A. The Example of Abraham (vv. 20-24)

²⁰ You foolish man, do you want evidence that faith without deeds is useless?

As if his point still lacks sufficient support, James offers to provide additional *evidence that faith without deeds is useless.* His evidence, however, will be drawn from Scriptural examples.

²¹ Was not our ancestor Abraham considered righteous for what he did when he offered his son Isaac on the altar?

The writer of Hebrews examines the faith of *Abraham* in some detail (Hebrews 11:8-12, 17-19). The one incident from Abraham's life that James chooses to emphasize is God's command that Abraham sacrifice *his son Isaac.* It is difficult for us to imagine a greater test of faith than this. God was telling Abraham to put to death his only son—the one through whom the covenant promises that had been given to Abraham would be fulfilled; at least that is the way Abraham must have viewed God's command. Yet he obeyed God regardless, and God provided a substitute sacrifice, sparing Abraham's son.

²² You see that his faith and his actions were working together, and his faith was made complete by what he did.

Faith and *actions* are not in opposition to one another: they complement one another. Works, in order to be acceptable to God, must be based on faith in him. Faith, if it is to be *complete*, must result in a life committed to actions that glorify God.

²³ And the scripture was fulfilled that says, "Abraham believed God, and it was credited to him as righteousness," and he was called God's friend.

Here James quotes the *scripture* found in Genesis 15:6. The previous verse tells how God sent Abraham out to look at the starry heavens and asked him to count the stars. He then assured him that his seed would be as numerous as the stars. At that point, Abraham had wondered how such a promise could be fulfilled; for he had no children (Genesis 15:2, 3). In spite of this, *Abraham believed God*. Abraham's willingness to obey God by offering Isaac as a sacrifice demonstrated that his faith was "made complete by what he did" (James 2:22).

Because of his obedient faith, Abraham *was called God's friend* (see Isaiah 41:8). We can enjoy a similar friendship if we also trust and obey God. To his disciples, Jesus said, "You are my friends if you do what I command" (John 15:14).

²⁴ You see that a person is justified by what he does and not by faith alone.

Some have claimed that there is a contradiction between what James says here and what Paul affirms in Romans 3:28: "For we maintain that a man is justified by faith apart from observing the law." We need to remember that Paul is concerned with legalistic acts performed in an attempt to obtain justification; James writes of deeds of service growing out of our relationship to God through faith. Paul is dealing with one's *becoming* a child of God, while James is dealing with one's activity *as* a child of God.

B. The Example of Rahab (vv. 25, 26)

²⁵ In the same way, was not even Rahab the prostitute considered righteous for what she did when she gave lodging to the spies and sent them off in a different direction?

James may very well have concluded his argument with verse 24, but he chose instead to strengthen his position by citing another example in which a person was *considered righteous* through the combination of faith and works. *Rahab* was a *prostitute* in the city of Jericho. Her faith in the God of Israel moved her to risk her life by giving *lodging* to the two Israelite *spies* who had slipped into the city (Joshua 2:1-21). Perhaps James included such an example to demonstrate to the Jewish Christians to whom he is writing that the necessity of faith and works is not limited only to the Jewish people. Neither is the commission of Jesus to proclaim the gospel (Matthew 28:19, 20).

²⁶ As the body without the spirit is dead, so faith without deeds is dead.

God calls us to *faith*, but not to a passive and lifeless faith that sits idly by, doing nothing to impact the world. We are Christ's body, the organism through which he works in the world today. Let us be active and involved, willing to go where he leads and to do what he wants.

LIVING AS GOD'S CHOSEN PEOPLE (1 PETER 2:1-10)

Establishing the Groundwork

Not many heroes of the early church are as well known as Simon Peter! He was one of the first of Jesus' disciples (John 1:35-42) and was taught intensively through the years of Jesus' earthly ministry. Peter was the one who preached on that memorable Day of Pentecost when the church began its tremendous growth (Acts 2:1-41). Later, God chose Peter as the first to carry the gospel to the Gentiles (Acts 10:1-48). We know little about Peter's movements after this. The last time he is mentioned in the book of Acts, he was released from prison in Jerusalem and then "left for another place" (Acts 12:17). He appears to have remained a respected leader in the Jerusalem church (Galatians 2:9), but he traveled some as well. Paul mentions a trip to Antioch (Galatians 2:11), and apparently the church at Corinth was familiar with him (1 Corinthians 1:12).

Life, however, grew more difficult for Peter and for other Christians in the second half of the first century. By the time Peter wrote the letter that we know as 1 Peter, the government-sanctioned persecution of Christians under the emperor Nero was beginning to intensify. Peter himself was probably living in Rome when he wrote the letter; the mention of "Babylon" in 1 Peter 5:13 is generally recognized as a cryptic, or hidden, reference to the capital of the empire that rivaled ancient Babylon in both splendor and oppression. Since the persecution of believers does not seem to have yet broken out in full force, the most probable time of writing is sometime before the end of AD 64, just prior to the outbreak of persecution.

In this letter, Peter encourages fellow Christians to remain steadfast and hopeful in the midst of the approaching severe hardships. He assures them that such difficulties are not a sign that their faith is weak or misdirected; rather, their faith in Christ is more than adequate to sustain them through whatever trials may come. The recipients are described in the opening verse as "God's elect, strangers in the world, scattered throughout Pontus, Galatia, Cappadocia, Asia and Bithynia" (1 Peter 1:1). These areas covered the northern, central, and western provinces of Asia Minor (modern Turkey).

Examining the Text

I. Our Spiritual Health (1 Peter 2:1-3)
A. Shunning the Bad (v. 1)

¹ Therefore, rid yourselves of all malice and all deceit, hypocrisy, envy, and slander of every kind.

The word *therefore* links Peter's exhortations in this passage with his reminder that the people he addresses have been born again (1 Peter 1:23). Because they are new people, they must live like new people. Thus Peter urges them to *rid* themselves of the sins listed in this verse. Such characteristics as *deceit, hypocrisy, envy, and slander* should never be found among God's holy people.

Even though Christians were victims of slander from outsiders (1 Peter 2:12; 3:16), could it be that they were practicing it toward each other? Some students think so. Perhaps bickering and division arose among the believers because of the persecution directed toward them. However, this was a time for Christians to be united, not divided.

Other students see it differently, however. Perhaps these new believers were trying to wage spiritual warfare through human means (2 Corinthians 10:3). When slandered, they slandered in return (cf. 1 Peter 2:23; 3:9). Peter urges them to get rid of their old way of dealing with issues and, instead, to behave like new people in Christ.

B. Seeking the Good (vv. 2, 3)

² Like newborn babies, crave pure spiritual milk, so that by it you may grow up in your salvation,

Peter's description of his readers as *newborn babies* should not be considered an insult rebuking them for their immaturity. It is a description arising from their new birth described in 1 Peter 1:22, 23. The fact that they are babies in a spiritual sense demonstrates that they have been delivered from sin and its consequences, but also highlights their need to *grow up* in their *salvation*. Just as a nursing baby naturally craves his mother's milk, so should Christians naturally *crave* the *pure spiritual milk* of God's Word.

> [3] *. . . now that you have tasted that the Lord is good.*

To have such a craving for pure spiritual milk should not be difficult, since these Christians have already *tasted that the Lord is good*. This verse calls to mind Psalm 34:8, the context of which stresses that God delivers from affliction those who persevere in faith to the end. It was an appropriate message for believers who were facing their own afflictions from an increasingly hostile society. It also helps us understand the warning against apostasy in Hebrews 6:4-6.

II. Our Spiritual House (1 Peter 2:4-10)
A. The Materials (vv. 4, 5)

> [4, 5] *As you come to him, the living Stone—rejected by men but chosen by God and precious to him—you also, like living stones, are being built into a spiritual house to be a holy priesthood, offering spiritual sacrifices acceptable to God through Jesus Christ.*

Here Peter switches to another illustration to describe all Christians' relationship to Jesus. Jesus is *the living Stone* to whom we Christians, as *living stones*, come. All Christians are built *into a spiritual house* (the church). Adding to the imagery, Peter notes that we "living stones" are also *a holy priesthood*, meant to offer *spiritual sacrifices*. Now that the Old Testament era is past, there is no longer any need for a separate category of priests. We are all priests (Revelation 1:6; 5:10), and Jesus is our Great High Priest (Hebrews 4:14; 6:20).

Romans 12:1 helps us understand the nature of our spiritual sacrifices. That passage urges us to offer up to God our very bodies—not put to death at the altar like ancient sacrifices, but living and serving. Hebrews 13:15, 16 calls Christians to "offer to God a sacrifice of praise—the fruit of lips that confess his name" and "to do good and to share with others, for with such sacrifices God is pleased."

B. The Cornerstone (vv. 6-8)

> [6] *For in Scripture it says:*
> *"See, I lay a stone in Zion,*
> *a chosen and precious cornerstone,*
> *and the one who trusts in him*
> *will never be put to shame."*

The *Scripture* Peter quotes is Isaiah 28:16, a prophecy of Jesus as a *precious cornerstone* that was spoken some seven hundred years before Jesus' birth. In the original context, Isaiah addressed the rulers of Jerusalem who had rejected his advice and entered into a political alliance with Assyria. He stressed the need for these leaders to put their confidence in God (Israel's true leader), because he was their sure foundation.

Jesus is the *chosen and precious cornerstone* that God has laid in *Zion*. (Zion is another name for Jerusalem and the hill on which it stands.) The term *chosen* calls attention to Jesus' distinctive mission and to God's special delight in him (Isaiah 42:1; Matthew 17:5). The writer of Hebrews tells Christians that they have come to "Mount Zion" by having come to Jesus and his church (Hebrews 12:22-24).

To the *one who trusts in* Jesus as the cornerstone, he becomes a source of honor. That person will *never* be ashamed of his decision to trust Jesus. Those who reject Jesus and associate him with shame or scandal stumble over the stone to their eternal ruin.

> *7 Now to you who believe, this stone is precious. But to those who do not believe,*
> *"The stone the builders rejected*
> *has become the capstone,"*

This quotation is taken from Psalm 118:22. That passage describes a building *stone* rejected by *builders* whose efforts God overruled. That *rejected* stone became the chief cornerstone, the most important stone in the building. Long before Peter wrote this letter we are reading, he presented that portion of Psalm 118 as a fulfilled prophecy of Jesus (Acts 4:8-12). Jesus was rejected by the official *builders* of Israel—the priests and scholars and teachers. But God overruled them (note Jesus' use of this Psalm in his parable of the tenants in Mark 12:1-11). He had another plan in mind (Acts 2:23, 24).

We who believe in Jesus understand how *precious* he is: the secure cornerstone of the eternal church to which we commit ourselves. No other foundation is necessary or possible (1 Corinthians 3:10; Ephesians 2:20). *Those who do not believe,* the non-Christians, take their stand with the mistaken builders who rejected him at his first appearance on earth. Unbelievers may be loud in their denial now, but in the end they will be confounded, discredited, and put to shame.

> *8 . . . and,*
> *"A stone that causes men to stumble*
> *and a rock that makes them fall."*

They stumble because they disobey the message—which is also what they were destined for.

Peter now cites Isaiah 8:14. The *message,* the good news of Jesus and salvation, was told in Peter's time and is told now in our century. Each person who hears it has the same opportunity to submit to Jesus as Lord. Those who do so are built into a spiritual house with him, saved for eternity. Those who refuse to do so *stumble* and *fall* for eternity. God has not *destined* anyone to reject Christ. But those who do reject Christ of their own free will are indeed destined to stumble over him.

C. The Building (vv. 9, 10)

⁹ But you are a chosen people, a royal priesthood, a holy nation, a people belonging to God, that you may declare the praises of him who called you out of darkness into his wonderful light.

We are not only a spiritual house (v. 5), but also *a chosen people,* a group of people related by being born again (1 Peter 1:3, 23). We are *a royal priesthood,* a group of priests (2:5) associated with Jesus the King. As *a holy nation* we are dedicated to God's service. Being *a people belonging to God* indicates that we are his distinctive possession, an honored status that once belonged to Old Testament Israel (Exodus 19:5, 6; Deuteronomy 7:6). All of these titles mean that we ought to *declare the praises of him who called* us *out of darkness into his wonderful light.*

¹⁰ Once you were not a people, but now you are the people of God; once you had not received mercy, but now you have received mercy.

Here Peter cites Hosea 1:6, 9, 10; 2:23. The reference to God's *mercy* links this verse with the preceding one, for by his mercy we are called to leave sin's darkness and come into God's light.

Multitudes of people in our world have an identity crisis; they do not know who they are because they do not know God. Such is not the case with Christians; we know who we are, and we know what we should do. Someone in the darkness needs our light; let's keep it shining.

SUFFERING FOR CHRIST (1 PETER 3:13-17)

Establishing the Groundwork

The verses in 1 Peter leading up to the next passage being examined include a variety of teachings that focus on how Christians are to live as "aliens and strangers in the world" (2:11). Peter highlights how our loyalty to Christ should affect our relationships with civil authorities (2:13, 14, 17), people on the job (2:18), our spouses (3:1-7), our brothers and sisters in the church (3:8), and those who insult us (3:9). The primary motivation and example of our conduct is Christ himself (2:21).

In the following passage, Peter addresses the issue of how Christians are to conduct themselves when their status as "aliens and strangers" brings them face to face with suffering and persecution. Peter calls what some of the Christians are facing a "painful trial" (4:12) and indicates that it is being inflicted on Christians elsewhere (5:9). What attitudes should Christians have? What actions should they take? These are the concerns Peter addresses in the following Scripture.

Examining the Text

I. Do Not Be Frightened (1 Peter 3:13, 14)
A. Principle (v. 13)

13 Who is going to harm you if you are eager to do good?

If we as Christians are *eager to do good*, that is, if we are zealous to live morally upright lives, people, especially the authorities, are not likely to *harm* us. After the events on the Day of Pentecost, the church in Jerusalem enjoyed "the favor of all the people" (Acts 2:47). Peter himself asserts in this letter that God has ordained governing authorities "to punish those who do wrong and to commend those who do right" (1 Peter 2:14). On the other hand, persecution is always possible. The more the early church witnessed, the more it was persecuted.

Peter may also be reminding us that if we are right with God, no *ultimate* harm can come to us. For the Christian, even death is not a tragedy but a triumph.

B. Priorities (v. 14)

14 But even if you should suffer for what is right, you are blessed. "Do not fear what they fear; do not be frightened."

Sometimes doing *right* is not enough to keep us from being mistreated. People may abuse us just because our conduct highlights their own evil. In that case their attack is a compliment. Rather than being upset or troubled, we should rejoice that our right conduct brings forth opposition (Acts 5:41). The commands not to *fear what they fear* and not to be *frightened* encourage any persecuted Christian to remember that "the one who is in you is greater than the one who is in the world" (1 John 4:4).

II. Be Prepared (1 Peter 3:15-17)
A. To Give an Answer (v. 15)

15 But in your hearts set apart Christ as Lord. Always be prepared to give an answer to everyone who asks you to give the reason for the hope that you have. But do this with gentleness and respect,

While the previous verse focuses primarily on what we should not do in the face of unjust suffering, this verse highlights what we should do. Rather than yielding to fear when faced with the possibility of persecution, Christians are to *set apart Christ as Lord* in their *hearts*. The presence of God with his people, even in the throes of the most severe trials, is reaffirmed.

The Greek word translated *answer* is one from which our word "apology" comes. While to us an apology usually implies being sorry for something one has said or done, this word means a "defense," in this case a defense of one's faith in Christ. *The hope that you have* refers not only to Christians' conviction about the future, but to the attitude of peace and serenity that they can possess even when threatened by their foes. Such a spirit would invite questions from curious observers. Each of us should ask, "Is my faith the kind that causes others to ask the reason for my hope?"

The words *gentleness and respect* describe the attitude with which we should defend our faith. We are not to browbeat others or become arrogant and obnoxious, but in compassion seek to lead them from darkness to light. Our mission is not to win arguments, but to win the lost.

B. To Counter Enemies (v. 16)

16 . . . keeping a clear conscience, so that those who speak maliciously against your good behavior in Christ may be ashamed of their slander.

The Christian must keep a *clear conscience* by doing right—doing it so continuously and so obviously that those who falsely *speak maliciously* of his good way of life will be *ashamed of their slander*. We are reminded that it is usually the quality of our conduct and behavior (more than our eloquence or logical explanations) that will convince questioners of the truth of our convictions.

C. To Suffer for Doing Good (v. 17)

17 It is better, if it is God's will, to suffer for doing good than for doing evil.

Most would agree that to *suffer* for *doing evil* is a good thing; perhaps the one suffering will learn to stop doing evil! But suffering for *doing good* is more difficult to accept. The best Christian witness is an honest life that refutes the defamation and slander of skeptics through its visible and consistent goodness. Peter calls Christians to suffer for their good deeds, as Jesus did (1 Peter 2:19-23). Those who do so are within *God's will* and "should commit themselves to their faithful Creator and continue to do good" (1 Peter 4:19).

PREPARING FOR THE DAY OF THE LORD (2 PETER 3:1-10)

Establishing the Groundwork

Peter's first letter to the Christians in Asia Minor was aimed at strengthening them against the rising tide of persecution engendered by the Roman emperor Nero. Peter's second letter was directed to the same general audience (see 2 Peter 3:1). Its purpose was primarily to warn against the influence of false teaching and the teachers who were promoting it. In particular, chapter 2 calls attention to false teachers within the church who are contradicting sound doctrine, while chapter 3 speaks of scoffers outside the church who are maligning the belief of Christians in the return of Christ and the end of the world.

It should be noted that there are significant similarities between the contents of 2 Peter and Jude. (Compare 2 Peter 2 with Jude 4-19.) Some have suggested that one borrowed from the other or that they both drew from a common source. If any borrowing occurred, it was not a slavish borrowing but one that adapted the material to suit the writer's purpose. With the threat of false teaching prevalent in so many places, the same instruction would have been appropriate to use in more than one setting. (Consider the comments on Ephesians as a "circular letter" in the "Establishing the Groundwork" section on Ephesians 2:8-22 in chapter 9.)

By the time he wrote 2 Peter, Peter was an old man expecting to die rather shortly (2 Peter 1:13, 14). He reminded his readers of his experience with Jesus on the mount of transfiguration (1:16-18). He also indicates an acquaintance with the writings of Paul and considers them to be on a level with the inspired Scriptures (3:15, 16). The date was probably in the year AD 67 or 68.

Examining the Text

I. What We Are Hearing (2 Peter 3:1-4)
A. Sound Advice (vv. 1, 2)

¹ Dear friends, this is now my second letter to you. I have written both of them as reminders to stimulate you to wholesome thinking.

This verse establishes a clear link between 1 and 2 Peter. It tells us the order of the two books, and that both epistles were written to the same group of churches (identified in 1 Peter 1:1). It also indicates that Peter had a key theme that he was trying to develop within both epistles: *to stimulate* the readers *to wholesome thinking*. The first letter had encouraged such thinking in areas such as holy living, responsibility to government, relationships between husbands and wives, confronting persecution, and leadership in the Lord's church. The particular topic about to be covered in this chapter is the return of Jesus.

² I want you to recall the words spoken in the past by the holy prophets and the command given by our Lord and Savior through your apostles.

Peter does not tell us the specific *command* of the *Lord* that he wants his readers to *recall* at this time. If we assume that this command is one associated with the second coming of Christ, the one that naturally comes to mind is that we always watch and stay ready. This is the theme of Matthew 24:42–25:30, a portion of Jesus' discourse on his second coming. Jesus' advice on how to prepare for his return is to practice daily a godly lifestyle in service to him and to others. This kind of readiness through godly living is often mentioned in the writings of the *apostles* as well as in the Old Testament *prophets*.

B. Foolish Talk (vv. 3, 4)

³ First of all, you must understand that in the last days scoffers will come, scoffing and following their own evil desires.

Biblically speaking, *the last days* are all the days of the Christian era, all the time between Jesus' first coming to his second coming (see the use of the term in Hebrews 1:2; 1 Peter 1:20; 1 John 2:18). *Scoffers* have been busy throughout most of this era, trying to turn God's people away from the truth. Their foundational problem is that they follow *their own evil desires* instead of following Jesus. They are concerned about their own profit, pleasure, and pride, and not about the kingdom of God and his righteousness (Matthew 6:33). It is not in their selfish interests to accept that history might come to an end at any time.

⁴ They will say, "Where is this 'coming' he promised? Ever since our fathers died, everything goes on as it has since the beginning of creation."

By the time Peter wrote this letter, some 35 years had passed since Jesus promised that he would return. *"Where is this 'coming'?"* the scoffers ask. The *fathers* may mean the scoffers' own fathers—the first generation of Christians, the men who had come to Christ in the initial days of the church. They had believed the promise that Jesus will come back; they had lived out their lives expecting to see him. But now they are dead. The scoffers are claiming that it is silly for the next generation to continue believing a promise that has not been kept. And since Jesus has not kept his promise, they say, it is pointless to be bound by his teaching.

In fact, say the scoffers, nothing has changed since long before the fathers lived: *everything goes on as it has since the beginning of creation.* It must be time to abandon Christianity, because the passing of time has proven it to be a failure.

II. What We Should Remember (2 Peter 3:5-10)
A. God's Powerful Word (vv. 5-7)

5, 6 But they deliberately forget that long ago by God's word the heavens existed and the earth was formed out of water and by water. By these waters also the world of that time was deluged and destroyed.

There is nothing wrong with ignorance when it cannot be helped. Everyone is ignorant of some things. But willfully ignoring the truth that one ought to be aware of is, in essence, a rejection of the truth. This is the sin of the scoffers: *they deliberately forget* the fact that it was *by God's word* that the *heavens* and *earth* came into being in the first place! This same word of God, as expanded by Jesus, is what promises an end to that old creation. Peter's statement that *the earth was formed out of water and by water* seems to refer to the creation account in Genesis, which describes how the waters on earth were separated from the atmospheric waters and how the "water under the sky" was "gathered to one place" so that dry ground appeared (Genesis 1:6-10).

Furthermore, the scoffers are wrong when they claim that the ordinary course of nature has gone on "since the beginning of creation" (v. 4). Long after the creation, the normal course of nature was interrupted by another spectacular event: the great flood of Noah's day. *The world of that time* was *deluged* with water, and most of humanity was *destroyed* in a judgment scarcely less spectacular than the one promised in Matthew 25:31-46.

7 By the same word the present heavens and earth are reserved for fire, being kept for the day of judgment and destruction of ungodly men.

The present heavens and earth came into being by the word of God (v. 5). By his word a flood destroyed most of the conscious living things of that world (Genesis 6:13). *By the same word* the creation we see is *reserved for fire*. It will be burned up (v. 10), and the *ungodly* will perish.

Thus Peter has offered a powerful refutation of the scoffers' argument that a universal destruction by fire is impossible because it is without precedent. There is a clear precedent for supernatural activity on a universal scale. It now remains for Peter to respond to the argument that the long delay in Christ's return implies a forgotten promise.

B. God's Amazing Grace (vv. 8, 9)

8 But do not forget this one thing, dear friends: With the Lord a day is like a thousand years, and a thousand years are like a day.

Limited as we are by time, it is hard for us to grasp eternity. Eighty years is a long time to a person on earth, for it leaves him or her only a few more years to live. But when God has "lived" *a thousand years,* he has as many years to live as he had when the thousand years began; for his life has neither beginning nor end (Psalm 90:2). Thus when Jesus says, "I am coming soon" (Revelation 22:7, 12, 20), we should not doubt his promise as the years pass by, but should assume that he speaks from his divine perspective.

It should also be noted that Peter's statement should not be understood as a prophetic key for determining the timing of Christ's return. Many have tried to use the "day equals 1000 years" formula to calculate the date of the second coming, but all attempts have proven futile (and ultimately embarrassing). Reading this verse in its context tells us that Peter has no interest in prophetic speculation. His focus is on the reality of Christ's promise and our appropriate response to that promise.

9 The Lord is not slow in keeping his promise, as some understand slowness. He is patient with you, not wanting anyone to perish, but everyone to come to repentance.

Perhaps you find yourself frequently disturbed and alarmed by the evil reported almost daily in the halls of government, in places of business, in schools, on the street, and in homes. Do you ever wonder why God hasn't destroyed this wicked world before now? Here is the answer: God is waiting for more people to repent. God's patience is an important biblical theme (Exodus 34:6; Romans 2:4; 9:22); he does not want *anyone to perish.* Do we share that same passion for lost people?

C. God's Final Day (v. 10)

10 But the day of the Lord will come like a thief. The heavens will disappear with a roar; the elements will be destroyed by fire, and the earth and everything in it will be laid bare.

Peter echoes the words of Jesus in Matthew 24:43 when he says that *the day of the Lord will come as a thief in the night.* Of course, nothing criminal or evil is intended by this analogy. The point of comparison is that there will be no advance warning of the specific time Jesus will return. For the Christian who stays prepared, this presents no difficulty. For everyone else, the thief imagery should be seen as an urgent warning.

The day of the Lord, however, will not also depart unseen and unheard as *a thief* does. Peter's description of the destruction of the universe on the final day is a sobering one. There will be a *roar*, perhaps akin to the roar of a huge fire. Everything in *the heavens* (including the sun, moon, and stars) will disappear. *The earth and everything in it will be laid bare*; every physical element of life on earth will be consumed by the *fire*. Later Peter mentions the promise of "a new heaven and a new earth, the home of righteousness" (v. 13), which John saw fulfilled in the book of Revelation (21:1, 2).

GOD'S LOVE AND OURS (1 JOHN 4:7-16)

Establishing the Groundwork

It is generally agreed that John, the "beloved apostle," wrote the three epistles that bear his name. John was probably one of the two disciples of John the Baptist who listened to his testimony and "followed Jesus" (John 1:37). Jesus gave the name "Boanerges" to John and his brother James—a name meaning "Sons of Thunder" (Mark 3:17). Apparently this was because of the aggressiveness that both of them could and did show on certain occasions (Mark 10:37; Luke 9:52-54). Both men came to model the love of Jesus, especially John, whose writings (notably the Gospel and his three letters) are characterized by frequent references to love.

Records from church history indicate that after Jerusalem was destroyed in AD 70, John lived in Ephesus. It was probably from that city that he wrote the three letters known as 1, 2, and 3 John (and also the book of Revelation) between AD 90 and 95.

By this time, more than half a century had passed since Jesus rose from the dead and ascended to Heaven. The church was being influenced by a false doctrine known as Gnosticism. (For more information on this teaching, see the "Establishing the Groundwork" material on Colossians 1:15-20 in chapter 10.) In response to such teaching, John began his first letter with a strong declaration of his own personal acquaintance with Jesus and his accurate knowledge of Jesus' teaching (1 John 1:1-4).

Years before John wrote his letters, Paul warned Timothy concerning men whose teaching was perverted because their love was perverted. They loved themselves more than they loved their fellowman, they loved money, and they loved pleasures more than they loved God. Therefore they became bad characters indeed (2 Timothy 3:1-5). In contrast, we now hear John urging Christians toward a proper kind of love.

Examining the Text

I. God's Love for Us (1 John 4:7-11)
A. Source of Love (vv. 7, 8)

⁷ Dear friends, let us love one another, for love comes from God. Everyone who loves has been born of God and knows God.

Although God's children are to love their enemies (Luke 6:27-29), in this text John talks about loving *one another*—about loving our fellow Christians. *Love comes from God* (indeed, "God is love," v. 8), and all of God's children ought to be loving as he is loving. Such love in us is powerful evidence that we really are God's children. It is the trademark that identifies us to the world as followers of Jesus (John 13:35).

⁸ Whoever does not love does not know God, because God is love.

Sadly, the opposite is true as well. Unloving people do not even *know God*. He is a stranger to them.

B. Proof of Love (vv. 9, 10)

⁹ This is how God showed his love among us: He sent his one and only Son into the world that we might live through him.

One could suggest that God has shown his love for humanity in ways too numerous to count. But the clearest evidence of *his love* is that *he sent his one and only Son into the world*. God sent Jesus from Heaven to earth not only to live as a man among men, but also to be despised, rejected, persecuted, tortured, and killed! A loving God subjected his beloved Son to all that in order *that we might live through him*. How great, then, is God's love for us! It is beyond measure, beyond understanding. But thank God it is not beyond belief. It cannot be doubted, for God proved it by sacrificing his Son to pay sin's penalty for us (John 3:16, 17).

¹⁰ This is love: not that we loved God, but that he loved us and sent his Son as an atoning sacrifice for our sins.

Love in all its fullness, in all its power, in all its splendor is not seen in our puny love for God. It is seen in God's tremendous love for us. God demonstrated it by sending *his Son* to give his life *as an atoning sacrifice for our sins*.

C. Result of Love (v. 11)

11 Dear friends, since God so loved us, we also ought to love one another.

To despise a fellow Christian for whom God's Son died is unthinkable! In light of how much we have been loved, *we also ought to love one another.* We should be constantly thinking of how we can be more helpful and loving to fellow Christians, those here at home as well as those on the other side of the world.

II. Our Love for Others (1 John 4:12-16)
A. Our Status (vv. 12, 13)

12 No one has ever seen God; but if we love one another, God lives in us and his love is made complete in us.

In his Gospel, John also writes, *No one has ever seen God* (John 1:18). There, however, he adds that God's Son, "who is at the Father's side, has made him known." We can know God very well by learning about his Son, who walked the earth in the visible form of a man and spoke God's truth (John 6:46; 14:9). In a much smaller way, people who do not know Jesus form their idea of God from the way we, God's other children, imitate his love, for *God lives in us.* What a sobering thought!

God's *love is made complete in us* as *we love one another.* God's love completes its work when we copy his love and give help to one another in his name. In love God wants to give us help; he enables his loving people to give that help to others.

13 We know that we live in him and he in us, because he has given us of his Spirit.

John's observation that *we live in him and he in us* is a way of saying that our relationship with God is close and complete (see 1 John 2:24; 4:15). When we imitate God's love and help one of his needy people, God *in us* is doing it. But if we were not *in him,* we would not imitate his love and do his work. It is a mutual indwelling, but we do not live together as equals. He is God, the creator, the all wise, the all powerful. He lives in us as director and controller. We live in him as devoted and obedient servants. Let us pray, as Jesus did, "Not my will, but yours be done" (Luke 22:42).

We know we dwell in God *because he has given us of his Spirit.* God is the one who "set his seal of ownership on us, and put his Spirit in our hearts as a deposit" (2 Corinthians 1:22). The Spirit's presence in every Christian makes that Christian God's temple (1 Corinthians 6:19).

B. Our Testimony (v. 14)

14 And we have seen and testify that the Father has sent his Son to be the Savior of the world.

John and the other apostles actually had *seen* Jesus (1 John 1:1-3). They had been with him almost continually for approximately three and a half years. Both his miracles and his teachings provided clear evidence that *the Father* had *sent his Son to be the Savior of the world.*

Over and over the apostles have given that testimony through the Scripture of the New Testament. We have not seen Jesus, and we are not inspired as the apostles were; but we can repeat the apostles' testimony in Scripture as confidently as they: God indeed did send his Son to be the Savior of the world.

C. Our Confession (vv. 15, 16)

15 If anyone acknowledges that Jesus is the Son of God, God lives in him and he in God.

One who says *that Jesus is the Son of God* agrees with the truth, and agrees also with countless Christians who have made the same statement before. Of course, this agreement involves far more than merely mouthing words. If one really *acknowledges* that Jesus is the Son of God, then he or she will live a life in agreement with what the Son says. He or she will love, honor, and obey Jesus even as Jesus loves, honors, and obeys his Father. Thus such a person makes it evident that *God lives in him and he in God.*

16 And so we know and rely on the love God has for us.
God is love. Whoever lives in love lives in God, and God in him.

If we *know* Jesus and have faith in him, we *rely on* his promise. We are sure that we have everlasting life. To Jesus we turn over all we are and all we have, confident that in him we shall be more than we could be without him.

We know that *God is love.* But we know that God is more than that. He is also light (1 John 1:5), spirit (John 4:24), a consuming fire (Hebrews 12:29), our refuge and strength (Psalm 46:1), King of all the earth (Psalm 47:7), our help (Psalm 54:4), our fortress (Psalm 59:9), and our light and our salvation (Psalm 27:1). But in this text John is writing about God as love. Evidence of God's love is everywhere, from the sunshine and rain and bountiful harvests to the gift of his Son to rescue us from death and give us life everlasting. Every good thing that nourishes our lives or brings us joy is evidence of God's love. However, the greatest proof, the most compelling evidence, of that love remains the cross, on which God's sinless Son gave his life for sinful humans.

How to Say It

ABRAHAM. *Ay*-bruh-ham.

ANTIOCH. *An*-tee-ock.

ASIA. *Ay*-zha.

ASSYRIA. Uh-*sear*-ee-uh.

BABYLON. *Bab*-uh-lun.

BITHYNIA. Bih-*thin*-ee-uh.

BOANERGES. *Bo*-uh-*nur*-geez (strong accent on *nur*).

CAPPADOCIA. Kap-uh-*doe*-shuh.

CORINTH. *Kor*-inth.

GALATIA. Guh-*lay*-shuh.

GNOSTICISM. *Nahss*-tih-*sizz*-um (strong accent on *Nahss*).

ISRAELITE. *Iz*-ray-el-ite.

JERICHO. *Jair*-ih-co.

PENTECOST. *Pent*-ih-kost.

PONTUS. *Pon*-tuss.

RAHAB. *Ray*-hab.

SIMON. *Sy*-mun.

ZION. *Zi*-un.

Chapter 13

Visions of Hope: Studies in Revelation
Revelation 1:4-16; 3:14-22; 7:1-3, 9-17; 21:1-7, 22-27

"TO THE SEVEN CHURCHES" (REVELATION 1:4-16)

Establishing the Groundwork

God's people are no strangers to difficulty. They have frequently endured physical persecution, exile, and the demand that they renounce their God and swear allegiance to false deities, including the human rulers of lesser kingdoms. Apocalyptic (that is, highly figurative and symbolic) literature has often appeared as a kind of "code" writing during times of severe persecution. By this means, the faithful have been encouraged and instructed in terms that made no sense at all to their oppressors. The Old Testament books of Daniel and Zechariah abound in such language.

The earliest persecutions of the church came from Jewish sources that were familiar with the Old Testament apocalyptic material. Thus, for a time, plain language served best in strengthening the church. However, when the Roman Empire sought to require all its subjects to worship the emperor, and intensified its persecution of the church, apocalyptic symbolism again became the style in which God's Word was communicated to God's people. This is the style that is found throughout most of the book of Revelation.

Most students believe that Revelation was written during the persecution that was mounted by Domitian, the Roman emperor who reigned from AD 81 to 96. The writer of Revelation identifies himself simply as John. While that was a common name at the time, there can be little doubt that this is John the apostle. The style of writing differs considerably from that of his Gospel and his three brief epistles; however, one must keep in mind that the circumstances behind the writing of Revelation differed considerably. John was already separated from his friends by exile because of his preaching (Revelation 1:9). How would he communicate to them a written message of ultimate triumph over their Roman oppressors without getting himself and them into greater difficulties? The wise Holy Spirit provided John with visions of the victory of Christ in words and symbols familiar to those who knew the Scriptures, but meaningless to the literal Roman mind.

I. Greeting to the Churches (Revelation 1:4, 5a)
A. Writer and Readers (v. 4a)

⁴ᵃ John,

To the seven churches in the province of Asia:

John, who had served for years among the churches around Ephesus (the principal city of *the province of Asia*), was known well enough among them to require no further introduction. The province of Asia occupied much of the western one-fourth of Asia Minor, or modern Turkey. As part of the Roman Empire, Asia and its people came under the imperial edict that anyone who accepted the protection of Rome must participate in the forms of worship to the Roman emperor.

Churches were found in at least ten cities of Asia in New Testament times. The *seven* mentioned here and addressed individually in Revelation 2 and 3 may represent all churches in every place and time, since seven in the Bible frequently symbolizes perfection or completeness. The book of Revelation is applicable to all congregations, but its message speaks particularly to those suffering under conditions similar to those experienced by the seven churches.

B. Blessings and Their Source (vv. 4b, 5a)

⁴ᵇ, ⁵ᵃ . . . Grace and peace to you from him who is, and who was, and who is to come, and from the seven spirits before his throne, and from Jesus Christ, who is the faithful witness, the firstborn from the dead, and the ruler of the kings of the earth.

John's petition for *grace and peace* to his readers combines the Greek wish for goodness and beauty with the Jewish prayer for God's wholeness. The New Testament adds the assurance of God's love in Jesus Christ to *grace,* and the wholeness that can come only from Jesus to the idea of *peace* (John 14:27). The words *who is, and who was, and who is to come* are reminiscent of the name by which God revealed himself in Exodus 3:14, 15 (I AM WHO I AM).

The term *seven spirits* signifies the Holy Spirit, with the number seven (as noted above) implying completeness. Perhaps the number seven was used in conjunction with the seven churches to which this writing was sent. Yet just as the seven churches would be considered one body, the seven spirits designated the one Spirit (Ephesians 4:4).

The primary focus of the book of Revelation is *Jesus Christ* (see 1:1, 2). Here three aspects of his ministry are highlighted. First, he is *the faithful witness.* Jesus told Pilate that he had come "to testify to the truth" (John 18:37), and his faithful commitment to this mission led to his death. Death, however, could not hold him. Through his resurrection, Jesus became *the firstborn from the dead*. Similar titles are "the firstfruits of those who have fallen asleep" (1 Corinthians 15:20) and "the firstborn from among the dead" (Colossians 1:18). Jesus was the first to be brought back to life, never to die again. This triumph over death makes him *the ruler of the kings of the earth*. He is the supreme ruler over all earthly rulers—"Lord of lords and King of kings" (Revelation 17:14). This was a vital truth for the persecuted church to keep in mind when facing the threats of the Roman government.

II. Glory to the Savior (Revelation 1:5b-8)
A. He is Blessed (vv. 5b, 6)

5b, 6 To him who loves us and has freed us from our sins by his blood, and has made us to be a kingdom and priests to serve his God and Father—to him be glory and power for ever and ever! Amen.

Jesus Christ, the source of blessing to the saints in the seven churches, is now presented as the object of adoration among those communities of faith. *Loves* is in the present tense; Jesus has promised his continual presence with his dedicated disciples (Matthew 28:20). Does the might of the Roman Empire seem insurmountable? Followers of Jesus should take comfort in knowing that he has established his people as a *kingdom*. It is a kingdom "not of this world" (John 18:36), made up of *priests* (see 1 Peter 2:5) who have direct access to God in Jesus' name. All of this is reason to celebrate and to praise God's *glory and power for ever and ever*.

B. He is Coming (v. 7)

7 Look, he is coming with the clouds,
and every eye will see him,
even those who pierced him;
and all the peoples of the earth will mourn because of him.
So shall it be! Amen.

Just as a cloud was present when Jesus ascended (Acts 1:9), so will *clouds* be part of the background when he returns (Matthew 26:64). Paul mentions clouds in his description of Jesus' return in 1 Thessalonians 4:17.

That *every eye will see* Jesus means that his audience will include reluctant foes (*those who pierced him*, as predicted in Zechariah 12:10), as well as eager followers. The word *mourn* pictures the bitter cry of those *peoples of the earth* who must confront divine judgment unprepared (Matthew 13:42, 50).

C. He is Eternal (v. 8)

⁸ "I am the Alpha and the Omega," says the Lord God, "who is, and who was, and who is to come, the Almighty."

Alpha is the first letter of the Greek alphabet, and *Omega* is the last. Thus the *Lord God* declares himself to be the eternal one (as he is described in verse 4), living before all else began and after all created matter has been extinguished. Near the close of Revelation, Jesus describes himself with the words *the Alpha and the Omega*, and uses other titles that affirm his deity (Revelation 22:13, 16).

III. Assignment to John (Revelation 1:9-11)
A. The Man and the Place (v. 9)

⁹ I, John, your brother and companion in the suffering and kingdom and patient endurance that are ours in Jesus, was on the island of Patmos because of the word of God and the testimony of Jesus.

Although he was an elderly and respected apostle at this point, John did not consider himself above or superior to those he addressed. He was their *brother*, sharing their experiences. He understood what it was like to endure *suffering* for one's faith. He, along with Peter, had suffered persecution not long after the church began (Acts 4:18-21; 5:40-42). Later he had lost his brother James during the persecution initiated by King Herod Agrippa I (Acts 12:1, 2). Now, after many years, John had insisted on preaching that God, as revealed in Jesus Christ, was the only deity to be worshiped, while the emperor Domitian demanded that any worship be directed toward himself. For that reason, John had been exiled—separated from his people and confined to a desolate *island*.

Among the islands in the Aegean Sea, the island of *Patmos* is a rough and irregular cluster of three sections linked by narrow necks of land. Its total tortuous shoreline is comparable with its distance from the Asian coast—some 40 miles, though Patmos contains not more than 13 square miles in total area. John's exile there is believed to have lasted about 18 months and to have been concluded by the emperor Nerva after the death of Domitian in AD 96.

More meaningful to us is John's introduction of the threefold Christian experience of *the suffering and kingdom and patient endurance that are ours in Jesus*. These themes echo throughout Revelation: *suffering* for the faith, the triumph of Heaven's *kingdom* over worldly realms, and the *patient endurance* that enables the saints to achieve Heaven's victory. This triumphant trio makes the book of Revelation of special value in times of hardship.

B. The Preparation (v. 10)

10 On the Lord's Day I was in the Spirit, and I heard behind me a loud voice like a trumpet,

Following Jesus' resurrection on the first day of the week and the establishment of the church on the first day of the week (the Day of Pentecost), Christians chose that day to meet at the Lord's table (Acts 20:7) and to bring offerings for the needy (1 Corinthians 16:2). The term *the Lord's Day* does not appear in Scripture until this passage in Revelation, but soon afterward Christians in general were known to call the first day of the week the Lord's Day.

John's exile kept him from meeting with fellow believers for worship (Hebrews 10:25), but he could still engage in prayer and meditation. During such a time, he *was in the Spirit*; that is, he was drawn into a special spiritual experience that would result in the scene described in this and the following verses. The *loud voice* that he *heard behind* him reminded him in an impressive way that, though in exile, he was by no means alone.

C. The Assignment (v. 11)

11 . . . which said: "Write on a scroll what you see and send it to the seven churches: to Ephesus, Smyrna, Pergamum, Thyatira, Sardis, Philadelphia and Laodicea."

The order in which the cities are named where the *seven churches* were located formed a kind of circuit, from *Ephesus* northward, then eastward and southward to *Laodicea*, east of Ephesus, which is the last city mentioned. Thus the *scroll* on which John would *write* what he saw may well have been intended to be circulated among the churches. Why other cities in the region, such as Troas, Miletus, Colosse, and Hierapolis were omitted can only be surmised. Churches anywhere, however, could profit from the seven messages John was to receive.

IV. Description of the Savior (Revelation 1:12-16)
A. His Place with the Churches (vv. 12, 13a)

12, 13a I turned around to see the voice that was speaking to me. And when I turned I saw seven golden lampstands, and among the lampstands was someone "like a son of man,"

John gave immediate attention to *the voice* coming from behind him. Immediately he noticed *seven golden lampstands*. Revelation 1:20 states that these lampstands symbolized the churches to which the writing was addressed. One is led to think of Jesus' declaration that his followers are to be "the light of the world" (Matthew 5:14). Each congregation is responsible to bring the light of the gospel to its surroundings.

Among the lampstands was someone *like a son of man*. John's description is reminiscent of Daniel's night vision: "In my vision at night I looked, and there before me was one like a son of man, coming with the clouds of heaven" (Daniel 7:13). Jesus referred to himself frequently by this title (Matthew 8:20; Mark 2:10; Luke 22:69; John 1:51), emphasizing his identity with humanity while at the same time affirming his divinity.

B. His Robe of Authority (v. 13b)

13b . . . dressed in a robe reaching down to his feet and with a golden sash around his chest.

The *golden sash around* the *chest* of the figure before John would bring to mind the priestly garments to be worn by Aaron and his sons (Exodus 39:27-29). How fitting for our great High Priest, who "has made us . . . priests" (v. 6), to be clothed in such garments!

C. His Appearance of Purity (v. 14)

14 His head and hair were white like wool, as white as snow, and his eyes were like blazing fire.

Pure, glistening *white* is the symbol of utmost purity and of the holiness of God. Such an individual, whose *eyes were like blazing fire*, could see and understand the inmost thoughts of the human heart.

D. His Posture of Power (v. 15)

15 His feet were like bronze glowing in a furnace, and his voice was like the sound of rushing waters.

The appearance of the Christ's *feet* resembled *bronze glowing in a furnace*—refined and burnished to a glow. In addition, his words were spoken with authority. The *sound* of his *voice* was not an intimidating shout, but a naturally dominant sound, like that of waves crashing on a rocky seacoast or of a mighty waterfall.

E. His Concern for the Churches (v. 16)

16 In his right hand he held seven stars, and out of his mouth came a sharp double-edged sword. His face was like the sun shining in all its brilliance.

The *seven stars* are interpreted by Jesus in verse 20 as the "angels of the seven churches." Each of the seven letters was directed to "the angel of the church" in the designated city. Various explanations have been given as to who these angels were. The Greek word translated "angel" can also mean "messenger" and may designate a leader in the church such as a preacher or elder. It seems best to understand the "angels" as referring to these human messengers, who would, like John, have been special targets of persecution. What an encouragement to these individuals to know that the Lord of the church holds them *in his right hand!* (See Isaiah 41:10.)

The *sharp double-edged sword* coming *out of* the *mouth* of Christ represents the word of God, which is "sharper than any double-edged sword" (Hebrews 4:12; see also Revelation 19:15). That word cuts both ways, to protect and comfort the faithful and to defeat and destroy the enemy.

His face was like the sun shining in all its brilliance. Perhaps John's mind went back to what he and Peter and James witnessed at the transfiguration of Jesus, when "his face shone like the sun, and his clothes became as white as the light" (Matthew 17:2). Although John was in exile by the decree of the emperor, no emperor's edict could restrain the presence of Jesus in his glory.

JESUS' MESSAGE TO THE CHURCH AT LAODICEA (REVELATION 3:14-22)

Establishing the Groundwork

John makes clear from the outset of Revelation that this is a message revealed by Jesus Christ himself (Revelation 1:1, 5). But not only is the message from him, it is also about him. We see Christ in the midst of the seven golden lampstands in 1:20, which are identified as the seven churches of Asia. Christ is the one who knows the circumstances of the seven churches—their strong points, their weak points, everything! In the letters directed to the churches, he challenges them (and us) to be overcomers of those obstacles that would destroy a proper relationship with him.

Each of the seven letters is addressed to the "angel" of the church. It was suggested in the previous study that the Greek word translated "angel" can also mean "messenger" and may have designated one of the leaders of the church. Jesus then introduces himself to each church in a particularly striking way that is meant to capture the attention of the audience. Then (in most instances) come words of commendation, in which Jesus highlights the positive qualities within the church. These are followed by words of condemnation, in which Jesus calls attention to the weaknesses of the church that need to be addressed if that congregation is to be an effective "lampstand." At the close of each letter comes a challenge to the church to remain steadfast and a description of the reward awaiting those who are "faithful, even to the point of death" (Revelation 2:10). There is also this solemn warning: "He who has an ear, let him hear what the Spirit says to the churches" (2:7, 11, 17, 29; 3:6, 13, 22).

Out of the seven churches, only two do not receive any word of rebuke; they are Smyrna (Revelation 2:8-11) and Philadelphia (Revelation 3:7-13). Only one received no words of commendation and that was Laodicea, whose letter is the subject of the following study.

Laodicea was the richest city in the district of Phrygia. Its major commodity was a glossy black textile made from the soft black wool of a now-extinct breed of sheep. Its famous medical college developed a "Phrygian powder" that was used to make a widely exported eye salve. These and other businesses developed banking establishments that dominated the area and made Laodicea wealthy and influential. (Ironically, its site is now deserted.) The city, however, had a problem with its water supply; the water, delivered to the city by aqueduct, was tepid and distasteful.

As we study Jesus' words to the Laodiceans, we will see that many of these aspects of life in Laodicea were incorporated into the language that he used to address the church and appeal to its spiritual needs. He wanted the Laodiceans to see that the items in which they took such great pride were actually worthless when compared to what he could give them.

Examining the Text

I. Jesus' Concern for Laodicea (Revelation 3:14-18)
A. Who Jesus Is (v. 14)

14 "To the angel of the church in Laodicea write:
These are the words of the Amen, the faithful and true witness, the ruler of God's creation.

To the Christians in *Laodicea*, Jesus initially identifies himself as *the Amen*, a title based on a Hebrew word that means "in truth" or "truly." He also refers to himself as *the faithful and true witness*. The importance of both of these titles will be seen when Jesus unmasks the Laodicean church and confronts the believers there with the truth about their sad condition.

In addition, Jesus calls himself *the ruler of God's creation*. The Son of God was present at the creation of the heavens and the earth and was the instrument of their creation (John 1:1-3; Colossians 1:15-17). He is Lord of the church and Lord of creation!

B. What Jesus Knows (vv. 15-17)

15, 16 "I know your deeds, that you are neither cold nor hot. I wish you were either one or the other! So, because you are lukewarm—neither hot nor cold—I am about to spit you out of my mouth.

The church in Laodicea was not charged with any great wickedness, or even with tolerating false doctrine. The Lord of the church simply found this church disgustingly self-satisfied and lacking in genuine motivation and commitment. The phrase *neither cold nor hot* brings to mind the problems with Laodicea's water supply, mentioned earlier. The city's *lukewarm* water illustrated perfectly the spiritual condition of the church.

We can understand why Jesus would say, *I wish you were* hot. It is easy to relate spiritual heat to the kind of passion mentioned in Romans 12:11: "Keep your spiritual fervor, serving the Lord." We still speak of someone being "on fire" for the Lord. But why would Jesus say, *I wish you were* cold? How could this be more pleasing to God than a neutral, lukewarm stance?

Perhaps the bitter atheist or the hardened sinner, like the tax collectors and prostitutes in Jesus' day, may be led to recognize his need and turn to Christ more readily than the self-satisfied nominal Christian. It may also be that the nominal Christian is so unattractive that he hurts the cause of Christ more than does the outspoken enemy of the church. In any case, Jesus says that he is sick enough to *spit* this church *out of* his *mouth*, so disgusted is he at their bland version of Christianity.

An alternative explanation suggests that "hot" and "cold" have nothing to do with spiritual zeal at all. Relating the language to water, it is easy to see why hot water and cold water are both preferable to lukewarm water. Hot water is soothing, and cold, refreshing. But lukewarm water is neither. Jesus may be saying something like, "Don't just sit there, do something!" The Laodiceans are self satisfied and smug—and inert! We can serve the Lord in very different ways, hot or cold, but Jesus cannot stomach our inactivity.

17 "You say, 'I am rich; I have acquired wealth and do not need a thing.' But you do not realize that you are wretched, pitiful, poor, blind and naked.

When Laodicea suffered major damage in an earthquake some 30 years before this letter was written, the city was so financially secure that it refused assistance from the empire. They did not *need a thing*, or so they thought.

In reality, the Christians in Laodicea were sadly impoverished. They failed to recognize the need for the kind of wealth that their banks could not handle, the kind of eyesight that their "Phrygian powder" could not provide, and the kind of clothing not made from their fine fabrics. Until they learned to depend on God, they would be eternally helpless and pathetic. They would have no assets beyond the grave, no ability to see beyond temporary material things, and no covering for their sins.

C. What Jesus Advises (v. 18)

18 "I counsel you to buy from me gold refined in the fire, so you can become rich; and white clothes to wear, so you can cover your shameful nakedness; and salve to put on your eyes, so you can see."

Buy from me, invites Jesus, for he is the only source of the riches, clothing, and vision needed by the Laodiceans. Not from deposits in their banks, but from depending upon him, would come the riches of faith "of greater worth than gold, which perishes even though refined by fire" (1 Peter 1:7). Not from their supplies of black textiles, but from the Savior with whom they had clothed themselves at baptism (Galatians 3:27), could they receive the *white clothes*, signifying purity and forgiveness from the blackness of their sin and shame. Not from their famous eye *salve*, but from him who had given sight to a blind man with an ointment of mud and saliva (John 9:6, 7), could they receive the spiritual sight that Jesus will still bestow on any willing patient (John 9:39-41).

II. Jesus' Challenge to Laodicea (Revelation 3:19-22)
A. His Plea (v. 19)

19 "Those whom I love I rebuke and discipline. So be earnest, and repent.

Purposeful *discipline* is one of the clearest expressions of *love* (see Proverbs 3:11, 12; Hebrews 12:5-11). Thus, to this church that has made Jesus sick by bragging that it does not need him or what he has to offer, Jesus declares his love. It is the love that prunes the fruit-bearing branch to make it still more fruitful (John 15:1, 2). Only when the Laodiceans' smug complacency was shattered could they effectively repent, shake off their apathy, and become *earnest* to serve the Lord with their considerable resources.

The command to *repent* is not only for the unsaved; this church needed to do it! The repentance that preceded baptism into Christ must be followed with repentance whenever the Christian has failed to follow his Lord faithfully.

B. His Promise (vv. 20-22)

20 "Here I am! I stand at the door and knock. If anyone hears my voice and opens the door, I will come in and eat with him, and he with me.

There is no more touching picture than the one that shows Jesus knocking patiently at a *door* that must be opened from within. This is not the *knock* of a stranger. This is not an appeal for sinners to be saved. Jesus is addressing a church, or perhaps a church member who has come to feel that he can get along just fine without Jesus. Jesus will not enter where he is not welcomed, even though he is the Lord of glory and is himself the door (or "gate") by which any person must enter life eternal (John 10:7). If the occupant does respond to the *voice* and the knocking, and *opens the door* to welcome Jesus, he will *come in* and will stay to *eat*, representative of the intimate fellowship that Jesus wants to have with those who are his friends (John 15:14).

> [21] *"To him who overcomes, I will give the right to sit with me on my throne, just as I overcame and sat down with my Father on his throne.*

The word *throne* indicates power and authority. Jesus *overcame* all opposition to the fulfillment of his Father's plan and was then "exalted" and given "the name that is above every name" (Philippians 2:9). He *sat down*, having completed that plan to provide for the salvation of humanity (Hebrews 1:3). Likewise, his disciples must follow the same path of first overcoming on earth and subsequently reigning with Christ in Heaven.

> [22] *"He who has an ear, let him hear what the Spirit says to the churches."*

In each of the first three letters to the seven *churches*, a promise to the faithful overcomers appeared *after* the admonition to listen to the divinely given message. In the letters to Thyatira, Sardis, Philadelphia, and Laodicea, these words constitute a firm and final command. It applies not only to the congregations immediately addressed, but to the Lord's people in all churches and in all times. Listen!

THE MULTITUDE BEFORE THE THRONE (REVELATION 7:1-3, 9-17)

Establishing the Groundwork

The vision recounted in Revelation 7 seems to interrupt a series of events recounted in chapters 4-6. Yet it is built on what is found in those chapters. Chapters 4 and 5 describe the glorious one who is seated on his heavenly throne. Accompanying him is the Lamb, having been slain and yet standing, who alone was found worthy to open the sealed scroll of eternal mysteries. Surrounding the throne appear four living creatures, suggesting the totality of created beings. Encircling all these are 24 thrones occupied by 24 white-robed elders, symbolizing either the leaders of believers from both old and new covenants or the believers themselves. Surrounding all of these is a throng of angels, joining in praise to God.

Chapter 6 presents a series of visions occurring with the opening of six of the seven seals on the scroll. Each of the first four visions consists of a horse with its rider. First comes a victorious rider on a white horse, followed by one on a red horse (representing war), another on a black horse (representing pestilence or famine), and a fourth rider (whose name was Death) on a "pale" horse. The opening of the fifth seal results in a vision of "the souls of those who had been slain because of the word of God and the testimony they had maintained" (Revelation 6:9). The sixth introduces the terrors of the final judgment, from which multitudes try to hide themselves.

The vision of the sixth seal closes (as does the sixth chapter of Revelation) with a penetrating question about who will be able to stand at the great day of the wrath of the one who sits on the throne and of the Lamb (v. 17). At this point, Revelation pauses from the opening of the seals to provide the answer. The seventh and final seal will not be opened until the beginning of chapter 8.

Examining the Text

I. Restraint and Seal (Revelation 7:1-3)
A. Angels Protect the Church (v. 1)

¹ After this I saw four angels standing at the four corners of the earth, holding back the four winds of the earth to prevent any wind from blowing on the land or on the sea or on any tree.

The picture of *the four winds of the earth* creates an image of "fullness of opposition" to God's people, just as the four horses and their riders did in the opening of the first four seals of the sealed scroll (Revelation 6:1-8). God's protection is seen as *four angels standing,* ready to serve God and his people. To make the picture all-inclusive, they are positioned *at the four corners of the earth.* Such a description is not meant to convey the idea that the earth is flat. Rather, the figure shows a firm defense from all directions.

The series of the potential targets of the wind seems somewhat unusual: the *land,* the *sea,* and *any tree.* In identifying the realm where people live, John probably uses this series so that the reader will not be tempted to take it too literally and try to cite a particular geographical location at a certain time in history. A tree is a natural object to select for observing the symbol of opposition, the wind. What do we do if someone asks us whether the wind is blowing, or how strong it is? We look to the nearest tree to check the movement of the leaves or the branches. Thus, the use of *tree* helps us to know that the expression is figurative, but real.

It is the ministry of the angels to hold back the wind. Hence, the Christian perceives that there is no way any opposition need destroy one's relationship with Christ. It is foolish to ask what would happen if the angels were to let go. We know that God is in control, and the four angels will not weaken.

B. Angels Seal the Church (vv. 2, 3)

² Then I saw another angel coming up from the east, having the seal of the living God. He called out in a loud voice to the four angels who had been given power to harm the land and the sea:

The spotlight now falls on *another angel,* who comes *from the east.* This phrase could be translated more literally as "from the rising of the sun." This angel's mission was one of light and preservation. His *loud voice* relays instructions to *the four angels* seen holding back the four winds from the servants of God. There is no mistaking the commanding nature of this voice. The next verse helps us understand the meaning of *the seal of the living God.*

³ "Do not harm the land or the sea or the trees until we put a seal on the foreheads of the servants of our God."

When we read *do not harm the land or the sea or the trees,* our thought is not on "place," but on "people," as the context indicates. This *harm* is delayed until God's servants can be sealed and protected. Thus we see why the opening of the seventh seal had been delayed. The pause was a pause of grace, allowing the angels to *put a seal on the foreheads of the servants of our God.* Ezekiel 9:3-6 tells of a similar marking of the faithful before the punitive slaughter of those who were guilty of abominations in Jerusalem. Both markings are reminiscent of the procedure followed during the institution of the Israelite Passover. A mark was placed on the doorposts of the Israelites' homes in Egypt before the Lord struck the Egyptians with the plague of death on the firstborn (Exodus 11:1–12:30).

The forehead was an appropriate place to carry the seal identifying those belonging to God. Associated with the intellect, the forehead indicates a willing commitment. It is prominent and easy to see. Deuteronomy 6:6-8 directs that God's people take his words and "bind them on your foreheads." Sealing is also a figure used in the New Testament of the presence of the Holy Spirit (cf. 2 Corinthians 1:22; Ephesians 1:13; 4:30). It is a mark of ownership, and thus provides authentication, security, and protection.

Verses 4-8 describe those who were sealed as 144,000 descendants of Jacob, with 12,000 from each of twelve tribes. The twelve tribes named are not identical with the ones who were assigned territories in the Promised Land. This, along with the precise pattern of exact numbers, suggests that these numbers are symbols rather than literal statistics.

What do these numbers symbolize? Some believe that the 144,000 (vv. 4-8) are saved Jews, while the "great multitude" (v. 9) are Gentiles who have turned to Christ. It is more likely that the 144,000 and the great multitude are the same group. This understanding is in line with the tendency of the New Testament to apply Old Testament language to the church (see Hebrews 12:22-24; 1 Peter 2:9). Those who belong to the "Israel of God" (Galatians 6:16) are pictured in Revelation as the Israel of God in glory with him.

II. Multitude and Proclamation (Revelation 7:9-12)
A. Appearance of Many (v. 9)

⁹ After this I looked and there before me was a great multitude that no one could count, from every nation, tribe, people and language, standing before the throne and in front of the Lamb. They were wearing white robes and were holding palm branches in their hands.

Whether we think of this *great multitude* as "numbered" (144,000) or as a group *that no one could count*, we should not miss John's message: Christians throughout the centuries (including the twenty-first century) are just as much a part of this group as those in John's day. For this multitude, nationality and language are irrelevant! As we see them *before the throne and in front of the Lamb*, they are ready to worship.

Part of being ready for this festive celebration is wearing the right clothes (see Matthew 22:11, 12). To be dressed in *white* is a common characteristic of those who overcome through Christ (Revelation 3:4, 5, 18; 6:11; 7:13, 14). Their actions involve having *palm branches in their hands*. Palm branches are often a part of a scene of festive joy (John 12:13). They are appropriate for the expressions of praise and worship that follow.

B. Ascent of Praise (vv. 10-12)

¹⁰ And they cried out in a loud voice:
"Salvation belongs to our God,
who sits on the throne,
and to the Lamb."

When Christians see what their relationship with *God* and *the Lamb* really means, the natural reaction is praise and worship. The Lamb has provided our *salvation*, which includes forgiveness, righteousness, and assurance with the presence of the Holy Spirit.

¹¹ All the angels were standing around the throne and around the elders and the four living creatures. They fell down on their faces before the throne and worshiped God,

All the angels are described in Revelation 5:11 as "numbering thousands upon thousands, and ten thousand times ten thousand." The twenty-four *elders* mentioned previously (4:4) are present, along with the *four living creatures* described in 4:6-8. At this point, the angels join the redeemed multitude in praise. Jesus described them as rejoicing whenever a lost person joins the number of the saved (Luke 15:10).

¹² . . . saying:
"Amen!
Praise and glory
and wisdom and thanks and honor
and power and strength
be to our God for ever and ever.
Amen!"

The angels' sevenfold tribute of praise is nearly the same as that recorded in Revelation 5:12, where their praise is given to the Lamb.

III. Identity and Service (Revelation 7:13-17)
A. John Questioned (vv. 13, 14a)

¹³, ¹⁴ᵃ Then one of the elders asked me, "These in white robes—who are they, and where did they come from?"
I answered, "Sir, you know."

At this point, John's role changed from that of an observer of the events in Heaven, and he became an invited participant. An otherwise unidentified member of the twenty-four *elders* may have noticed some confusion in John's expression, so he left the assembly around the throne to help this observer understand what was happening. He spoke the question that was evidently on John's mind: *Who are* these vast numbers of people *in white robes*, and *where did they come from?* John could have suggested an answer, but he preferred to learn from one who knew. So with appropriate respect he said, in effect, "I'm listening; tell me."

B. Elder Replies (vv. 14b-17)

¹⁴ᵇ And he said, "These are they who have come out of the great tribulation; they have washed their robes and made them white in the blood of the Lamb.

The reply of the elder, who serves as spokesman in the scene, then reinforces the meaning for the reader. The ones clothed in *white* robes are overcomers. *The great tribulation* is a "trial" they have experienced or are experiencing as their faith is tested. They are clothed in righteousness in God's presence because of their faith in the salvation provided by Christ. In casting their allegiance with him, they have *washed their robes* in *the blood of the Lamb.*

Daniel 12:1 speaks of a great "time of distress," and Matthew 24:21 also warns of "great distress." These passages may refer to specific periods in history. But before we get carried away with too much speculation of "when" and "where," let us remember that all Christians are tested. Each of us goes through some kind of *great tribulation*. Each of us has personal struggles in a sin-cursed world, as John had in his day. But those struggles will come to an end, as we see in the next verse.

> ^{15} *Therefore,*
> *"they are before the throne of God*
> *and serve him day and night in his temple;*
> *and he who sits on the throne will spread his tent over them.*

The uncountable multitude from verse 9 is observed *before the throne of God,* eager to *serve him day and night*. It is difficult to know exactly how the saints will serve God in Heaven, beyond expressions of worship and praise. Since there will be no poverty or pain, acts of mercy to the needy will not be necessary. The eternal activities are a part of the divine provision that we cannot begin to fathom.

> ^{16} *"Never again will they hunger;*
> *never again will they thirst.*
> *The sun will not beat upon them,*
> *nor any scorching heat.*

The elder found it easier to describe Heaven by its relief from familiar problems and difficulties than by its positive provisions. We know what hurts us here on earth; Heaven is a place where none of that will be present. *Hunger* and *thirst* are universal and sometimes critical problems. There will be no such deprivations in Heaven.

In many areas where John had ministered, the discomforts and dangers of desert *heat* were closely related to hunger and thirst. But the new Jerusalem is later described as having no need of the sun, "for the glory of God gives it light, and the Lamb is its lamp" (Revelation 21:23).

In circumstances of deprivation or need, or when we feel especially burdened or discouraged because of living in a sinful world, the presence and the protection of the Lamb can seem far away and not quite real. The image from our next verse gives us something to hold on to in such times.

> *17 "For the Lamb at the center of the throne will be their shepherd;*
> *he will lead them to springs of living water.*
> *And God will wipe away every tear from their eyes."*

The reason there is no more hunger or thirst (v. 16) is that *the Lamb* will be the *shepherd* of his people. He will provide for their needs, including leading them to *springs of living water*. Here the promises of Psalm 23 reach their ultimate fulfillment.

It may seem paradoxical that the Lamb can also be a shepherd. But in chapter 5, the Lamb is described by another paradox: "looking as if it had been slain," yet "standing in the center of the throne" (v. 6). It is the nature of apocalyptic language to move quickly from one image to the next.

Perhaps the most touching picture presented in the Bible is that of Almighty God tenderly caressing one of his faithful ones and wiping away his *tears*. This was foretold in Isaiah 25:8: "He will swallow up death forever. The Sovereign Lord will wipe away the tears from all faces."

THE NEW JERUSALEM (REVELATION 21:1-7, 22-27)

Establishing the Groundwork

The previous study from Revelation 7 considered God's "sealing" or identifying his people as those who have emerged from the "great tribulation" (v. 14), which is part of the continuing warfare between God and Satan. Chapters 8-18 depict that warfare in dramatic visions that are puzzling in detail but very clear in showing the ferocity of the conflict. Chapters 19 and 20 depict the end of that warfare through Christ's coming in glory and judgment. The outcome is eternal joy for his people and the consignment of his enemies to the eternal lake of fire.

Our challenge today, then, is to be as faithful as John wanted his first-century readers to be. If we are, then our lives will demonstrate godliness to this generation and to the next. If we are not, then judgment awaits. The book of Revelation makes all this clear to us. The closing scenes of this book bring this message to a climax and motivate us to faithfulness. Rather than seeking more revelation, as some today foolishly do, may we devote ourselves to understanding and applying the revelation that God has already given us. When we do, rich blessings surely await.

Examining the Text

I. In a New Situation (Revelation 21:1-7)
A. New Creation (vv. 1, 2)

¹ Then I saw a new heaven and a new earth, for the first heaven and the first earth had passed away, and there was no longer any sea.

The phrase *then I saw* marks an important transition. Throughout Revelation, we have been alerted both to what is seen and what is heard; for the message is the combination of these two (see Revelation 5:1, 2, 6, 11, 13).

This scene here is that of *a new heaven and a new earth* in contrast to *the first heaven and the first earth.* In John's vision of the future, "the old order of things has passed away" (v. 4). This present world has been good, but it is not sufficient for the eternal order. It groans under the weight of sin (Romans 8:22). In 2 Peter 3:10, 12, the apostle tells us how this physical world will be destroyed. Even the Garden of Eden was not complete enough to provide the fullness of relationship that God has in view for his people.

We see another contrast between the old and the new creations with the statement that *there was no longer any sea.* The sea was a very ominous realm in the minds of ancient people. The sea separated John from his brothers and sisters in Christ as he was exiled on the island of Patmos (Revelation 1:9). It is from the sea that "the beast" of Revelation 13:1 comes with his purpose of overcoming the saints. For John and his contemporaries, the sea was the epitome of evil, of all things bad and harmful.

Thus the situation that John pictures is one in which all opposition is gone—anything that would trouble the servants of God or anything that would separate them from God.

² I saw the Holy City, the new Jerusalem, coming down out of heaven from God, prepared as a bride beautifully dressed for her husband.

The scene of "renewal" continues in a marvelous way. John's first-century readers know about old Jerusalem, of course, with all its unholiness and injustice. Even now in the early twenty-first century, we can see that earthly Jerusalem is a place torn by violence and fear. What a refreshing contrast it is, then, to anticipate *the new Jerusalem!*

This *Holy City* stands in vivid contrast to Babylon, the "unholy city" representing all wickedness, which had been destroyed in God's judgment (Revelation 18:1-8). To the new Jerusalem, God gave a purity and a beauty like that of a radiant *bride* on her wedding day. That bride appears *beautifully dressed,* prepared for the great wedding supper of the Lamb (Revelation 19:9). Her radiance and purity present a stark contrast to the corruption of Babylon the Great (17:5), to whom God promises, "The voice of bridegroom and bride will never be heard in you again" (18:23).

B. New Relationship (vv. 3, 4)

³ And I heard a loud voice from the throne saying, "Now the dwelling of God is with men, and he will live with them. They will be his people, and God himself will be with them and be their God.

The desire of God to be *with* his *people* is one of the most prominent themes in all of Scripture. The purpose of the tabernacle in the wilderness was to provide a place where God's presence would be recognized by the Israelites (Leviticus 26:11, 12). Later God's presence was associated with Solomon's temple (1 Kings 8:12, 13). After this temple was destroyed by the Babylonians, the prophet Ezekiel reassured God's people that this did not mean that God had forsaken his people (Ezekiel 37:27, 28).

When Jesus came to earth, he was designated as Immanuel, meaning "God with us" (Isaiah 7:14; Matthew 1:23). Christians are to recognize that the Spirit of God dwells in them, making their bodies his temple (1 Corinthians 6:19). The perfect and eternal fulfillment of God's plan to dwell with his people will come only when his presence is directly experienced, without the limitations of time or space.

⁴ He will wipe every tear from their eyes. There will be no more death or mourning or crying or pain, for the old order of things has passed away."

Here we see the fullness of God's care as God himself wipes *every tear from our eyes* (Isaiah 25:8; Revelation 7:17). John also describes the removal of the sources of those tears—those experiences that are part of living in a sin-cursed world. The words *death, mourning, crying,* and *pain* bring to mind issues of suffering and separation. But the time is coming when the enemy who brought us such woes will be no more! All of those characteristics of *the old order* will have *passed away.*

C. New Assurance (v. 5)

⁵ "He who was seated on the throne said, "I am making everything new!" Then he said, "Write this down, for these words are trustworthy and true."

The source of the message—*he who was seated on the throne*—underscores the extreme importance of what is *said.* What is *new* implies a contrast with what was "first" (v. 1). This is an important point regarding what it means for God to be with his people. The old creation will not just be "fixed up." It will be new!

As we hear along with John the command to *write*, we recognize the value and the usefulness of the message. Just as the one who gave them is "Faithful and True" (Revelation 19:11), so also are his *words*.

D. New Inheritance (vv. 6, 7)

⁶ He said to me: "It is done. I am the Alpha and the Omega, the Beginning and the End. To him who is thirsty I will give to drink without cost from the spring of the water of life.

The God who introduced himself as *the Alpha and the Omega* in Revelation 1:8 now uses the same title, as the making of all things new for the children of God is complete: *It is done.* Jesus refers to himself by the same title (Revelation 22:13). The phrase *the Beginning and the End* carries the same meaning; Jesus described himself as "the First and the Last" in Revelation 1:17.

However, the protection of Christ is only for those who take their thirst to *the spring of the water of life.* The idea of "water" as a figure of God's care is not new. (See Psalm 65:9; Isaiah 41:17, 18; 55:1; Jeremiah 2:13; Zechariah 13:1; John 4:13, 14; 7:37, 38.) This figure was also found in the previous study from Revelation at the close of a grand scene depicting God, his people, and the absence of all opposition (7:17).

⁷ "He who overcomes will inherit all this, and I will be his God and he will be my son."

We must stress again that the blessings described in this passage are only for those who overcome through the power of the Lamb. Not all will accept or keep a place in God's family as Christians, the church. It is noteworthy to check the listing in Revelation 21:8 of those whose end is the second death. That end is eternal separation from God. It is the direct opposite of what the faithful inherit—God with his people.

II. In the Presence of God (Revelation 21:22-27)
A. Temple and Lamb (vv. 22, 23)

²² I did not see a temple in the city, because the Lord God Almighty and the Lamb are its temple.

The focal point of Old Testament worship was the *temple.* God put his glory there (1 Kings 8:11), but also took that glory away because of the wickedness of his people (Ezekiel 10:18-22). The laying anew of the temple's foundation in Ezra's day was a time of great joy and weeping (Ezra 3:10-13). The completion of the second temple in 516 BC was an emotional occasion as well (Ezra 6:13-18). But no temple experience of the old covenant could match what is being described here! The fullness of this picture includes the presence of the *Lord God Almighty and the Lamb*. There is no "curtain" to separate God from people as in the old temple. The Lamb has removed it (see Mark 15:38). This is the great worship experience we desire—all barriers are gone. Now we are in the very presence of God.

²³ *The city does not need the sun or the moon to shine on it, for the glory of God gives it light, and the Lamb is its lamp.*

God provided the *light* of the *sun* and the *moon* to benefit humanity (Genesis 1:16). Heaven, however, will not need such sources of light, for it will offer a manifestation of *the glory of God* unlike anything ever witnessed by human eyes. Here is eternal safety and security!

B. Nations and Gates (vv. 24, 25)

²⁴ *The nations will walk by its light, and the kings of the earth will bring their splendor into it.*

The light of the gospel will have made it possible for those of many *nations* to experience the *light* of God shining in the holy city. The presence of these peoples indicates once again the multinational composition of God's eternal family (Revelation 7:9). *The kings of the earth* are in attendance as well, acknowledging that they are in the presence of the King of kings. As is the case with many details of the new Jerusalem, the prophet Isaiah foretold this (Isaiah 2:2; 60:3).

²⁵ *On no day will its gates ever be shut, for there will be no night there.*

How dark a city often was in ancient times! City *gates* would be *shut* securely at *night* lest enemies plunder the defenseless inhabitants under cover of darkness. Our scene reminds us that the threat of enemies is gone for those who are in the presence of God. He offers constant light and complete protection. The prince of darkness, Satan, has no place here (Revelation 20:10).

C. Glory and Honor (vv. 26, 27)

²⁶ *The glory and honor of the nations will be brought into it.*

Because of the Lamb, all the *nations* have been blessed. Salvation has reached "the ends of the earth" (Acts 1:8). Grace given to the faithful returns from them as *glory and honor* to the Lamb upon the throne, for he is "King of kings and Lord of lords" (Revelation 19:16).

> *²⁷ Nothing impure will ever enter it, nor will anyone who does what is shameful or deceitful, but only those whose names are written in the Lamb's book of life.*

The holy city has nothing *shameful or deceitful*. Everything about this city is pure and holy, as God and redeemed humanity live together. There is complete separation from all wickedness. The *names* that *are written in the Lamb's book of life* gain the promise of Revelation 21:7: "He who overcomes will inherit all this."

While much of Revelation may leave readers mystified, there is no mystery to the final outcome: God's people will reign victoriously with him—forever!

How to Say It

AARON. *Air*-un.

AEGEAN. A-*jee*-un.

AGRIPPA. Uh-*grip*-puh.

ALPHA. *Al*-fa.

APOCALYPTIC. uh-*pock*-uh-*lip*-tick (strong accent on *lip*).

ASIA. *Ay*-zha.

BABYLONIANS. Bab-ih-*low*-nee-unz.

COLOSSE. Ko-*lahss*-ee.

DOMITIAN. Duh-*mish*-un.

EGYPTIANS. Ee-*jip*-shunz.

EPHESUS. *Ef*-uh-sus.

EPITOME. ih-*pih*-tuh-me.

EZEKIEL. Ee-*zeek*-ee-ul or Ee-*zeek*-yul.

HEROD. *Hair*-ud.

HIERAPOLIS. Hi-er-*ap*-o-lis.

IMMANUEL. Ih-*man*-you-el.

ISRAELITE. *Iz*-ray-el-ite.

JACOB. *Jay*-kub.

LAODICEA. Lay-*odd*-uh-*see*-uh (strong accent on *see*).

LAODICEAN. Lay-*odd*-uh-*see*-un (strong accent on *see*).

MILETUS. My-*lee*-tus.

OMEGA. O-*may*-guh or O-*mee*-guh.

PATMOS. *Pat*-muss.

PENTECOST. *Pent*-ih-kost.

PERGAMUM. *Per*-guh-mum.

PHRYGIA. *Frij*-e-uh.

PHRYGIAN. *Frij*-e-un.

SARDIS. *Sar*-dis.

SMYRNA. *Smur*-nuh.

SOLOMON. *Sol*-o-mun.

TABERNACLE. *ta*-ber-*na*-kul (*ta* as in *tan; na* as in *nap;* strong accent on *ta).*

THYATIRA. *Thy*-uh-*tie*-ruh (strong accent on *tie; th* as in *thin*).

TROAS. *Tro*-az.

ZECHARIAH. *Zek*-uh-*rye*-uh (strong accent on *rye*).